LISTENING
TO THE
LAND

DERRICK JENSEN

Listening
to the
Land

CONVERSATIONS ABOUT

NATURE, CULTURE,

AND EROS

Sierra Club Books

SAN FRANCISCO

The Sierra Club, founded in 1892 by John Muir,
has devoted itself to the study and protection of the earth's
scenic and ecological resources—mountains, wetlands, wood-
lands, wild shores and rivers, deserts and plains. The publishing
program of the Sierra Club offers books to the public as a nonprofit educational service in the hope that they may enlarge the
public's understanding of the Club's basic concerns. The point
of view expressed in each book, however, does not necessarily
represent that of the Club. The Sierra Club has some sixty
chapters coast to coast, in Canada, Hawaii, and Alaska. For
information about how you may participate in its programs
to preserve wilderness and the quality of life, please
address inquiries to Sierra Club, 730 Polk Street,
San Francisco, CA 94109.

Interviews of John Keeble, Neil Evernden, and Thomas
Berry were originally published in *The Bloomsbury Review*.

Library of Congress Cataloging-in-Publication Data
Jensen, Derrick, 1960–
Listening to the land : nature, culture, and Eros
/ Derrick Jensen.
p.   cm.
ISBN 0-87156-417-3
1. Nature—Religious aspects.   2. Human ecology—
Religious aspects.   3. Twenty-first century—Forecasts.
I. Title.
BL226.J46   1995
304.2—dc20   94-35086

Production by Susan Ristow
Book and cover designs by Sandy Drooker
Composition by Wilsted & Taylor

Printed in the United States of America on acid-free paper
containing a minimum of 50% recovered waste paper, of which at
least 10% of the fiber content is post-consumer waste
10 9 8 7 6 5 4 3 2 1

CONTENTS

INTRODUCTION

WE ARE MEMBERS of the most destructive culture ever to exist. Our assault on the natural world, on indigenous and other cultures, on women, on children, on all of us through the possibility of nuclear suicide and other means—all these are unprecedented in their magnitude and ferocity. Why do we act as we do?

I began this project because I wanted to understand our culture's pervasive destructiveness and to know if it is possible to live another way. Perhaps, I thought, what we are doing is natural, instinctive, and no different from the expansion of bacteria on a petri dish. Or perhaps the cause of the destructiveness is more specific to our being human; our adaptability and capacity for critical thinking guarantee that we will "outcompete" every other species.

But if that's the case, how do we explain the existence of the Hopi, the Inuit, the Ladakhi, the !Kung, and other groups of people who fashioned ways of living that were in dynamic equilibrium with their surroundings? How do we explain the continued survival until a century ago—at least twenty thousand years after humans arrived on this continent but a mere three hundred years after the arrival of Europeans—of flocks of passenger pigeons that darkened the sky for days at a time? How do we explain the possibility of humans living side by side with 70 million buffalo, 40 million pronghorn antelope, with grizzly, wolf, and salmon?

I determined that I would gain understanding from those people actively searching for answers—those environmentalists, feminists, theologians, psychologists, and indigenous philosophers who have dedicated their lives to exploring and countering the destructiveness of our culture and to promulgating more peaceful ways to live. Our conversations raised yet more questions: What is the relationship between technological innovation and human misery? Is there a direct relationship between environmental destruction and other forms of oppression, such as misogyny or genocide? Given that humans are causing the greatest mass extinction in the history of the planet, can there be hope? How can we, as a culture and as individuals, rediscover our connections to ourselves, to our neigh-

1

bors, to the rest of the natural world? Would these connections help us to better realize our potential as human beings?

What has emerged from this questioning is a book about listening. Early in the course of the project, Thomas Berry said to me, "The universe is composed of subjects to be communed with, not objects to be exploited. Everything has its own voice." He went on to say, "Somehow we have become autistic. We don't hear the voices."

How do we remember how to listen? Would we live differently if we listened to the voices of the species we are causing to go extinct? What lessons can we learn from the women who are raped, the children who are beaten? What do indigenous peoples worldwide have to teach us?

What would happen if each of us began listening to our own needs? In our conversation, Terry Tempest Williams said that "our needs as human beings are really very simple—to love and be loved, a sense of connection and compassion, a desire to be heard. Health. Family. Home. The dance, that sharing of breath, that merging with something larger than ourselves. One plus one equals three."

What will it take for each of us to remember how to dance?

There has never been a more crucial time for us to ask that question. Dave Foreman pointed out, "All of us alive now are members of the most important generation of human beings who have ever lived, because we're determining the future, not just for a hundred years, but for a billion years. When we cut a huge limb off the tree of natural diversity, we're forever halting the evolutionary potential of that branch of life."

Not only is evolutionary potential being destroyed, but as Christopher Manes told me, "We have to realize the same forces that hack up the wilderness, put fences around it, and call this progress also shepherd us down meaningless paths, frustrate our talents, impoverish our internal lives."

I didn't understand that when in 1983 I graduated from the Colorado School of Mines with a degree in mineral engineering physics. I had what it seemed everyone wants: the opportunity for a large paycheck from a not-too-meaningless job. My economic future was secure. Yet I was miserable and wondered if I was insane; thirty thousand dollars a year, as it had been presented to me, was supposed to mean a lot of happiness.

Now I understand that there are other models for happiness. During our conversation, Arno Gruen said, "With the Mbuti—the pygmies of the former Congo—for example, or many of the Native North or South Americans, what is of central importance is how people feel with one another, how they get along, how they can sustain and help one another." Many of these cultures exist, or existed prior to contact with our culture, without rape, without war, without child abuse. This is true of the Okanagans of British Columbia, who reject the use of aggressive force. As Jeannette Armstrong told me, "To us as Okanagans, for a person to do anything in that way is unacceptable, unheard-of. Not only is it unethical, but since you have so many other tools, it doesn't make sense."

The recognition that nonaggressive and synergistic ways of living exist raises a whole new series of questions. Is there a relationship between nonaggression and happiness? Why does a culture, or a person, become aggressive? What can those who have survived this aggression teach us? Is it possible to live a life based on cooperation within a culture that is essentially competitive? Where does love fit in?

I believe each of us already knows the answers to these questions. We just need to remember that we know. As Susan Griffin told me, "We are on the verge of destroying material life. One of the ways I think we can avert that is to recognize the profundity of material existence, to deeply respect our own process of knowing in the world, knowing with heart and mind and body and sensuality all at the same time. This involves a deep self-respect for that process of knowledge that has evolved over millions, even billions of years, and it involves entering that process with full passion."

It is possible—indeed imperative—for each of us to enter that "process of knowing in the world," that process of deep listening, with full passion. Linda Hogan said, "You know those moments you have when you enter a silence that's still and complete and peaceful? That's the source, the place where everything comes from. In that space, you know everything is connected, that there's an ecology of everything. In that place it is possible for people to have a change of heart, a change of thinking, a change in their way of being and living in the world." This book has helped point me to that quiet space of connection, and I can only hope it may do the same for its readers.

* * *

Two summers ago I helped John Keeble build a rock retaining wall against the foundation of his house. We talked about my questioning as we searched for rocks to fill different-shaped spaces in the wall. I realized I was using a similar sorting process to increase my understanding and to create this book. I was searching for people to fill specific gaps in my knowledge—Reed Noss could help me to understand the role of conservation biologists in stemming the destruction of biodiversity, Jerry Mander could help me to make sense of the necessary connection between technology and totalitarianism, Catherine Keller could help me with the question of why revolutionary movements based on love, such as Christianity, often get co-opted and turned to the advantage of those already in power.

I realized also that the interviews, just like the rocks in the wall, were building on one another. Themes begun in one interview might not be resolved until several interviews later, or might be resolved from several different perspectives. Thus, although the conversations in this book make sense when read in any order, if read sequentially they tell a coherent story. It is the story of a return to knowledge, the knowledge each of us holds in our bodies, which comes from appropriate forms of relationship with self, other humans, work, technology, eros, time, the rest of nature.

I chose the dialogue form instead of the single-voice narrative in the hope the reader would experience the story for what it is—a communal effort at working through some of the greatest and most difficult questions ever faced by human beings.

The most recent gift this book has given to me is the certainty that even within our culture, a culture often seemingly hell-bent on self-destruction, it is still possible to fashion a life based, as Paul Shepard puts it, on "cooperation, sharing, and mutuality." It is possible to find a niche from which to do everything within your power to stop the destruction around you. It is possible to carve out a life based on love, which after all is the only life worth living.

Dave Foreman

For more than twenty years, Dave Foreman has been at the forefront of the conservation movement, working where political activism intersects with ecological philosophy. In the 1970s, believing that the best way to preserve wilderness was to work within the system, he became the Southwest regional representative of The Wilderness Society. *In 1980, disillusioned by the inability of mainstream conservation organizations to halt the destructive forces within our culture, he cofounded Earth First! The goal of Earth First! was to help develop a biocentric worldview and to translate that philosophy into action by fighting with uncompromising passion for the Earth.*

More recently Dave Foreman helped to found The Wildlands Project, an effort bringing together grassroots activists and conservation biologists to design and establish linked areas of wilderness extensive enough to support large mammals. In addition to being chair of The Wildlands Project, he is executive editor of Wild Earth *magazine and author of* Confessions of an Eco-Warrior *and* The Big Outside *(with Howie Wolke).*

DERRICK JENSEN: You've written that the defense of the Earth is not "Lord Man protecting something less than himself. Rather, it is a humble joining with Earth, becoming the rain forest, the desert, the mountain, the wilderness in defense of itself."

DAVE FOREMAN: Our desire to protect wilderness comes from passion, from an emotional identification with wilderness. It's a sense of expanding the concept of the self to include the landscape around us and identifying with that landscape.

This may seem an alien concept on first blush, but for somebody who knows a place, who can sit in the desert, watch it and accept it for what it is, who does not need to experience it on a dirt bike, or for somebody who can go into an old-growth forest and sit underneath a five-hundred-year-old tree and try to pick up some wisdom from it, I don't think it is alien. We *are* place. We *are* connected to everything, and we are open to the world around us.

Aldo Leopold wrote that there are those who love wild things and sunsets, and those who do not. I think we all fundamentally and early on love wild things and sunsets, but some of us have it socialized out of us. We forget that love. There might be a point you can't turn back from. I feel sorry for people who don't have that identification with nature, because they're living half a life.

DJ: When are you happiest?

DF: When I'm not thinking abstractly. When I am being fully an animal, when I'm in the middle of a rapid on the river and having to respond to the river.

I'm happiest when I experience the moment entirely for what it is. I'm happiest when I'm bird-watching, or when I'm walking down a trail in the wilderness and the internal dialogue finally ceases—I'm just there in the place. Our physical adaptation is for running or moving through wild country. That's when we're truly human and truly alive.

I am a large mammal, a child of the Pleistocene, the age of large mammals. It's natural to want to see other large mammals. I recently had the joy of my life when I came in contact with a Jaguar on the Monkey River in Belize. Rationality ceased, abstraction ceased. We ignore the fact that we need wilderness around us to be mentally healthy.

DJ: Let's talk about abstraction. Elsewhere you've said that while deep ecology is your ethic, it's still an abstraction.

DF: All ethics are abstractions. The map is not the territory. The Western intellectual tradition really began, I believe, when Socrates told Phaedrus, "I am a man who loves learning, and trees and open spaces can't teach me a thing, whereas men in town do." We've been on the wrong path ever since, and deep ecology is an attempt by those of us from that tradition to try to get back to a more fundamental wisdom. This means it's going to be an abstraction for a while, until we are able to somehow reinhabit the Earth in some kind of future primitive.

How that's going to happen, I don't know. My job, which I do with The Wildlands Project, is to conceptualize a new kind of reserve system that does deep ecology on the ground, because deep ecology isn't deep ecology when it's just academic intellectual masturbation. Deep ecology becomes something real when it motivates our day-to-day actions, and there is no more honorable thing any of us can do with our lives than to work to put part of the world off-limits to the activities of human beings.

DJ: Why?

DF: Right now human beings are agents of biodiversity destruction on the order of an extraterrestrial comet. Leading biologists tell us we may lose one-third of all species on Earth in the next forty years. Michael Soulé, the founder of the Society for Conservation Biology, says for all practical purposes vertebrate evolution is at an end, and that the only large mammals left in another decade or two will be those we consciously choose to allow to exist. We are destroying the building blocks of nature that have been building for nearly 4 billion years.

In this country, wilderness preservation has focused on scenic rocks and ice above timberline, while giving up more important lower elevation forests. We've ignored grassland areas, river bottoms, places that might not be as spectacular or as suited for recreation but that are more important from a biodiversity standpoint.

The result is that the national parks and wilderness areas have failed to protect the biological and natural heritage of North America. W. D. Newmark, in his study of national parks about ten years ago, found that even Yellowstone National Park and the surrounding area was too small to maintain viable populations of Grizzly Bears or Gray Wolves.

Because we might not have any places big enough for large predators except in Alaska or northern Canada, Reed Noss and other conservation biologists have begun working with metapopulations. That involves preserving corridors which link, for example, the Yellowstone National Park ecosystem with the Glacier/Bob Marshall ecosystem and the central Idaho ecosystem, as well as the Canadian Rockies. In the East, we want a connected chain of wilderness areas from the Everglades to northern Maine and into Canada, so the Eastern Cougar and the Florida Panther will be once again connected. And then of course we need east-west corridors.

We need to preserve more than little outdoor museums, snapshots in time. The Wildlands Project is fundamentally about protecting the evolutionary process, the potentiality for future speciation. For that we need areas large enough to have stochastic events, like forest fires or the hurricane that went across the Everglades.

DJ: You seem to focus on large predators.

DF: If there isn't room for large predators—for Wolves and Bears and Saltwater Crocodiles and Harpy Eagles—human beings have clearly exceeded local carrying capacity. Educated people in the world today nearly all accept evolution as a scientific fact. But very few people have accepted the social implications of Darwinian natural selection—that we are animals. You get cornucopians of the right and the left, whether they take their economic theories from Adam Smith or Karl Marx, that refuse any notion of limits, or the idea of carrying capacity, as it's applied to human beings. The Wildlands Project is a way to come to terms with that. And if we can protect viable populations of large predators, we can figure 90 percent of all biodiversity is being protected.

DJ: Why protect biodiversity?

DF: For its own sake. We have no right to destroy the biodiversity of this planet. These other species and ecosystems exist for their own sakes. When I saw that Jaguar in Belize, she did not consider herself watchable wildlife, or a source of joy for me. She has a life just as full of meaning and joy to her as mine is to me.

All this goes to the heart of what kind of people we are. I can't imagine the legacy of destroying large mammals on this Earth, destroying coral reef ecosystems, songbirds, amphibians. It's a burden I can't bear. We need to come to terms with what we're doing, and we need to think about our legacy.

If you want to put it in somewhat religious terms, fighting to save biodiversity, the process of evolution, is a way for us to save our souls.

DJ: How will The Wildlands Project be implemented?

DF: The first thing is to talk about it, prepare a draft proposal for the entire North American continent with lines on maps and throw it on the table. That will be helpful because it will expand the terms of the debate, expand the possible.

On a practical basis, we start with what we have. The Klamath Forest Alliance has proposed corridors between wilderness areas in northwestern California and has filed lawsuits and appeals to protect those corridors from Forest Service timber sales. Folks with the Southern Rockies Ecosystem Project are mapping all remaining old growth in Colorado and figuring how to connect it into a single linked reserve system.

When we're constantly wrapped up in brushfires, it's hard to look at the big picture. Tying local battles into a continental wilderness recovery network will help frontline conservation activists determine their priorities. And it gives folks a vision, encourages them, gives them more energy.

It also helps us do things like look at northern Maine, where 10 million uninhabited acres are owned by paper companies. That land is available for two hundred dollars or less an acre. Ten million acres essentially for the price of a Stealth bomber. By putting it in the context of this continental system, we can argue better for the money to acquire it. If we acquired it, we could have an Alaska-size wilderness wildlife refuge in New England, and in twenty years there would be Wolves and Caribou and Lynx and Eastern Cougar there.

The Wildlands Project is audacious. It's big not only in terms of space but also in terms of time. If we identify, say, a private ranch in Montana that's between two wilderness reserves, and we feel that fifty years from now it will be necessary as a corridor for Wolves to go from one area to another, we can say to the rancher, "We don't want you to give up your ranch now. But let us put a conservation easement on it. Let's work out the tax details so you can donate it in your will to this reserve system." When it's needed as a corridor, it will be there.

DJ: How does the possibility of a socio-industrial crash impact your conservation strategies?

DF: I've tried to develop a strategy where it doesn't matter. I personally believe there's going to be a crash. I don't know when or how it will take place, whether it will be a pandemic, a massive economic crash, a clash of centralized state governments, a massive famine, or whatever, but I do know industrial civilization cannot go on. The anthropologist Marvin Harris talks about the industrial bubble. As this bubble expands its skin becomes thinner. It is going to pop.

From that perspective, The Wildlands Project is trying to protect as much land as possible, and to protect breeding stocks of all species, so that after industrialism collapses there will be enough building blocks of natural diversity to recolonize the world.

On the other hand, if we come to our senses, build some kind of sustainable society, control overpopulation and see a steady decrease in human population, develop a steady-state economics, develop the kind of agriculture Wes Jackson, Wendell Berry, and others are working on, the kind of forestry Orville Camp is working on, and reinhabitory communities like folks in northern California or the Oregon backwoods are trying to create, the results are the same. This kind of North American wilderness recovery strategy becomes a key element in that new society, and becomes sacred space where the new people will fully become human beings.

DJ: Where does fun fit into this?

DF: There's incredible fun in working with people you connect with and feel close to. Fun comes from going into the wilderness and experiencing it on its own terms. Fun comes from learning humility and respect. My friend Doug Peacock says we need Grizzly Bears to teach us humility, and he jokes that while he might think about packing a pistol in a city, he never would when he's in Bear country. You need to go without a gun so you aren't on top of the food chain.

Fun comes from the privilege of being born into this blue-green living planet, no matter how bad the situation gets. Fun has to motivate it all, or as I prefer to say, joy. Joy in living. Joy in fighting the good fight. Even sometimes joy in saying, "Today is a good day to die," and going for it.

And joy has to motivate your activism. We need to walk in respect on the earth, not out of a sense of duty, but out of a sense of joy. A couple of years ago Wendell Berry said to me that deep ecology needs to be careful not to just establish rules. It needs to be something that wells up from within. By respecting the land you walk softly on it.

DJ: You were one of the founders of Earth First! and helped make famous the phrase, "No compromise in the defense of Mother Earth."

DF: I'm all for compromise. It's just that our opportunity for compromise passed about one hundred years ago. We're down to the last 5 percent of old-growth forest. We could have compromised at 50 percent, but we didn't. We've got to save all that's left and begin to restore some. Paul Sears, one of the great botanists of America back in the thirties, forties, and fifties, said we needed to protect 25 percent of the United States in inviolate condition. Conservation biologists today are saying it's more like 50 percent, if we are going to have the whole range and diversity of species. When we're down to the last 4 percent of the redwood forests, we're way beyond that kind of compromise.

What we *can* do is be concerned about the poor bastards who all along have been misled by the logging companies. We can try to retrain them.

We can do something for community stability. The timber-dependent communities in the Pacific Northwest have been destroyed by the timber companies. The people have been exploited, and they continue to be exploited. Bernard DeVoto, editor of *Harper's*, saw that nearly fifty years ago when he said that the West, for all its emphasis on individualism, is the part of America most dominated by outside economic interests. The rugged individualists of the West, whether they're cowboys or loggers or miners or farmers, have always been more than ready to sell themselves to the corporate bidder with the most money and then to blame somebody else when the corporation cuts and runs.

Let's face it, the loggers of the Pacific Northwest have had the wool pulled over their eyes by the corporations, and in their natural frustration and rage at having seen their lifestyle and communities destroyed, are lashing out at the handiest scapegoat, be it conservationist or Spotted Owl. If they would quit beating us up and quit killing Spotted Owls, maybe they would realize that conservationists who are working to create a sustainable economy in the Pacific Northwest are their best friends.

DJ: Do you see any way either to reform or get rid of the idea of corporations?

DF: The whole notion of corporations has to be radically redefined. Big corporations must have a deeper community interest, something beyond making a profit for their stockholders.

I get pissed off at the so-called conservatives today who prattle on about property rights—rights this and rights that—without any sense of responsibility. With rights come responsibilities and accountability. The only time they want to talk about responsibility is when Dan Quayle goes after some poor, uneducated, trodden-down teenage mother in a Saint Louis slum. I want to talk about the responsibility of Armand Hammer for murdering people at Love Canal, I want to talk about the responsibility of Harry Merlo and other timber company barons for destroying communities and the land base on the Pacific Coast.

Our priorities are insane. When I went to Washington, D.C., fifteen years ago to be a lobbyist for The Wilderness Society, a senator took me aside. He told me to put my heart in a safe-deposit box and replace my brain with a pocket calculator. He told me to quote only economists and engineers and said if I was ever emotional I would lose my credibility.

But damn it, I am emotional. I'm an animal, and I'm proud of it. Descartes was wrong when he said, "I think, therefore I am." Our consciousness, our being, is not all up here in the skullbox. It's our whole body we think with, and it goes beyond that. David Brower tells us that you can't take a California Condor out of the wild and put it in the L.A. zoo and still have a Condor, because the being of the Condor does not end at those black feathers at the tips of its wings. It's the rising thermals over the Coast Range. It's the rocky crag where she lays her egg. It's the carrion she feeds on. The Condor is place, and as we were talking about earlier, we are place, too.

DJ: What will it take for us to survive?

DF: Courage. In my speeches I talk about what Aldo Leopold called green fire. When Aldo Leopold was young he used to shoot any Wolf he saw, and years later, in *A Sand County Almanac*, he wrote how the death of one of those Wolves changed his life. He said, "We reached the old wolf in time to watch a fierce green fire dying in her eyes. I realized then, and have known ever since, that there was something new to me in those eyes—something known only to her and to the mountain. I was young then, and full of trigger-itch; I thought that because fewer wolves meant more deer, that no wolves would mean hunters' paradise. But after seeing the green fire die, I sensed that neither the wolf nor the mountain agreed with such a view."

We need that green fire in our eyes. Somehow we've got to remember how to think like a mountain, and somehow we have to speak for Wolf.

Each of us is an animal, and a child of this earth. Each of us has responsibility to all other animals and plants and to the process of evolution that created us. All of us alive now are members of the most important generation of human beings who have ever lived, because we're determining the future, not just for a hundred years, but for a billion years. When we cut a huge limb off the tree of natural diversity, we're forever halting the evolutionary potential of that branch of life. That's what it fundamentally comes down to.

Nobody has ever lived who is more important.

A reporter once asked me what I thought my nephew's and niece's children would think of me. Would they consider their great-uncle an ecoterrorist, a radical, a lunatic conservationist? I said, "No. They're going to ask, 'Why the hell didn't you fight harder? Why weren't you more radical? Why weren't you more militant? Why didn't you save *more* forests?' "

That's what I ask, too. Goddamnit, where are the 70 million Bison, where are the Passenger Pigeons, where are the Carolina Parakeets? Where's the Sea Mink, the Labrador Duck, the Heath Hen? Where's the tallgrass prairie?

The conservation movement has failed to challenge people with an ethical mandate. We seem to have gotten the notion we have to make it palatable for people, make it easy for them. "Oh, you can have your cars and your freeways, and we can protect nice scenic national parks, too."

A new vision must be articulated. Martin Luther King saying "I have a dream" energized the country. People responded to that dream. But since that dream was institutionalized, sort of, in the Civil Rights Act and the Voting Rights Act, the dream has never been explicitly stated again. That's really sad, and that's why even though the civil rights movement has had great successes, there have been great failures.

By the same token, I think conservationists had a wonderful dream with the Wilderness Act, but then we fell into the comfortable reaction.

DJ: Is The Wildlands Project then essentially the articulation of a new dream?

DF: Absolutely. A totally audacious dream.

CHRISTOPHER MANES

Well versed in classical, modern, and postmodern philosophy, Christopher Manes is perhaps best known for his book Green Rage: Radical Environmentalism and the Unmaking of Civilization, *which is an urgent plea for us to reconsider our industrial way of life. He has written that "industrial society may indeed be the most deleterious and unsustainable economic system the world has ever seen, since it constantly eats into the ecological systems on which it depends."*

Why did we industrialize? What choices have we made that have led us down this "deleterious and unsustainable" path? What options, political and philosophical, are open to us now? These are some of the questions he considers in his work.

Christopher Manes is a former associate editor of The Earth First! *Journal and a contributing editor to* Wild Earth, *a journal of conservation biology. In* 1990, Green Rage *was nominated for a* Los Angeles Times *book award in science. Manes has also produced a documentary,* Earth First!— The Politics of Radical Environmentalism, *excerpts of which have appeared on* 60 Minutes *and* MTV.

CHRISTOPHER MANES: Today's environmental problems are symptoms of deeper problems in our culture and how we view the world. Fortunately, we are in the midst of a broad philosophical reevaluation of our history and our place on this planet.

The view that somehow our industrial society is inevitable no longer holds much credence with anthropologists, philosophers, or historians with any sophistication. Our industrial way of life is a choice—other cultures have chosen different, often less destructive, roads. The Yanomami Indians, for example, don't feel the same urge we do to cut down their forests and obliterate nature. This tells me that the impulse for industrial "progress" may hold for our very limited culture during a very limited time period, but other, perhaps more humane, ways of living are open to us.

Before we can change, we first have to recognize we have choices, that we can remake our culture, perhaps in line with our older, reverential traditions toward nature. And up until the second half of the twentieth century, we lacked the mind-set to do so. But the death of nature we see around us, with one ecological disaster after the next, has sparked deeper questions about our place in nature.

And of course powerful forces in our society are trying to smother this reevaluation, co-opt it, commercialize it so it becomes a trend you can sell basketball shoes and beer with. That's basically what the greening of American corporations is about. The point is to absorb environmental dissent by employing its images for an ulterior purpose. That's the special genius of our consumer society: it takes rock 'n' roll, civil rights, the labor movement, and turns them into a medium for selling beer.

I doubt this will happen to environmentalism because, unlike other historical movements, it's rooted in a pressing reality. That is, environmental issues are not just based on social structures and conflicts. Different types of societies, whether capitalist, communist, or despotic, create all sorts of consequences—often grave consequences—for their members. And some societies are simply better than others. Nevertheless, there's a kind of unreality to social systems, which come and go over time, often, it seems, at random.

Nature, on the other hand, is absolute. It persists beyond our ideologies, underlying them, limiting them. Our particular culture has become so inimical to life that in the next generation it's going to destroy one-third to one-half of the species on this planet. This is what conservation biologists like Michael Soulé and Norman Myers are saying, and no one can scientifically challenge their conclusions. A society can't simply destroy and re-create its ecological foundation as if it were some institution like the local supermarket.

So nature rises up to act as a physical boundary to our social theory and practice in a way not seen in the capricious history of injustice humans have been making for themselves over the past few millennia.

The history of the world has been a parade of doomed civilizations, some noble, some corrupt, all of which thoughtlessly destroyed their ecological base. We may be following that same march to oblivion, unless we have the courage to change.

DERRICK JENSEN: Where does technology fit into this? In *Green Rage,* you make clear that we can't pick and choose "good" technology. Solar energy, for example, doesn't happen in a vacuum.

CM: I believe it's naive to think modern technology is simply a tool. Rather, it's a social system that springs from and also yields a particular relationship with the world. Technologies like solar power don't just pop up out of nothing. They require a system of factories, roads, government, currency, schools, and police. If you want fluoride toothpaste, you probably have to take nuclear arms and toxic waste and all the things we are now finding incompatible with the natural world.

I see a real distinction between technology and craft. Technology confronts the world, forces it to do things it wouldn't do naturally. Craft belongs to a humbler, more ancient relationship with nature—going with the flow. The earth gives up clay and fire, and we make ceramic pots from this bounty. The earth and its nonhuman communities aren't diminished or banished by the process of craft. Craft fits human needs into the existing landscape, whereas technology attempts to alter and deny the landscape at an ever accelerating pace with no recognition of nature's limits.

I can imagine an extreme scenario in which we are forced to completely deindustrialize without being able to keep the good things in our culture, like Bogart movies and Mexican food.

But on the other hand, we can try. We can reevaluate what is truly important to us, and I think we'll find the answer will be baseball and jazz and children's birthday cakes. We could try to arrange our affairs to keep important things like these, while putting to rest the crazy industrial monster that is thrashing around destroying life on this planet. But to do so requires vision.

The popular press often conjures up a vision of the future dominated by advanced technology, all running smoothly. I personally find this an unappealing, dehumanized vision, void of spontaneity and freedom. A high-tech society comes with costs we are all becoming painfully aware of. A cost to the integrity of nature. A cost to the integrity of our spiritual life.

On the other hand, a growing number of people have a vision of a natural, re-enchanted world, dominated by wild nature rather than by technological artifacts. And when we talk about wildness, we should consider not only the wildness of nature and the wonderful blossoming and efflorescing of life that goes on around us, but also the wildness Thoreau speaks about in our own lives, the independence, freedom, and deeper emotional participation in life that our overwrought and regimented culture can't tolerate.

We have to realize the same forces that hack up the wilderness, put fences around it, and call this progress also shepherd us down meaningless paths, frustrate our talents, impoverish our internal lives. In a real sense, we're already one of the most constrained societies in the history of the world. Michel Foucault, the French philosopher, called it a carcereal society, that is, a prison society, subject to constant supervision by anonymous managers. In fact, the government probably has more data on me and you and the guy next door than the worst tyranny in history ever accumulated on any of its citizens.

And not only the government. Compared to other modern institutions, the state today pales in its ability to form our knowledge of who we are, to create the imagery and symbols that define us. That power now resides with Coca-Cola and Apple Computer, Inc. The real threat to liberty and the environment now stems from commercial institutions. And there is nothing in the classic liberal thought that gave birth to our Constitution that can handle this danger.

We have to find new ways to protect our disappearing freedoms, because it's not a threat that registers on the radar scope of our Enlightenment philosophy. We have to forge a new trail to free not only nature but also human nature from the stricture of modern supervised society.

DJ: I have a habit of asking people if they like their jobs. About 90 percent say no.

CM: Societies like ours, modern consumer societies, are tremendously effective at controlling the behavior of large populations. How do you get people to do crazy things like drop atomic bombs on cities, or cut down forests, or become a stripper in a night club? We set up a hierarchy where money represents the only index of a person's value and participation in the good things of our culture. Then, through the media, those with capital generate the powerful images that define us. And finally, institutions such as universities produce an endless barrage of knowledge—economic, political, psychological—proclaiming that any understanding outside these confines, such as reverence for nature, doesn't constitute knowledge.

Roland Barthes writes about this. If you can constrain the universe of discourse, make sure that only certain ideas can be discussed, you can effectively control a population's thoughts and actions. In our society, the ways we can relate to each other and to nature have been narrowly defined by a debased economic and political language. The wild, the poetic, the numinous, the irrational are all dismissed as nonknowledge, if not insanity. To say nature speaks to me strikes most people as semipsychotic. And yet most past societies believed just that, that nature was filled with speaking subjects other than humans.

The result of our diminished view of the world is a society of pseudochoices. We don't get to choose how we are going to live our lives, or the images that define us, or how we relate to this vast continent we live on. But we do get a choice of colors for our cars—Do you want a red Miata or a blue Miata?

Barthes's analysis defines the real issue environmentalism must face: Who owns our society's discourse? Right now, it's the media, the universities, the corporations, and other distant institutions with a stake in the domination and diminution of nature.

To appreciate the uncanny effectiveness of how our discourse is manipulated, you merely have to look at our understanding of ethics. We in the West have developed a notion of transcendental ethics—a peculiar idea, really. Transcendental ethics asserts that certain obligations hold true everywhere at all times for all people. This, of course, is a powerful tool for manipulating the behavior of a modern citizenry. For instance, images of patriotism can induce a whole generation of Germans to invade Russia. Or the flattering idea that God gave us dominion over the earth justifies the cutting down of forests, transforming the desire to maximize profits into something moral, if not sublime.

Which is really the point. There are always institutions in the background that have produced—not necessarily on a conscious level—ideas that are to their benefit and that increase their power. And these institutions, whether they are universities, churches, parties, or Coca-Cola, go to the bank at the end of the day.

DJ: In the essay "Nature and Silence" you write that we now interact with writing the way people historically have interacted with nature.

CM: David Abram, a friend and philosopher, observed that we talk about texts as if they were speaking subjects. "The book says . . ." is how we describe a text's contents. The book isn't talking, but we experience it as if it were. His point is that for most cultures throughout history—including our own in preliterate times—the entire world used to speak. Anthropologists call this animism, the most pervasive worldview in human history. Animistic cultures listen to the natural world. For them, birds have something to say. So do worms, wolves, and waterfalls.

And animistic cultures were clearly right. Step outside and listen for yourself. Under the traffic and the noise of the city you'll hear birds and insects and a world humming with unique voices. Not just human voices, but all kinds of speakers.

When texts were invented—a recent invention—our relationship to the world changed in profound ways. Suddenly we began to believe that meaning resided in texts instead of nature, in human words instead of the language of the world. Thus, the animism that once pervaded the world has now collapsed into the narrow realm between the covers of a book.

More and more thinkers are coming to believe that our troubled relationship with nature began with this silencing of the world. As Foucault points out, social power operates through a regime of privileged speakers, from priests to kings to authors, intellectuals, and celebrities. These speakers are taken seriously, as opposed to the discourse of "meaningless" and often silenced speakers, such as women, minorities, children, prisoners, the insane. For human societies, moral consideration seems to fall only within a circle of speakers in communication with one another. So if we heard the trees speak, we might not cut them down.

DJ: Or we would ask permission.

CM: Which is exactly what primal people do. They ask permission before they cut or hunt. There's nothing wrong with cutting down trees or hunting. Let's just do it the right way, which requires that we *listen* to what the ecosystem needs to continue.

To ask permission symbolically acknowledges the needs and intents of the trees. If we could hear trees talk, they might tell us not to clearcut, to use selective cuts only, to respect the forest.

Scientists—at least the best of them, like Michael Soulé, Reed Noss, and other conservation biologists—might say that this listening means attending to the functions of an arboreal ecosystem. This is done through field studies and observations of the complexities of a natural area. I think the science of ecology may reinvigorate our power to listen to nature.

But very few people are listening anymore, because of this strange and almost hallucinatory notion that only humans have anything to say. But the world resounds with speaking subjects, from dugongs to flamingos to quaking aspens, all signifying the complex intents and desires that make up the biosphere.

The idea that only humans have discourse is such a radical and ridiculous notion that it's taken a thousand years of really bad language philosophy to convince us. Nevertheless, birds sit talking to each other, communicating their knowledge and feelings and interests. I can't think of any substantive difference between birdsong and the discourse of linguistics, except perhaps that fowl often make more sense.

A great deal of our ideology, by excluding nature and fixating on human discourse, is hallucinatory. One of the most important things for us to do is get back to our senses, in the palpable sense of responding directly to physical nature. That's why I'm so interested in the Enlightenment. It was when philosophy went off on this curious tangent where moral consideration became the sole possession of "rational beings," that is, eighteenth-century Europeans in white wigs.

You can see the pathologies that sprang from this, from the "dark Satanic mills" of Blake's London to the defoliation of North America. These became possible through a labyrinth of discourse in which human society no longer listened to the real world of nature.

But increasing numbers of writers, activists, philosophers, religious leaders are realizing we can no longer ignore the real world and its intents. And that real world consists of old-growth forests, deserts, and saltwater marshes, not the New York Stock Exchange. The urban landscapes we've created are probably mere specters on the natural landscape. Fleeting. Doomed.

DJ: What about people who say that urban landscapes are natural, since evolution gave us a brain and the brain created paving materials?

CM: We all know the difference between a living forest and a parking lot. One's natural, the other a cultural artifact. In making the distinction, we could foolishly follow traditional philosophy into a vast epistemological thicket. But we should remember that epistemology is just one language, one that grew primarily out of the Enlightenment. It doesn't trump all other languages.

The argument that cutting down forests is somehow natural merely masks the fact that it's a political choice. And choices have histories. Calling a particular history inevitable—"naturalizing history," as Barthes describes it—has been a prime task of philosophy for two thousand years. But after two world wars, Chernobyl, the Exxon *Valdez*, we have no excuse for being so naive. Our environmental problems are a result of a series of choices, many of which have to do with powerful institutions of all kinds: religious and political and economic. Some choices have been stupid. For instance, deforesting the world.

I suggest we simply forget traditional epistemology. As men and women in the world who care about our children and our well-being and our future, we have come to conclude that there's a problem with our relationship with nature. Our culture is overwhelming nature through pollution, habitat destruction, the assault on biodiversity, and simply the spread of ugliness. In this real world, where people sit across kitchen tables and talk, nature makes perfect sense and there is nothing problematical about distinguishing it from culture.

Philosophers such as Julian Simon, who build their whole philosophical agenda, usually an anti-environmental agenda, on the act of confusing epistemological arguments with everyday language, should simply be laughed at by sensible people who want to address a meaningful problem, not a logical puzzle.

DJ: How do you respond to charges of being against "progress"?

CM: Progress is a myth. One of those ideas I mentioned earlier that justify social behavior. A convincing argument can be made, and has been made by people with far more scholarship than I, that in any substantive sense societies don't progress; they merely change. What are the usual things we talk about when we talk about progress?

DJ: Medicine. Leisure.

CM: We hear how people used to suffer terribly from diseases in the past. But we can see through this line of argument. Anthropologists, for example Stanley Diamond, have demonstrated that primal people work less, have healthy diets, don't get run over by BMWs, and don't have their limbs severed in industrial accidents. When hunter-gatherers shifted to agriculture, life span actually decreased, health deteriorated, and infectious diseases ran rampant. Small isolated bands following migrating animal herds is probably the most effective defense against plagues and starvation ever devised.

It's true that fewer people die of tularemia today than in the past. But then, more people die in automobile accidents. Many horrible diseases have been eradicated, but then again "civilized" nations have fought a couple of world wars that exterminated 50 million people. Native Americans, for instance, weren't responsible for that little bit of progress. As to the uncertainties of nuclear holocaust, toxic wastes, ozone depletion, it is the industrial world of progress that has created these sublime anxieties.

I'm not advocating we go back to anything. I only suggest we think clearly and honestly about where we are and who we are. If we do that, progress will become a less seductive concept.

And you have to remember there are multiple realms of activity. If you want to build a physical house, look to the Enlightenment, where people developed empirical methods for improving structures and materials and engineering skills. Don't go to ancient Greek metaphysics.

On the other hand, if you want to build a cultural house, the residence of our values and how we relate to other people and nature, don't go to the Enlightenment. You won't find anything of use in the speculative principles of reason.

So we have progressed greatly in building physical houses. But have we progressed in more fundamental questions about learning to dwell on this planet? The answer has to be no.

DJ: What do you see for the future?

CM: I'm pretty optimistic right now, because I see an awful lot of bright young people on campuses just dying to do something related to the environment. I'm surprised at their enthusiasm, since it's hard not to be utterly self-centered in our post-Reagan cynicism.

In order to act, a person has to believe success is possible, and many young people have that belief. For a variety of reasons, mostly because they haven't had the experience of failure yet. So they'll take on projects that are just crazy. And the funny thing is, the crazy projects often work.

Without a vision nothing is possible. But young people have imagination and vision, and imagination is what will save us. That's all it takes, a vision, even though it seems impossible to attain. The impossible is exactly what's required to solve our environmental problems.

I suppose I have a schizophrenic attitude toward the future. I personally think our society is doomed because of its sheer folly. That's the Old Testament prophet in me. I also firmly believe that everything's going to be all right. That's the Coyote in me.

DAVID ORR

David Orr excels at asking questions. What does the dawning awareness of planetary limits and the interrelatedness of all life have to do with how we define, direct, and transmit knowledge? Barring miracles, how might we think about the transition to a world that is peaceful, just, and sustainable? If, two hundred years from now, we have achieved such a world, how might the transition appear to its historians? What industrial illusions and techno- logical fantasies were jettisoned along the way?

Given his talent for framing questions, it is not surprising that much of David Orr's work addresses the role of education in the transition that hu- manity is just now beginning to face. What will people need to know to live responsibly and well in a finite world? In response to questions such as this, in 1979 Orr cofounded the Meadowcreek Project, a "fifteen-hundred-acre laboratory for the study of environmentally sound means of agriculture, for- estry, renewable energy systems, architectural design, and livelihood."

David Orr is professor and chair of Environmental Studies at Oberlin College. He is also the Education Editor for Conservation Biology *and a member of the editorial advisory board of* Orion. *His books include* Ecolog- ical Literacy: Education and the Transition to a Postmodern World *and* Earth in Mind: Education, Environment, and the Human Prospect.

DAVID ORR: Many people believe that advancement of science and technology will solve all of our ecological problems. Fundamentally, though, the problem is not one of knowledge. It never has been. Even though we don't know all the linkages and mechanisms of nature, we have always known enough to do better than we are now doing.

So why do we act so destructively? Wes Jackson thinks it began with Descartes and Bacon. Others trace it to various technologies. Lynn White once proposed that the origins of our crisis are rooted in Judeo- Christian beginnings. No matter, there *was* a fork in the road where we began to define ourselves as above and beyond the natural world. At that point, which came about more as a long-term tectonic shift than as a historical event, a crisis of faith occurred. We no longer believed that we were participants in nature, but its master.

Many tribal cultures, I am told, didn't have a word for scarcity. But the whole supposition behind technology is that there *is* something profoundly unfriendly and threatening in nature. You simply don't find that in indigenous cultures. That doesn't mean life was always nice and happy, but that it would on balance be satisfying.

DERRICK JENSEN: If technology is founded on the idea that the world is unfriendly, the relationship between love and science will be strained.

DO: This pertains to how we educate people, how we train the minds that go on to develop our technologies and our policies. I've often wondered how many of the courses offered in the typical college curriculum threaten the ecological viability of this planet. How many are trivial? How many are important?

It is often presumed that good thinking is synonymous with science. But science is a subset of that larger category. In this regard there is an important distinction to be drawn between intelligence and cleverness. Intelligence is systemic and long-term. Cleverness tends to be fragmentary and focused on the short-term. The reductionist mind-set is fragmentary and short-term.

Now to your question. Wisdom, knowledge in the broadest sense, is always motivated by love. And love requires the capacity to say no as often as to say yes. It's defined as much by what it doesn't do and will not do as by what it does.

None of this is much talked about in education. That concerns me. We are unable to connect the most powerful human emotion, love, with our most powerful activity, science. That's not a small part of the crisis around us.

This connects with place. When Tom Midgley Jr. invented CFCs (chlorofluorocarbons) in 1930, science advanced. But Midgley was never held accountable for what that knowledge would ultimately do: suppress biotic activity, increase the cancer rate, damage the human immune system, and cause cataracts.

You could repeat that story again and again, at least partly because within this culture knowledge is driven fundamentally by possibility and profitability. No cultures that we consider "primitive" were as careless.

We, on the other hand, have taken knowledge out of the fabric of society and put it in universities, colleges, and schools. We justify this by saying these institutions are developing knowledge and research. But no one is ever asked to explain how their research promotes or retards the human prospect. Instead, the yardsticks we now use to measure knowledge are invariably abstract—for example, human progress and economic growth. The purpose of the environmental movement, and the broad movement for human survival, has got to be to bring these abstractions down to specifics: by which I mean their effects on specific localities.

I grew up in a little town in western Pennsylvania whose Main Street held the vestiges of a repair-reuse-recycle economy, including enterprises like a watch repair store and a shoe repair store. All the stores were locally owned. My mother used to buy vegetables and eggs from local Amish farmers.

Looking back I am struck by two things. One is what a nice place it was. The other is that we were unable to say why it was a nice place, and so were not prepared to defend it. Recently, at a reunion, I asked three of my high-school friends how they thought our education had failed us. Long silence. It was a question they weren't prepared to think about. But the truth is, we had learned only about other places, other things, and abstractions that allowed us to make our way in an industrial world. But, and here's the point, had AMAX decided to open a strip mine outside our town, we would not have been prepared to say why it should not be done.

DJ: How do we educate people to defend a place?

DO: It's not as hard as it might seem. For one thing, by law we have to educate everybody. This means society has access to the young. Presently we're training the young to further industrialize the planet, but there is a growing recognition of the limits to industrialization.

Place-centered education also means building in ways that fit particular places. For example, I led a class last year where we developed what architects call a "program" for an environmental studies center for our campus. During the course students worked with a dozen architects from all over the United States. We were asking whether we could design a building that (1) heats and cools itself with natural energy flows; (2) is built with nontoxic or recycled materials; (3) produces no waste products; (4) invites wildness into the environs; (5) has a positive cash flow. The answer to all of these questions, we discovered, is yes.

Place-centered education also means changes in curriculum. Right now, a student can graduate from college and know all about genetic engineering and nuclear engineering. We teach them these things before we know what places they are loyal to. If longevity is our intent, that's not smart.

We need to cultivate minds before they build nuclear reactors, shopping malls, and freeways. They could instead build bike trails and write poetry. Education could help by making sure that children mature into full adulthood. Indigenous cultures, for instance, did this through rituals, initiation rites, and celebrations, whereby the childish, self-centered phase of life is brought to a close, and the child is given a new identity as an adult, acknowledged by the whole community. At the same time the person is given recognition as a member of the community, they are also brought to a basic level of maturity.

Contrast that with our system. We send people through four years of higher education, but without making them members in a community. It should be no surprise that we end up with many childish adults, but now equipped with high technology. Much of the ecological destruction we see around us is a result of immaturity and the power of our knowledge.

Again, this transformation is related to place, because the way in which indigenous peoples certified adulthood was rooted in place. A child became an adult *in a place*. We don't do that. A person graduates from Harvard or Yale or the Colorado School of Mines with obligations to no place in particular. Their knowledge is mostly abstract, and equally applicable in New York or San Francisco. All too often college graduates are, in Wendell Berry's words, "itinerant professional vandals."

Education ought to allow for bonding to the natural world. E. O. Wilson believes we have an affinity for life, which he calls biophilia. In other words, nature tugs at us. Biophilia is the gravity that pulls us toward nature. We not only live on this planet, but this planet lives in us, in our minds, our imaginations, our dreams, and in our genes. The eruption of industrial-technological societies was in many ways unnatural. We don't feel comfortable with it, and we aren't likely to feel comfortable with it, because we're not wired to be at ease in industrial places. They're too noisy and too dangerous, with too many hard surfaces and too few green places. They're fundamentally alien to much of what has made us human.

As an experiment in place-centered education, I'm going to teach a course on the local watershed: the Black River. You could teach the same kind of course using a seashore, an island, a mountain, or a desert. I want to immerse students in a natural system. Water engages all of our senses. We drink it. Some people are baptized in it. We swim in it, bathe in it, listen to the sound of it. A river is a biological thing, a geological thing, a social thing, a legal artifact defined by laws and regulations, and it has a history. A course on a river acts as a good solvent for compartmentalized knowledge.

Your question of how to educate people to defend a place raises many other questions. What are the tools people need to be effective citizens of a place, in a biotic as well as a political sense? What should they feel? What should they think about? How do you recognize the health of a place? What is a healthy place-centered economy?

The students who come through Oberlin and every other college in the country are going to have to do what we have not done. They will have to control population—we're adding a quarter of a million people to the population of the earth every day. They will have to make a transition from fossil fuels to sunlight. They will have to control toxics, learn how to use energy and materials efficiently and how to use technology with much greater intelligence than we have. They will have to preserve biological diversity and begin healing the damage we have done in the past two hundred years of industrialization.

To equip them to do these things, education will have to change a great deal. It will need to engage the world more closely. For example, using what we know to solve problems: what is now being called "service learning." Imagine if colleges were to allocate just 25 percent of faculty and student time to solving *real* problems: helping to clean up environmental messes, build local economies, and restore place-centered human societies that function within the limits of ecosystems.

It may even be profitable to do this. For example, my students worked on two problems here in Oberlin. The city schools had a deficit last year of about $880,000. At the same time, the town spent about $4.5 million on electricity. If the town were to cut electricity use by using cost-effective technologies now available, it could reduce the total use by as much as $2 million. If the city could recapture some percentage of these savings and apply this to the school deficit, both problems could be reduced. The students got really fired up about this project.

DJ: How could these changes be implemented on a large scale?

DO: This will require a renaissance of citizenship and rethinking our cultural and historical heritage. Europeans came to this continent not for spiritual enlightenment but to get rich. They didn't worry much about how to distribute that wealth. Politicians could always say to the poor, "Your relative share isn't getting bigger, but your absolute share is." This is no longer true. Blue-collar wages have actually retreated since 1973.

Circumstances now suggest to me that we should resuscitate the classical republican ideals of civic virtue, acknowledging that you can't run a good society with selfish and short-sighted people.

This means we have to reckon with the kind of people we've become. We've got a whole culture locked in the first stage of Abraham Maslow's five stages of human development: infantile self-gratification. Advertisers, who spend $120 billion a year to tell us the world is limitless, intend to keep us there. Technologists reinforce the message, telling us they can solve whatever problems come up.

Who is there to tell us that the collective interest and long-term obligations to our children require us to be good citizens, family members, and community members?

This will be tough because we'll have to talk about such things as natural debt. When politicians talk about growth or jobs, they will also have to talk about lost biotic capital. Can you imagine a presidential debate about our debt to the biotic world? How would the candidates handle the fact that if forced to pay full costs, we could not have afforded to industrialize?

That debate can't take place because some of the key concepts are not in the public mind. This again goes back to education. We have to produce an ecologically literate citizenry, capable of discussing ecological issues seriously.

DJ: You've written, "We cannot expect to act with virtue if we cannot think clearly about it or articulate it well."

DO: Alasdair MacIntyre argued in his book, *After Virtue*, that while we've kept the language of virtue, we've lost its substance. The ideas of virtue and the virtuous person are in decline.

Part of the difficulty is that we've accepted a view of ourselves as purely economic creatures. And this *is* a problem, because the bottom line for self-maximizers is nowhere near the bottom line for ecosystems. We're much more complex critters than those portrayed in the model of "economic man." But we've accepted that vision of ourselves at the expense of a full, mature, human identity. We are capable of courage, virtue, and altruism. We can write poetry and prose, tell stories, and we can die for each other. None of these, however, are economically rational.

Even many of the people who argue for and teach neoclassical economics don't think like that in their private lives. They are often good parents and community members, not simply self-maximizers.

The goal of education ought to be to equip people to live well, with faithfulness and love and charity, and to think ecologically.

DJ: A theme that runs through all of this is integrity, in the sense of being integral.

DO: I've always been impressed by the similarities between ecology, as a study of the biophysical linkages of living systems, and the word *religion*, one of the roots of which means to bind together. By being bound to others, a person is drawn out of him- or herself. When that happens, the edge between altruism and self-interest begins to blur. To act in the best interests of children who will be born seven generations from now would be very good for our stature as people, our peace of mind, and our sense of accomplishment. It would be *good* for us as a species to shelter life, to begin to acquire a conception of ourselves as protectors of life. It would, help us mature.

DJ: What binds communities together?

DO: Well, for one thing our common dependence on energy, water, materials, resources, and waste. I've been asking how the organization of those flows retards or promotes both community and individuals. It's clear, for example, that an Amish community organizes those flows differently than other communities. And I'm realizing, too, that one of the underlying conditions of a truly successful community is that it cannot prosper at the expense of other communities.

We're going to have to redefine the word *prosperity*. It's not possible for us to continue in a world radically divided between the very wealthy and the increasingly impoverished. We not only have to redistribute wealth, but we have to count ourselves wealthy in large part by what we hold in common. We are wealthy if our town or neighborhood has a good park, a good school system, a good symphony orchestra, a great softball team, and opportunities for good work.

But I haven't answered your question, which in a lot of ways is *the* question of our time. Industrial civilization destroys communities. For one thing, it's frantic, and community begins to fail when you increase the velocity of people and goods beyond a certain level. I mean velocity in every sense of the word, from cars on freeways to the velocity of information.

We also have to simply reconnect people. Capitalism and technological society have atomized us. We have few obligations, few bonds, lots of cash in our pockets, and lots of time on our hands. That has ecological implications. Atomistic people will be destructive of the earth. They cannot be otherwise. Until we make ourselves homecomers, in real communities, we will be tempted to substitute motion and consumption.

One way to build communities is through stories. Some of those flooded communities along the Mississippi River may find themselves morally strengthened in coming years because they can tell stories about the great flood of 1993, when rich and poor joined shoulder-to-shoulder in the wee hours of the morning, filling sandbags at the levee. We have become impoverished at the story level, and that too has ecological implications. Stories bind us to places because they are about specific people in specific localities. People with a storied past tend to be placed people.

DJ: What's the role of the natural world in these stories?

DO: I remember a cold spring day years ago in the Ozarks, watching my twelve-year-old son and a friend of his jumping into a pond, then coming out and rubbing mud all over themselves. My first response was, "Your mother is going to be upset!" But then I realized they were enacting something primal: bonding with the landscape, literally absorbing the place through their skin.

Much of our sense of a place is somatic. A good farmer will pick up soil in his field and feel the dirt on his hands. And all of us as kids are tree huggers and tree climbers.

I once asked a group of senior environmentalists how they had come to do the work they did. There was a long awkward pause, after which they tried to describe the factors that had influenced them intellectually and rationally. Finally one of them said, "What happened to me was . . ." and proceeded to describe a near-religious and deeply personal experience. It was a story he'd never told publicly, and toward the end of it, tears were coming down his cheeks.

If the earth is something more than inert matter whirling through space, perhaps in some sense alive, how would it communicate that to us? What would our antennae pick up? Is there something that transcends our intellect and our experience?

Some people, perhaps all people, *feel* something beyond what we can say in words. As we evolved on the earth, did we develop some deep resonance with all life? We have a great affinity for life, and the environmental movement is a manifestation of that affinity.

DJ: Gary Snyder has written, "Find your place, dig in, and defend it." Once again, how do you defend your place? What would a place-centered economy look like?

DO: Growing indigenous businesses, it seems to me, is one of the keys. We think of economic development as a way to entice business into our communities. But of course if capital is footloose enough to come to a town, it's footloose enough to leave when it suits it to do so.

There are solutions to that problem. If a business wants to come to an area, and if you're smart, the community sets the terms. If the business refuses to meet the terms, they can go someplace else. A company could be required to post a bond, and if it stays for twenty or twenty-five years, it gets the whole thing back. Or perhaps it has to spawn ten or twenty other locally owned enterprises, so if it leaves, the region still has an economy.

The Canadians, on the other hand, have stumbled on a perfect formula for poverty. Mitsubishi plunked down a billion dollars to build a pulp mill in northern Alberta. This mill will buy up timber in a 100- or 150-mile radius, pulp the lumber, ship it to Japan, and then export finished paper products back to Canada. They'll destroy a culture, an ecosystem, and their economy. It's pretty hard to do all those together, but they've done it.

Why? "Jobs," they say. That four-letter word has caused more destruction in the last twenty-five years than virtually any other thing I can think of. We simply have to think in terms of companies giving something tangible and lasting back to the communities in which they locate.

DJ: A community which includes the natural world.

DO: Industrialization has been a Faustian bargain. We traded off what were often elegant place-centered economies and societies, sufficiency, competence, and beauty. The industrialized world is ugly. No one defends it because it's pretty. In exchange we got mobility, but we also got restlessness. We got consumer products, but we also got huge amounts of junk. We got health care systems, along with modern industrial diseases. The fine print indicates that it has not been a bargain. Now, even though we can't throw it all out and start over, at least we can learn to be intelligent about how to readapt it.

How? I've always liked John Todd's line about "elegant solutions predicated on the uniqueness of place." These sorts of solutions require a different set of skills and a different mind-set. I think of my friend David Kline, an Old Order Amishman who farms one hundred acres with horses. One of my students once asked what he did for fun. He thought a long time, scratched his head, and said, "I farm." He's a happy man, with a sense of self and satisfaction that the modern seldom offers.

Modernization wasn't intended to give us that. It was intended to give us dissatisfaction. Because it can only work as long as people are dissatisfied. Only the person off-balance makes a dependable consumer.

The commercial, industrial, technological society sits like a heavy burden on our shoulders. It has driven out, *systematically*, alternatives that were communal, low-resource-using, ecologically sound, and spiritually rewarding. It's *possible* to still go out and buy forty acres of farmland someplace, but for most people life in industrial society is pretty constrained. That's why the industrial system has worked—it has driven out possibilities while appearing to multiply our "options." I can buy twenty-five kinds of toothpaste at the local supermarket, but I can't easily get to Cleveland, twenty-five miles away, by train or bicycle.

All that said, though, I do have a sense of realistic hope. We are entering an enormously difficult era, but one which at the same time has great potential. Life resonates within us at a much deeper level than materialism.

THOMAS BERRY

Thomas Berry has devoted his life to understanding the dysfunction of the Western story and to telling a new story that brings together the findings of modern science and the human search for meaning. This devotion has led him to become a historian of cultures and a writer with special concern for the foundation of cultures in their relations with the natural world.

Thomas Berry was a director of the graduate program in History of Religions at Fordham University from 1966 until 1979. Founder of the Riverdale Center of Religions Research in Riverdale, New York, he has been its director since its beginning in 1970. He has published a book entitled Buddhism and one entitled The Religions of India. More recently he has written The Dream of the Earth *and (with Brian Swimme)* The Universe Story. *He is currently writing a book on the twentieth century as the terminal phase of the Cenozoic era (the most recent 65 million years in the biological history of the earth) and the twenty-first century as the emergence of a recovery phase of the earth in what might be called the Ecozoic era.*

DERRICK JENSEN: Why is story important?

THOMAS BERRY: Narrative is the basic modality in which the human mind functions. We come to understand things through the sequence of changes that take place and are best presented in story form.

The universe is the great story. That's why peoples generally build their cultures on some story that tells how things came to be in the beginning, how they come to be as they are, and the human role in this story.

We're in difficulty now because the biblical story we live by has become dysfunctional. So we're very confused. And the modern story of the universe that comes from the scientific traditions doesn't carry meaning.

DJ: If that story doesn't carry meaning, our lives . . .

TB: Are meaningless. Nor can the people committed to the biblical story find any meaning. So life is without direction, without meaning, without fulfillment.

DJ: And you're working toward the telling of a new story.

TB: It's a coherent telling of the story of the universe that comes to us through empirical observations, but which the scientists have not dealt with in any significant way. To the scientists, the story is not in itself meaningful; it's mechanistic, an essentially random process going nowhere.

If scientists only understood their own data, they would have a most remarkable story, because the emergent evolutionary process is a truly grand way of experiencing the universe. The difficulty is that it can be understood only if a person has some sense of how the universe functions as articulated entities that have their own spontaneities, their own voices, their own ways of expressing themselves.

The universe is composed of subjects to be communed with, not objects to be exploited. Everything has its own voice. That's why primordial peoples have a deep sense of relatedness to all natural phenomena. Thunder and lightning and stars and planets, flowers, birds, animals, trees—all these have voices, and they constitute a community of existence that's profoundly related.

This community of existence has a celebratory aspect; the sun shines, the flowers bloom, the birds sing, the trees blossom, the fish swim through the sea. And humans respond to the universe with a sense of awe and wonder at the majesty of it all, with entrancement. In the earlier stages of humans this was the great liturgy.

Our primordial spontaneities, which give us a delight in existence and enable us to interact creatively with natural phenomena, are being stifled. Somehow we have become autistic. We don't hear the voices. We are not entranced with the universe, with the natural world. We are entranced instead with domination over the natural world, with bringing about violent transformation. We have for some reason developed the idea that anything in its natural state is wasted, that things are sacralized by use. The truth is exactly the opposite. To use it is to waste it.

Somebody said, "If nothing is sacred, nothing is safe." This has to do with human sensitivity. The forest can only become so many board feet of lumber when a certain part of the human mind goes dead. Humans couldn't kill the forest unless there was something already dead in the human intelligence, the human sensitivity, the human emotions. It's like needlessly burning the great artistic productions of the world.

It's a killing of inner experience. If we lived on the moon, our sense of the divine would reflect the lunar landscape. We wouldn't have any imagination. We would have minimal intellectual development, because there would not be many things to name.

DJ: Many environmentalists have pointed out the shortcomings of the mechanistic worldview that emerged from the Enlightenment. But couldn't Descartes and Bacon have been merely manifesting a pathology that already ran deep within the culture?

TB: Much deeper, absolutely. It runs deep in the biblical world and in the preoccupation with divine-human and interhuman relations at the expense of human-earth relations. The Bible establishes a transcendent personal monotheistic deity creating a world outside himself, in opposition to a prior attitude toward the divine as expressed directly in the natural world.

And it comes from the Greeks. Anthropocentrism is associated with that. So this alienation from the natural world comes from biblical, Christian, Western humanist sources, with the deepest roots of the pathology being anthropocentrism.

DJ: On the way here, someone handed me a religious tract that promised to save me from loving the world.

TB: Christianity was never alienated in theory from the natural world, but in actual practice there was a certain suspicion of it. You followed the law and the prophets—the love of God, the love of neighbor. There's nothing there to indicate a love of existence or a capacity for intimacy with the natural world for its own sake. Not to use it for monetary or even spiritual purposes but to be present to it.

As human beings we become present to each other and meaningful to each other. We complete ourselves in each other. And so with the natural world. Humans are completed in the natural world. We find ourselves there. Become inwardly enriched and fulfilled. That's why we go to the sea coast, to the mountains.

The fact that we have to talk about these things in this way shows we've lost something. The question becomes: How do we get out of this pathological process of self-destruction and destruction of the natural world?

DJ: How did you find your own way free of the cultural entrancement with violent transformation?

TB: I grew up in an undeveloped area of the South, and I saw the beginnings of the automobile age and, to some extent, of industrialization. By the time I was eight or nine years old I already saw something was happening that I didn't like. I decided that to do something about it, I would have to find out what happened to the Western thinking process.

That's why I went to a monastery when I was twenty. For ten years we were up at two in the morning for liturgy, and from three on I studied, with time out for meditation and work sessions and so forth. That continued without a break for about ten years. Then I went to a university from 1943 to 1947, and after that I went to China to teach.

All this has been an effort to understand something about the pathology of the Western mind and how to deal with it. I learned Chinese and Sanskrit so I could find out how the Chinese dealt with things, how the Indians dealt with things, how the Buddhists dealt with things.

DJ: What do you see for the future?

TB: When I was born, in 1914, there were fewer than 2 billion people in the world. Younger people alive today are going to see a population of 8 to 10 billion people. That's just in two lifetimes. When I was born, there were fewer than a million automobiles in the world. By the end of this decade there will be 600 million. I remember the discovery of the Arabian oil fields in the 1930s, and the development of the petrochemical age after the Second World War. The next generation is going to be in a tragic situation, particularly as regards petroleum. Our food depends on petroleum, and in a sense is transformed petroleum, just like energy, our transportation, our clothing, our utensils, our plastics. What are people going to do when the petroleum is gone? It's awesome to see a generation devour and needlessly glut itself on something like petroleum that's a one-time affair. There will never be any more petroleum, on any scale. The planet can't make it anymore.

What the next generation is going to have to face in dealing with all this makes a person think. And my thinking is largely an effort to provide a way in which the next generation can deal with the tragedy, with the ruins of their world. How do you prepare people for this? How do we stop it from happening? And what are the possibilities of taking on a constructive program that would enable the human community to envisage an attainable new mode of fulfillment? How can we respond to the situation creatively?

I talk about an Ecozoic era. The first principle of this new era is to recognize that the universe is a communion of subjects, not a collection of objects. That's the most basic statement a person can make about the universe or the future.

The second idea is that the universe is a single sacred community. There's no way the human can be fulfilled apart from the natural world. The human and nonhuman live or die, are fulfilled or not fulfilled, as a single community. We will go into the future as a single community, or we will both fail in our efforts at fulfillment.

The third principle of the Ecozoic era is that the human is derivative and the planet is primary. Everything human must envisage itself in its derivative status. This means, for example, that the first purpose of medicine is not to serve the human. Instead it must be to take care of the health of the planet, because if the planet is not healthy, humans can't be healthy.

Same with economics. We have the most absurd economics—trying to increase our gross national product while diminishing the gross earth product. It should be totally clear that the first law of economics has to be to preserve the integral economy of the planet. At present the whole of our economics is absurd and terribly vicious.

Politicians talk about getting America back on track, which, if it could happen, would be the worst possible thing. But it's not going to happen. America's never going to be back on track that way. This recession is never going to be over, because it's not a financial recession or a recession of productivity. This is an irreversible recession of the functioning of the planet Earth. As such the human economy will have a few ups and downs, improvements, disimprovements, but it's inevitably a down process until humans begin to see to it that the earth is healed, that the economy of the earth comes back. So long as we try to develop a human economy that doesn't sit well with the earth economy, we'll just progressively extinguish our only hope.

DJ: How can we see to it that the earth is healed?

TB: In the last century particularly we've developed enormous powers, and we have wounded the earth in many of its basic functionings. In the future, there's nothing going to happen that humans will not be involved in. That doesn't mean we can manage things, but it does mean there's no longer true wilderness. Instead there are only patches of semi-wilderness. And we cannot simply withdraw. We cannot make a blade of grass, but there's liable not to be a blade of grass unless we accept it, protect it, defend it, foster it.

While there is a lot we can do, we must not impose something on the natural world. The natural world has to heal and develop itself from within. That's not something we can do, any more than you can cure another person who is ill. We can help, but we can't heal.

DJ: How do we listen to the earth?

TB: The earth's language is not clear in our times, but when I talk to indigenous peoples, that's their language. I spoke to the Ojibwa a couple of years ago, and I didn't know what to say, but I asked the moon and the moon said tell them a story. I said, "What I say here is not important, but what the mountain says is important, and what the rivers say, and what the stars say."

These things speak out of a certain validity and with a certain power and a certain truthfulness humans need. They tell us something of existence, just like the sequence of the seasons deals with the mystery of life and death and renewal.

And the wind bears a certain mystery to it; a person can't see the wind, but the wind whistles and the wind passes through the trees and the wind helps carry the pollen. The birds soar in the winds. The winds awaken us to a sense of spirit, because they carry the sense of the invisible world.

How does the wind speak to us? A biting wind on a winter's day tells the person of harshness and the challenge of existence. It wants to make a person strong. And the softness of a summer breeze tells us of the compassionate dimension of the universe.

People say, "Oh, that's poetic. That's romantic." But it's the most scientific thing there is. If someone says to me, "I don't hear the voice of the wind," I say, "You better learn." The wind can tear your house to pieces, or it can cool you in the evening. One of the most important things about the wind is that it is uncontrollable, and therefore beyond human calculation. It tells us we don't have control even over our own lives. It says, "I know something you don't know, and I have a lot more control over your life and death than you. If I bring the rain, I will allow you to survive with food." The wind tells us a lot of things, if we have the capacity to respond to it, to reflect on it.

DJ: This leads to the idea of connection, of coevolution.

TB: Things constantly shape each other. The child teaches the mother while the mother teaches the child. By the same token, the pond shapes the dragonfly, and the dragonfly shapes the pond. The pond, and the richness of life in the pond, depends on the dragonfly. Something supplies food for the fish in the pond, and at the same time the water is purified by various forces of the gravel and the sand, and the whole symphony comes together. If any element drops out, everything else has to adjust. I couldn't be what I am without everything else being what it is; life is never an isolated process.

The students of Confucius asked him once, after they'd been with him for several years, if he could reduce his teachings to something very simple.

He said, "I can reduce everything to one word. Reciprocity."

If you take, you must give. Nothing is received unless there's a giving. That's where we go wrong. We take from the soil without giving to the soil something it can use integrally. It gives us nourishment, and we give it poisons. We should return to it nourishment, according to its mode.

Everything needs to move in a circle of mutual influences, a giving and a taking. If you break that circle, everything dies.

We put our wastes into the rivers or into smokestacks. We feed them to the winds, and let the winds do what they can with them. That breaks the circle.

DJ: You've written about genetic and cultural coding.

TB: For most life forms the genetic coding is adequate for almost everything a being does. Genetic coding teaches a bird its song, how to build a nest, how to find food. It puts the coloration on the wings, and even forms the wings. With many animals, especially some of the mammals, there is a certain amount of teaching, or acculturation, that is necessary.

Humans are genetically coded in a way that is not articulated adequately except through teaching, acculturation, invention. We have to invent ourselves more than other beings. That's what I call the cultural coding.

We are genetically coded, for instance, to think. We don't have a choice about that. We do have a choice, however, about what we choose to think, how we choose to think, and in general the type of world we choose to construct with our thinking.

The same is true with speaking. We're probably genetically coded to speak, but we invent our language. Through these activities we invent our total cultural processes.

DJ: Where do archetypes fit in?

TB: How does an individual activate the depths of the possibilities within the genetic coding? We still can't invent ourselves unless we have an inborn direction in which to do so. This is provided by archetypal images, as was discovered by Carl Jung.

All these basic symbolizations—the great mother archetype, the mandala archetype, the tree of life, the journey symbol, the centering symbol—help us to organize and direct our psychic world. These are our guides to being a healthy individual.

Unfortunately, although they guide us on our journey of progressive enrichment through childhood, adulthood, and old age, they don't give a person a story of the universe.

In that sense Jung lived in what I call a spatial world of consciousness, where life moves in a pattern of ever renewing seasonal sequence. What I'm dealing with is an emergent irreversible universe—a time-developmental mode of consciousness—where we experience the universe in a sequence of irreversible transformations.

The universe is attaining an expression of itself. This expression has three basic directions—differentiation, interiority, and bonding—that make the universe a universe.

There is differentiation—one thing the universe does not permit is duplication. Every leaf on every tree, and every snowflake, is unique.

There is interiority—everything expresses the deep mystery of existence. Whether it's a particle or whatever, there's that mysterious element of existence and inner spontaneity.

And there is bonding—every least particle is bonded with every other least particle. Everything is integral and interacts with everything else. This means that nothing is itself without everything else. There is a commonality, an integrity, an intimacy of the universe with itself.

And that intimacy, I think, is the fulfillment of the universe, with the intimacy conditioned on the uniqueness of things. Saint Thomas has a wonderful phrase, where he speaks of difference as the perfection of the universe.

Uniqueness in communion with. That's what the universe is about.

DJ: Does the universe then have a purpose?

TB: The purpose is simply existence. And the glory of existence. That's the ultimate purpose of everything—existence and self-delight in existence.

CHARLENE SPRETNAK

While modernity, with its faith in "value-free science" and the power of technology, has in some ways improved material conditions for many people, it has also led to Auschwitz, Hiroshima, and worldwide ecocide. There have been other costs as well—we have lost our connections to ourselves and to our communities, we have lost a perception of our own embeddedness in the rest of the natural world, and we have lost a sense of meaning in our lives. Much of Charlene Spretnak's work is concerned with reawakening in us our "meaningful human participation in the unfolding story of the Earth community and the universe."

Her writing has been central to the framing of Green politics, ecofeminism, and the women's spirituality movement. She is author of Lost Goddesses of Early Greece, Green Politics *(with Fritjof Capra),* The Spiritual Dimension of Green Politics, *and* States of Grace: The Recovery of Meaning in the Postmodern Age, *in which she developed "ecological postmodernism."*

DERRICK JENSEN: What is involved in the experience of grace?

CHARLENE SPRETNAK: "Grace" is what I call the experience of nonduality, the perception of the unitive dimensions of being in the cosmos. Modern cultures regard such experiences—which can either be cultivated through spiritual practice or come at unexpected moments—as "supernatural" and generally deny their existence. I think it's more accurate to call them "ultranatural": it's as if the cosmos suddenly bursts through our mundane level of consciousness and reveals to us another dimension of reality, the unbroken continuity of life. I think this is when we come closest to grasping our participatory relationship to ultimate mystery.

We know the universe lays out before itself trillions of possibilities every microsecond. Certain paths are taken and others not. Why? It's creativity in the cosmos, ultimate mystery, the divine.

Some cultures facilitate access to these experiences of grace, of nonduality, more than others. A traditional Native American elder, for instance, lives much of his or her waking hours in an unbroken awareness

44

of nonduality, the connectedness of all being. The indigenous elder's experience of life is quite distant from our experience as modern Westerners because we are socialized to perceive reality in a dualistic mode. Dualism has been a formative concept of Western philosophy at least since the Pythagoreans. The dualistic split—male/female, public/private, culture/nature, body/mind, and especially the core discontinuity between self and the rest of the world—plagues Western thought, causing layers upon layers of alienation. In addition, patriarchal cultures, including our own, foster the belief that all relationships have a dualistic structure: dominance and submission.

I feel that the changes called for by the crises we face—as well as by the possibility of living in awareness of nonduality—are best realized through a deep and broad understanding of nonviolence. The Gandhian sense of nonviolence as not simply the absence of punching someone in the face or launching a nuclear missile in their direction but, rather, a positive and constructive sense of caring about all being. Violence against other nations, societies, classes, races, ethnic groups, nature, and ourselves can all be seen as a failure to understand the richness of *ahimsa*, nonharming. Nonviolence, as I have come to understand it, means the evoking of the richest possible unfolding of the person, not in an isolated, atomized way, but in relationship to the rest of the natural world around her or him and to the community. This is a difficult concept for us because we live in a situation in which an organic sense of community has come to seem ephemeral. And what's real instead are the artificial constructs of the emerging global oligarchy of transnational corporations, the centralized state, and other constructed systems.

The callousness of the modern condition is so constraining as to make nearly impossible the personal and communal unfolding that would otherwise be conceivable. Hence, awareness of the profound interconnectedness of life and the accompanying sense of nonviolence leads to a subversive consciousness, in the best sense of the word. It opens the possibility of an *ecological* postmodernism.

It is crucial that people attempting to challenge the status quo take the lessons of nonviolence to heart, especially as concerns their fellow activists. Right now, care about *the person* is not central to most agendas, so actual working conditions in social-change movements are not far from what you find in the dominant culture. One hears quite often, "That kind of examination of consciousness, behavior, and organizational structure is too much of a luxury for us right now." Yet, such a dismissive attitude is clearly a counterproductive response because those movements lose people, especially women, in huge numbers. That's a brain- and talent-drain the movements cannot afford.

It wouldn't be a bad idea to begin activist meetings with a simple observation like the following: "We're all gathered in this hall tonight to address a social crisis. Half of us—and there is a general though not precise gender correlation as to which half—have been socialized to be very uncomfortable in somewhat undefined, egalitarian situations. Because of their socialization, these persons will tend to bend any social-change work to feed their psychological need for hierarchy, chains of command, and power or status over other people. Others, through conditioning and experience, find that type of structure preposterous and insulting. It holds people down and is against all the values we're trying to evolve. We need to be aware that the latter group, in general, simply won't work in that way. They'll just leave."

I don't believe, however, that the people insisting on and enforcing hierarchy and dominance are the sole cause of the problems facing social-change movements. There's a larger denial at work: many people marginally involved in these movements seem to view social-change efforts as a dress rehearsal. The level of involvement doesn't match the level of concern.

DJ: That air of unreality extends into the population at large. Last spring I read on page 24 of a newspaper that conservation biologists say we are causing the greatest mass extinction in the history of the world. Page 24. Other newspapers, of course, entirely failed to pick it up.

CS: Thomas Berry says that right next to the stock market report should run the "State of the Earth" report: "The market was up five points today; the Earth was down sixteen points." After all, economism seems to be the point of reference for what is real to most people in modern society.

DJ: Would the perception of grace help people treat social-change work as more than a dress rehearsal?

CS: It may seem unrealistic to base the change that's needed—a deep re-conceptualization of the nature of being—on a chance occurrence of experiencing the unitive dimension of being. That state, however, is not so esoteric and rare. Most young children experience a feeling of un-broken continuity with a special tree or animal. If they are born into a traditional native culture, with an earth-based spirituality, that sense of interconnectedness will be cultivated throughout their lifetime via in-creasingly sophisticated levels of symbolization and ritual communion. If a child is born into a modern Western culture, that awareness will most likely be crushed and denied from kindergarten on. Around that time, children's art usually changes into stick figures, and they learn to stop mentioning their earlier perceptions of unbroken connectedness.

William James wrote in 1903 in *The Varieties of Religious Experience* that moments of experiencing unitive dimensions of being are biologi-cal functions of the human. The body/mind's experiencing of nondual-ity hasn't exactly been a prestigious area of physiological research since then, but in the 1970s the biologist Sir Alister Hardy set up a research program at Oxford to study this type of experience. Using public an-nouncements, he and his staff asked people throughout Britain to send in accounts of spiritual or "mystical" experiences, whether or not they had anything to do with "God." They initially received four thousand accounts, which are reported in *The Spiritual Nature of Man*. Nearly all of the respondents noted that they had never told anyone about their experience. This reflects the modern denigration of spiritual matters, resulting in self-censorship. The reason these experiences *seem* so pre-cious, esoteric, and rare is not because they *are* rare but because the cul-tural denial is so strong.

DJ: Once someone accepts that there are other ways to be, they may still argue that no way is better than any other. What do you say then?

CS: That's the standard deconstructionist line. Deconstructive post-modernism (which is also called constructionism, poststructuralism, or constructivism) presents itself as being a radical break from Western philosophy and the resolution to the problem of the dualism inherent in it. It's very clear, however, that deconstructionism continues some of the most pernicious streams in Western philosophy. Far from being a radical break, it's a continuation of the assumed discontinuity between self and the rest of nature: the disembodied, solipsistic, alienated, and autistic view of the human in the Earth community.

The main critique deconstructionists have of modernity is the oppressive but hidden nature of what they call its "metanarratives," the overarching concepts that were sold to everyone as universal but which, in fact, serve purposes of conformity and control. Analyzing the social construction of concepts is indeed crucial to understanding the dynamics of the status quo—*but* deconstructionists then make the leap to declaring that since concepts are socially constructed, there is *nothing but* social construction in human experience. There is nothing inherent, they insist, to be repressed by one's social conditioning. Rather, conditioning (or "discourses," systems of knowledge and logic) is all there is. They declare, "No body without discourse!"—meaning we cannot know anything about the body except what our social constructions tell us, meaning that the culture into which one is born at a certain time and place determines what is experienced as sexually pleasurable, for example, and how the body is perceived.

This ideology is convoluted. If everything is strictly a social construction, who do they think is doing the constructing? To their "No body without discourse!" I declare, "No discourse without body!" The body is a source of nonlinguistic and noncognitive knowledge—*as well as* conceptual and abstract thought. Most of the latter is structured by metaphors, many of which are based on *bodily experience*, not purely arbitrary social construction. To constrict the modern Western humanistic box even further by insisting that nothing but social constructions matter and even those are merely "language games" (self-referential, closed systems) is to move in the wrong direction. We need to get rid of the solipsistic box of narcissistic humanism altogether by reconnecting with the rest of the Earth community and realizing the profound nature of our embeddedness therein.

Besides being a theory that presents humans as disembodied and disembedded, thus perpetuating the modern belief that we live on top of nature, there are other problems with deconstructionism. It is very patriarchal in its conceptualization of relationship as inherently oppressive, making no distinctions between relationships that *are* oppressive and those that evoke and nurture the unfolding of the person and the deep subjectivity of every entity on the planet.

Michel Foucault, who contributed much to the understanding of the dynamics of power, viewed the body as a battleground into which warring discourses try to put their socially constructed views of reality. He believed that after all such discourses had been exposed, one could then create oneself in autonomy. But, in fact, nothing in this interdependent universe exists in pure autonomy, although that has long been the patriarchal dream in the West. A person who opts for such an atomized view of human existence has detached him- or herself from the grand communion. That is a profoundly alienating state in which to live. Hence it's very troubling that so many young people are taught the extreme relativism of the deconstructionist worldview in universities today and cannot figure out any way out of it.

The path I would like to take beyond the mechanistic, dualistic, anti-nature, anti-spiritual orientation of modernity is a postmodernism that leads not into the nihilism of extreme relativism but, rather, to an ecological postmodernism. Such an orientation would emerge from the sense that our social construction is grounded in the fact that we are embodied organisms embedded in subtle processes of nature.

We exist in profound interrelatedness—in ways we barely apprehend in the West. We now know we are linked at the molecular level to everything in the universe, but there is also an amazingly complex interaction of self-organizing systems and emergent properties, all existing within the cosmological embrace of gravitation. We are affected, often at very subtle levels, by the fact that we are *embodied* and *embedded*. That's an emphasis we need to keep in mind as we dissect social construction. That, along with acknowledging nonduality, is the core of what I call ecological postmodernism.

The more puzzling question for me is not what's wrong with deconstructionism, but why it was embraced by so many hundreds of thousands of intellectuals. Some say it was the power game inside academia, that you had to learn the decon jargon and accept that worldview to get your degree and then to get hired. But it seems there is an emotional correspondence between the "death of the subject" and the "denial of meaning," which are core to deconstructionism, and the highly destructive assaults on the truly grand "subject" in which we once perceived our embeddedness: the Earth community, Gaia. If there was one thing that could be taken for granted before the modern era, it was the "life support systems" of the planet. That is no longer the case. There is something behind the denial of meaning that is deeply linked with the breakdown of our physical context.

DJ: Why would an organism create a society so inimical to its own processes?

CS: Western culture experienced what I would call a fall from grace when it lost the subtle sense of interrelatedness with the rest of the natural world, which traditional members of indigenous cultures have maintained. Once you perceive yourself as cut off from the web of life, all kinds of compensatory systems grow up. The name of the game is to dominate nature. The theme of an influential stream within Renaissance humanism, for instance, was that (male) humans can come into their true nature as terrestrial gods by imposing their will on the natural world. This agonistic orientation toward nature is deeply embedded in modernity. It was a core theme of the Scientific Revolution and, later, of the construction of "reason" as the touchstone of the Enlightenment. I have a clipping from a *New York Times* editorial baldly stating that nuclear-power protesters fail to understand that "human culture develops *in opposition to* nature." This "advanced"—and quite arrogant—thinking would appear completely pathological to a traditional native person. In the context of all cultures that have ever been studied, the intensity of the modern Western break from nature is rare, strange, and highly eccentric. There is no reason to uncritically accept our modern way of being as the "natural" way to relate to the rest of the Earth community.

This is especially true now, at the end of the twentieth century, when we are looking directly at the possibility of ecocide and species suicide. Dr. Rosalie Bertell, who has studied issues of nuclear waste and toxic buildup, says the most likely prognosis for the human species is slow death by poisoning.

DJ: Or perhaps, as you suggested in *States of Grace*, slow death by alienation.

CS: One can make the case that the constraint of our psyche has turned us into the Earth's walking wounded. Brian Swimme says the modern condition—alienation and loneliness—comes from unarticulated rage that we have been so profoundly cut off from the larger reality, the universe, the sacred whole.

DJ: The impact of Reverend Martin Luther King's "I Have a Dream" speech on you seems to apply to this.

CS: I was an adolescent watching the March on Washington on television and hearing his crescendo, "Free at last! Free at last! Thank God almighty, we are free at last!" Suddenly I understood that he wasn't talking "only" about getting African-Americans into colleges, or getting service at lunch counters, or getting to ride in the front of buses. He wanted *all of us* to be *free* of participation in the sin of oppression.

To opt out of caring about others is morally reprehensible. It's a slide into what Gandhi called the great callousness and cruelty of the twentieth century. Not that there hasn't always been cruelty, of course, but today you see it on shocking scales of modern efficiency.

DJ: How can the cosmic processes outlined by Thomas Berry—differentiation, subjectivity, and communion—be used by us as ethical guides?

CS: I believe that Thomas means *differentiation* as the honoring of diversity, *subjectivity* as the unfolding or deep interiority of an entity, and *communion* as the profound interrelatedness of all life in the Earth community. Regarding ethics, one could ask whether a given society is honoring all three processes. Analyzing a fascistic society by using these guidelines, we find that while it might construct a holistic structure (a pseudocommunion) for people, it certainly fails to honor diversity and to cultivate the unfolding of the individual. On the other hand, a culture consisting of 250 million atomized consumers might in some very skewed way pay attention to the (grossly constricted) subjectivity of the person, while utterly failing to cultivate any real sense of communion. In this last case, diversity and subjectivity are manipulated, of course, and constructed to serve the interests of the corporations.

The ecological grounding we need for this kind of analysis could become our salvation because the ecological way of thinking is the holistic way. It is the refusal to deny the interconnectedness that is disallowed by modernity. Modernity—and its hypermodern offspring, deconstructionism—take us far from wisdom.

It's inaccurate to claim that there are no *realities* of interconnectedness that should be acknowledged in thinking about social construction. They ground human existence. Awareness of the subtle implications of embodiment, embeddedness, and nonduality can lead us to a rich and endlessly dynamic participation in "the cosmologic," the great unfolding of the Earth community and the entire universe. Humans can be either oblivious, self-absorbed, and destructive life forms—or aware, attentive, and respectful participants in the cosmos. Aspiring to a depth of awareness of the sacred whole has always been the path to wisdom and grace.

John A. Livingston

As a lifelong naturalist and nature advocate, John A. Livingston has spent his career questioning cultural assumptions. More than twenty years ago he wrote, "Time is fast running out for the dismantling of the institutions which have kept us so grimly locked in step with 'progress,'" and, "While we should be unraveling the threads of tradition, we are weaving ever more elaborate curtains of rationalization. Every avenue of questioning closed off is another route to intellectual and spiritual freedom barricaded forever." Livingston's books, including One Cosmic Instant: A Natural History of Human Arrogance, The Fallacy of Wildlife Conservation, *and* Rogue Primate: An Exploration in Human Domestication, *have been crucial in shaping modern environmental philosophy.*

He is a professor emeritus in the Environmental Studies graduate program at York University, where he taught from 1970 to 1992. He has been president of the Canadian Audubon Society (now Canadian Nature Federation) and of the Federation of Ontario Naturalists. He was the first executive producer of the CBC television series The Nature of Things, *has produced many radio and television documentaries, and is the author of ten books, as well as many articles and reports in both academic and popular journals.*

DERRICK JENSEN: Why preserve wildlife? Is it merely to preserve my nature experience when I visit a national park?

JOHN LIVINGSTON: Wildlife preservation isn't merely preserving my experience. It's preserving my very *being*. The experience is a point of reference from which you can recall and reexperience that which makes you whole—identification with the greater whole, with nature. So when wildlife is not preserved, when it is destroyed, one's being is destroyed along with it.

Those of us who feel the most pain about this destruction seem to have had a childhood identification with nature. I'm a great believer in the idea that Edith Cobb put forward years ago in her book *The Ecology of Imagination in Childhood.* When one reencounters some element of nature to which one was bonded as a child, it's not merely the remembering or recovering of that experience, it's recovering the joy and ineffable beauty of that cross-species leap—one's very being in some bird or toad. So long as the bond gets some modest nourishment along the way, it is lifelong. It doesn't require as much reinforcement as one might think.

DJ: What's the difference between this connection with nature and an intense connection as a child with another human being?

JL: The latter is socializing, bonding on mother, bonding on parents, the group, the extended family. It's species-specific, and it's basic. It's how you know you're a human, or a humpback whale, or a chipmunk, or whatever.

The former is the entertaining of the other, the extraspecies adventure. To bond to nature, you've got to be free of mother, free of that kind of primary dependence. You've got to be ten or eleven years old in the human case, maybe a bit younger. Some say quite a bit younger. Prepubertal, anyway.

Now to have that experience, to bond to a beautiful animal, I have to be open-minded, as a child is open-minded. Open to all kinds of possibilities. Soon enough, alas, kids are conditioned to shut down any possibilities that lie outside the culturally accepted version of reality. As an adult, to open up to those "culturally incorrect" possibilities can be terribly difficult. For a child, it's dead easy.

People are culturally conditioned to fear opening up to the unknown. They've got a plastic shell of received wisdom, belief structures, and ideologies that was created around them.

That's because they have not had the childhood experience of being wide open to all possibilities. Instead, we're taught to be competitive, fiery-eyed achievers. You can't be a fiery-eyed competitive little achiever and open up and accept anything.

We train our children to be a certain way, and it's awfully difficult after a certain age to get back to that point where there's the possibility of accepting something else. If that experience of being wide open has been denied to you, and nature doesn't enter into that welcoming embrace, then it's not going to in the future. There's nothing to recall, to recollect. To reconnect to.

DJ: Early in *The Fallacy of Wildlife Conservation* you say, "In the broadest sense, wildlife preservation is a catastrophic, heart-breaking disaster."

JL: I say that simply on the evidence of what's happened during my lifetime. If you want some quantitative measure, you've got the shrinkage of natural places and the extirpation of populations of plants and animals. We've been going on and on about this since the turn of the century. There have been some successes, but the natural world has shrunk, almost like a time-lapse cinema in front of our very eyes.

And it's speeding up. You need only see a contemporary phenomenon like "sustainable development," the oxymoron of our day, and the way it's so vigorously pushed by governments everywhere both in the first world and third world, to see there is an imperative propelling the juggernaut of destruction.

I have no problem with my corporeal being going down the drain. I have a terrible problem with seeing everything wild and beautiful obliterated. We seem to have no concern whatever for the consequences of our actions, which I believe makes us a sociopathological society.

For the sociopath, the feelings of the person attacked don't exist. It's not that they're irrelevant; they're not even there. That's what I mean about our society, our civilization, being utterly pathological and sociopathological. We say the sociopath is sick and should be put in the hospital, but what do we do with a sociopathological species? There's no hospital to put us in, and no hospice to take care of us. Maybe we just have to be the architects of our own demise. Which we're surely doing. Our self-destruction would seem to be inevitable—even natural, at least on the evidence. The destruction of nature, on the other hand, is not natural or inevitable. In my view, it's evil. But when you postulate evil, then you must also postulate good, because it's a binary concept. If the good simply represents the untrammeled operation of natural events to their own purpose in their own direction and in their own time, then I could accept that, I suppose.

DJ: So would good be defined as "life-serving," or perhaps "life-loving"?

JL: Life-permitting. Just get out of the way and let it happen. Evolution is good and death is good and predation is good and epidemics are good and everything is good so long as it happens without external influence, artificial influence, if you like.

DJ: Does that mean we're artificial?

JL: We're outside the natural system. We have no ecological place, and we have no interspecies social place. We're like sheep and cattle and goats. We are as domesticated as they are. Any sense of either kind of place has been bred out of our domesticated animals by artificial selection and has been lost to us by cultural selection. The destructiveness of our behavior is the same as that of goats on the Galápagos Islands or sheep in Australia. We have moved outside and beyond natural constraints, just as they have.

DJ: Can the connection to other be a means to rid us of our domestication?

JL: So long as the other represents other species, it allows us to be in some considerable measure freer of our ideological straitjacket. In place of our biology (by which I mean our natural sense of ecological belongingness) we have substituted a crutch—ideology. Civilization cripples the mind and cripples the heart by offering a humanistic ideology in place of our evolved naturalness or wildness.

All domesticated animals have this piece missing; all of us are prosthetic beings. The animals depend utterly on us. We depend utterly on ideology. My dogs depend on me and on whatever I offer them. I depend on what ideological crutch my culture offers me. Ideology is my master.

Now, if my crutch is ideology, my way of life is abstraction. And as it turns out, virtually all of that abstraction is technical. Technical abstraction is my whole raison d'être. Storable, retrievable, transmissible technique is the hallmark of our species. It's not just how to kill a chicken or how to change a tire. We also know and transmit how to solve a problem in logic and how to solve a problem in theology. We are indentured to technique.

DJ: As a species or a culture?

JL: As a species. The structure of the human brain, hand-eye coordination, and all that. But it's emphasized by our own particular culture. Of course aboriginal cultures are also about how-to-do-it, whether it's expressed in myth, magic, lovely metaphors, whatever.

The coin of all human cultures is solutions. They just frame and express their questions differently. In our own technoculture, it's raised to a fine art. If the solution doesn't fit the problem, all you have to do is redefine the problem to fit the preferred techno-remedy.

DJ: If reliance on technique is part of our biological heritage, why do we as environmentalists spend so much time talking about it? We have to ask ourselves what exactly it is we're trying to accomplish.

JL: I sometimes ask myself that question too. Our thinking rarely moves beyond mechanistic problem definition, so that technical solutions can be brought to bear. Even when we look at our ethical systems, we rarely back off far enough to escape human chauvinism, expressed in binary logic. Our technical skills are extraordinary; why do we persist in using them in such bizarre ways?

In effect, all we are really doing is rearguard action. The captive breeding in zoos of endangered species, for God's sake. They're not even animals anymore. Incarcerated gene banks. That's the ultimate rearguard action, because most of the time it serves the species nothing. Reintroduction to the wild is impossible, because the habitat is gone.

DJ: Many environmentalists think there will be some sort of cataclysmic change soon and view themselves as simply trying to keep options open. If the grizzly bear hangs on until then, its evolutionary potential is still alive. If not, then the option has been forever foreclosed.

JL: A qualitative change is due. Yes, modern nature protection is trying to offer a few opportunities for nature to survive the human cataclysm, to somehow recover and renew itself. When the cataclysm does come (or has the Dreadful already happened?), without those opportunities there won't be any nucleus for the beautiful and wonderful to resurrect itself.

DJ: How do your students respond to this?

JL: I teach only graduate students. Some of the first-year students are shattered. They've never heard this kind of stuff before. But others say, "Geez, this is what I've been thinking all along and somebody has finally said it."

I used to hedge, many years ago. Now I don't hold anything back. But I just don't know whether that's constructive or not. The young people have to think positively. They have no option. I sometimes think I have no business mucking around with young minds anymore and feel that morally I should withdraw.

So the question we ask ourselves is: Do we have any right to tell the truth as we understand it to be?

DJ: In your essay "The Dilemma of the Deep Ecologist" you suggest that competition may be overrated as a biological force.

JL: It goes back to Darwin and before. The pervading social theory of the mid-Victorian imperial age was progress through struggle, through overcoming the less advanced peoples. We northern Europeans are the heroic expression of the titanic developmental struggles of the past. Darwin simply took the social theory of his day and applied it to natural selection. Every critter that's on earth has won in a competitive struggle.

Darwin didn't need to invoke competition, but he did, and that infected, permeated, all of biological science from that day onward. More's the pity.

No one in his right mind denies natural selection. But the fuel of it doesn't need to be competition. He could have used some other principle. However, he didn't. And here we are with competition and territoriality and social dominance and all the rest of the rubbish we're fed by mechanistic biology and the Sunday supplements. Social dominance in gorillas and whales and wolves and elephants? And anywhere else, for that matter? Come on! I have often wondered how Darwin's argument would have looked had he invoked cooperation, or compliance. Even more persuasive, I would think.

Take, for example, succession to climax. In succession, first there is bare rock, then lichens come, and then grasses, shrubs, and all that. Ecologists such as Eugene Odum actually say it's like two businesses striving—get that word *striving*—for the same goal, competing for space under those conditions. The aspens outcompete the grass, then the spruces outcompete the aspen, and the goddamn hemlock outcompete spruce, and on and on.

Why can't it be said that the lichens prepare the way for the grasses and the grasses prepare . . . and so on. Because that's exactly what they do. Each effectively prepares the soil for the next stage. It's insane to talk about competition there. Not even that they "effectively" prepare, they *do* prepare. I watch it work all the time when I'm out looking at trees and shrubs coming into new places. Don't give me competition!

DJ: Politicians talk in one sentence about "family values," seemingly trying to connote cooperation, love, and acceptance, and then in the next sentence they invoke the need for America to be competitive. That creates a terrific bind. Which way do I turn? What do they want? If we invoke compliance everywhere, there is no bind.

JL: I've loved sports all my life, and what I've loved is the game itself. You'd be horrified if you were to hear how hockey coaches try to build physical aggressiveness into little kids. On the one hand, the youngster is supposed to be playing a game with his friends, trying to do as best he can in the game and enjoying playing it well, while on the other he's being dragooned into behaving like a goon.

DJ: I'm thinking about softball. We agree to rules when we play—even competition involves compliance.

JL: Some of us play into adulthood. And many other animals do too, whether it's eagles or bears or wolves or whatever.

DJ: How about when two bull wapiti fight to breed with a female? Isn't that competition without compliance?

JL: It's ritual. They can't live without it. It looks spectacular because the wapiti have such enormous appendages. Wildebeest do exactly the same thing, but they come and stand with their foreheads together for maybe ten minutes without making a move, then they shake and walk away. Or there's the kongoni, which is a species of hartebeest. Two males get down on their knees, press their horns together, and rest on their knees. That's the ritual fight—double insurance that nobody gets hurt.

DJ: What are they doing?

JL: They're observing an essential ritual. Ritual is absolutely basic and fundamental. In human cultures, ritual is elaborately circumscribed with all manner of formal meaning. Which rather defeats the purpose. Ritual is supposed to be fun, it's supposed to be a social bonding agent, and it's supposed to be good for all concerned.

My wife and I have two dogs, and they have a morning ritual. They stand outside and call for my wife and/or me to go walking with them. When that's done, the ritual need is satisfied, and for the rest of the day they do their own thing. But it's essential to have that reaffirmation of the social bond every morning. Every species has its own ritual observances.

DJ: I've been taught that the point of the "fights" around rutting is to "earn" the right to breed with the females. Perhaps instead the point is the play of the contests themselves. Perhaps the whistling of the wapiti is a call to play.

JL: It is in the evolved nature of wapiti that they reproduce in groups of one male to several or even many females. That is the way it is, and no human judgment on it is possible. I fully believe that the apparent contests (or fights) we see are ritual performances that *must* be carried out before mating can begin. They may well help the herd bull to come into full rutting condition. The males we anthropomorphically like to see as "losers" are just those that are not yet fully developed or are getting a bit over the hill. In either case, they are not "beaten." After the ritual contest, they socially *defer* to the herd bull and shove off. They comply with his imperative. Sometimes, it must be said, somebody gets hurt. Accidents do happen, that's all. But not often.

I think the whistling of the wapiti is sheer exuberance. He is in the prime condition of his life, he feels great, and he lets the mountain valleys know it. Other males hear him and come to ritualize. Females hear him and come to be bred.

DJ: Tell me about territoriality.

JL: This is one of the places where compliance can be very favorably substituted for competition. Meadowlarks, for example, are alleged to be territorial. Song is supposed to be a defense of personal turf and a threat to other males of the same species. The weaker male, in the Darwinian sense, will retreat—a craven loser. You know all that claptrap.

And claptrap it is. It projects upon a bird, of all things, a drive for proprietorship, a drive for competition, a drive for status! I believe that when the neighboring male meadowlark hears the song at the border of the so-called territory, he respects and complies with the prior presence of the singer. He complies also with the personal distance of the singer. In the springtime, the personal distance of a nesting songbird expands to encompass whatever physical area is needed to feed and bring off a brood of young. We all have personal distances. Even among humans there are differences in different cultures. We Anglos (Nordics, whatever) are a bit standoffish and require a lot of room. Others don't appear to mind being cheek by jowl.

After the young have been raised, that extended personal distance diminishes. In the wintertime, when most birds are in flocks, it shrinks back to little more than their actual wingspread.

DJ: So is the meadowlark singing because he enjoys it?

JL: As the bull wapiti is impelled to whistle, the songbird is impelled to sing. In some species, both sexes sing. In that case, it is part of the bonding imperative. Where only males sing, I believe it is celebratory—for the same reason as the wapiti. The bird is celebrating not only his state of physical being, but also his seasonally extended self, his universe, and all that is in it. He's enjoying himself, obviously. And just as obviously, it advertises his availability to passing females and his presence to neighboring males. But even after the pair bond is made and the young have been gotten off, many birds continue to sing through the season. No way to ascribe a "function" to that, the mechanists notwithstanding. The bird just feels good. Some birds sing in the winter, in the snow. There's no "function" to that, either. Presumably they wouldn't do it if they didn't like to do it.

DJ: In *The Fallacy of Wildlife Conservation* you state, "I believe we live in a society of sensory deprivation, with all the bizarre imaging that that implies."

JL: Nowadays most of us live in cities. That means that most of us live in an insulated cell, completely cut off from any kind of sensory information or sensory experience that is not of our own manufacture. Everything we see, hear, taste, smell, touch, is a human artifact. All the sensory information we receive is *fabricated*, and most of it is mediated by machines.

I think the only thing that makes it bearable is the fact that our sensory capacities are so terribly diminished—just as they are in all domesticates—that we no longer know what we're missing. The wild animal is receiving information for all of the senses, from an uncountable number of sources, every moment of its life. We get it from one only—ourselves. It's like doing solitary in an echo chamber.

People doing solitary do strange things. And the common experience of victims of sensory deprivation is hallucination. I believe that our received cultural wisdom, our anthropocentric beliefs and ideologies, can easily be seen as institutionalized hallucinations.

DJ: Think about corporations. The United States Supreme Court has ruled on numerous occasions that corporations have the rights of human beings.

JL: And I guess ships and cities and nations have legal standing also. But not a redwood grove. And by the way, I don't think I want the redwood grove to have rights. Rights are political instruments—legal tools. We hear a lot of talk about "extending" rights to nature. How bloody patronizing! How patriarchal, for that matter. How imperialistic. To extend or bestow or recognize rights in nature would be, in effect, to domesticate all of nature—to subsume it into the human political apparatus. Political organization is a very real kind of domesticated pathology, hierarchically oriented and in utter contradiction to the compliant social behavioral impulses we carry (or maybe used to carry) in our genes.

The only way to deal with rights for nature is to subtract our own perceived right to use any and all aspects of the nonhuman world for any and all purposes, from recreational to industrial.

DJ: More hallucinations: Why does a government do things even when it has to lie to its citizens in order to do them?

JL: To support commerce.

DJ: But the bottom line should be human happiness.

JL: No, the bottom line should be peaceful interspecies and multispecies coexistence. But the bottom line of the human world enterprise is unending commercial growth. Not even jobs. Growth in financial return. That's the kind of belief system in which our so-called leaders have been raised, and it is the worldwide hegemony of modern industrial society—Euro-American style.

DJ: The belief in unending commercial growth is clearly a giant pyramid scheme. It's going to be extremely painful for the individual human beings who are around when the pyramid scheme collapses.

JL: It's going to be painful too for multitudes of individual nonhuman beings. Will there be a cataclysm? I think so. I may live to see it. And things will change. The only way that things will really change is through either total collapse or—just maybe—conscious total rejection and uprooting of the industrial growth ethos. I'm not holding my breath for that one.

DJ: Where does individual responsibility fit into this?

JL: That's very tough. You don't hold the individual European rabbit responsible for what its species, in its hordes, visited upon Australia. Neither can you hold the individual human being responsible for what the human species, in its hordes, is now visiting upon the planet. That would be neither logical nor ethical.

Of course, if you're a captain of industry in the hamburger business and cutting down Amazonian forest to put Brahma cattle in its place, that's different.

DJ: You're not going to allow them to escape personal culpability.

JL: No, and one must not. The cattle baron who is doing that kind of thing on the grand scale is culpable whether he admits appreciation of the environmental consequences or not. I say this because his actions cause wounds that cannot be healed. He has effected qualitative change. But then again, since he is a human being, a domesticated animal with no sense of ecologic or interspecies social place, why should we expect him to behave differently?

DJ: Is it possible for us to reawaken wildness in others?

JL: We would if we could. I only know how on the individual level, with young kids—my grandchildren, let's say—but on a wider basis than that I don't know. Even the school system seems to be impregnable to the kinds of things we're talking about now.

DJ: The root of education is *e-ducere*, which means to lead out or bring forth. Originally it meant "to assist at the birth of a child." School systems, though, seem much more interested in inculcation, which comes from *in-culcare*, "to stamp in with the heel."

JL: Think of how utterly pervasive the word *training* is in education—from kindergarten to graduate school. When did you last hear a politician utter the word *education* in the sense you have just used it? Both politicians and the educational bureaucrats talk almost exclusively about R and D—research and development—and that means *technical training*. That's where the big bucks are. That's where the country has to be, boys and girls, because it's a dog-eat-dog (don't you love that one?) competitive world out there, and without the right training the nation will be *left behind*.

DJ: How do you *not* train the people in your classroom?

JL: I try my best to encourage them to think on their own. I give them what resources I can. My style of teaching has always been to try to nourish the questioning process. I ask them questions, I try to provoke argument, try to get them to ask questions. I bear down hard, always, on problem definition. Are we sure we're asking the right questions?

DJ: Does the feeling of the extended self, lack of self/nature dichotomy, come and go, or do you feel it always?

JL: It comes and goes, depending on the situation. If one is in the right circumstances, then it's there. At other times it takes an effort of will to retrieve it. But I think we may be addressing the wrong side of the self/other split.

What about the concept of "the other"? Maybe that's the problem, not self. I think the self/other dichotomy may be so pernicious because we spend all our time concentrating on self, and we seem to take other as given. If there were no other, we wouldn't need the idea of extended self.

I don't think the coyote sees the bunny rabbit as other. She is what she eats, and before she eats it. No doubt the rabbit sees the coyote similarly—another part of the same being. When I scratch my head, which is "other," my fingers or my pate? Coyote and rabbit similarly. Gazelle and cheetah. Whatever.

DJ: A transformation of parts of self.

JL: Parts of a greater unit. Transforming, interacting, always toward new forms or levels of integration. Each death is the beginning of a new miraculous process of transformation. Always within the greater whole. So that butterfly is me. I *am* that frog.

DJ: What do you say to somebody who has three kids and says, "Don't bother me about a frog. I'm trying to get food on the table. We're in a recession, haven't you heard?"

JL: Well, that's the terrible downward spiral that we're into. That's why it will take some sort of cataclysmic event to break the cycle. If all the guy knows is what he knows, how do you expect the children to do any better?

DJ: What about overpopulation?

JL: It seems to be politically incorrect to talk about human overpopulation these days. I wonder why. I fear sheer human numbers more than I fear anything else. We haven't begun to see even a glimpse of its real potential yet. Now, there's your cataclysm.

There is something fundamentally *wrong* in a single species among millions locking up within its living, breathing biomass such a shockingly disproportionate share of the world's available nutrition and breeding so wantonly as to literally remove any ecologic potential for other species' recovery in the future.

We don't tend to notice human population pressure until there is social and political upheaval. But by the time that happens, the human support base has already been grievously eroded. And with it have gone those other members of the greater natural community that at one time peacefully coexisted there. Their places, and spaces, have been arrogated to anointed human imperialism. Nature preservation has fallen on pretty hard times.

DJ: What did you mean in *The Fallacy of Wildlife Conservation* when you wrote, "There is no reason for you to become a wildlife preservationist except for your entirely selfish individual experience"?

JL: If you can recall, or retrieve, awareness of your membership and participation in the greater life experience, then you can get rid of the twin millstones of self and other. When you have that broadening, widening, deepening experience, you're no longer alone. I think the human species, for all of its achievements, all of its abstraction and intellectualization, is the loneliest species on the block.

DJ: And you wrote, "Rationalization substitutes for qualitative experience. Once the experience has been incorporated into one's self, there is no need for either rationalization or proselytization. There is no reason for wildlife preservation. It is a state of being."

JL: I can't argue the case for nonhuman nature to you logically, or rationally, or clinically. But if you share my experience, I don't have to say anything.

DJ: Finally, you say, "The nature experience is entirely qualitative, not measurable, not rational."

JL: No peak experience is rational, or quantitative, or amenable to reductive fragmentation. I can't tell you why some piece of music has a particular effect on me, or some other work of art. There's a painting of

Saint Jerome, by El Greco, hanging over a mantelpiece in the Frick Collection. It gives me goose bumps. I don't know why. I get the same feeling when I hear the very first frogs calling from the icemelt in the spring. It's "My God—it's here. It's real."

DJ: Does the word *love* apply?

JL: I don't know. Does love require "other"? It's a feeling of elation, euphoria. Simple complete pleasure.

Lots of simple pleasures. The dogs' daily ritual is pleasurable to them, and they insist on having it. And it's pleasurable to me. It makes our day. "May I have the pleasure of your company?" That's what it is. That's what nature is, and what the selfless nature experience is. Belonging.

Matthew Fox

Called a "Green Prophet" by the archbishop of Canterbury, Matthew Fox is considered the "father of Creation Spirituality." His work has attempted to rescue Christianity from the destructive tendencies which now surround it. Matthew Fox brings back to Christianity the love, compassion, and political activism that gave the religion its energy in its early days.

Matthew Fox is founding director of the Institute in Culture and Creation Spirituality at Holy Names College in Oakland, California, where he teaches. The school is seen by many theologians as one of the most forward looking in the United States. In Fox's words, "It is a wisdom school where we are reinventing a transformed model of education, one that is committed to the personal and cultural transformation that occurs when people become awakened to spirituality. Our primary purpose of knowledge is compassion, which is understood as celebration and justice-making."

Matthew Fox has authored fifteen books, including A Spirituality Named Compassion, Original Blessing: A Primer in Creation Spirituality, The Coming of the Cosmic Christ, *and* The Reinvention of Work: A New Vision of Livelihood for Our Time.

DERRICK JENSEN: At the beginning of *The Coming of the Cosmic Christ*, you quote Albert Einstein as saying the most important question a person can ask in life is, "Is the universe a friendly place or not?"

MATTHEW FOX: Einstein's has always been an important question, and it was *the* question in the first century, when Christianity started. Believing angels are invisible forces that move the planet and move our psyches, the early Christians put it, "Are the angels friends or foes?" The tradition of the Cosmic Christ answered by saying that since Christ has power over the angels, the universe is benign no matter what the angels are doing.

However, as Thomas Aquinas points out, the lion eats the lamb, which lets you know there's a price to pay for being in the universe. Death is always there, especially for a species like ours that thinks about the future and worries about it. That's what makes every day so invigorating and such a miracle.

"Is the universe a friendly place or not?" Notice what a cosmological question that is. In all my years of education, no one ever asked that question. The universe hardly came into my education at all.

That's a result of this awful anthropocentrism our Western culture has burdened us with. It shows in education and religion, and it shows in the sadness of our souls, the cosmological loneliness.

I met an Australian who'd been lecturing in Ghana, I think it was, where they'd translated his talks. At one point he had said, "The number one spiritual problem in Sydney is loneliness." The translator stopped and said, "Repeat that." So he did. The translator thought for a while, and finally said, "I'm sorry, sir. There is no word for loneliness in our language."

That's stunning for Westerners. Loneliness is like food and drink for us, and I think the key is our lack of cosmology.

We have to recover that cosmic sense. Nation-states are not our home. Our home is the universe. And the universe is not just space. It's also time. Not only was the universe one trillion galaxies big before we humans came, but it was 18 billion years old, too. That's why we can't take any of it for granted, and why we shouldn't even take ourselves for granted.

Meister Eckhart says if the only prayer you say in your life is thank you, that would suffice. And Aquinas says the essence of religion is gratitude. How do we teach gratitude? What do you do with your gratitude? That's part of the mystical impulse. Our whole being, our existence, is a miracle.

I don't mean a miracle in the Newtonian sense. During the Newtonian era a miracle consisted of divine meddling into the universe's machinery, an interruption of the absolute mathematical laws of the universe. But in a creation theology, a miracle is not about interfering with nature's laws. It's the opposite. It's about realizing that nature's laws, or what Rupert Sheldrake calls habits, are miracles. What brought about our being here after 18 billion years of total drama is a miracle. And so existence itself is a miracle. All of us have a right to be grateful to be here.

Authentic self-love comes from the realization that the universe has made a lot of sacrifices and decisions along the way to bring us here.

There's this tremendous experiment called humanity going on in the universe. It's wild—pouring divine energy into this animal, offering it as much freedom, as many options as we have, and then standing back and saying, "What's going to happen?" It's awesome, and we're right at the brink of its being a total failure, because the way we're going obviously is going to kill us *and* most other life as we know it on the planet.

What we're doing is really embarrassing. It's embarrassing to us and it's embarrassing to the universe. I think the universe on most days regrets our coming.

Especially if you look at it anthropologically. Our species could have developed in very different ways. We could still be swinging from trees and be happier.

DJ: Or even as *Homo sapiens* we could still be connected to the earth. You quote Wendell Berry as saying, "Perhaps the greatest disaster of human history is one that happened to or within religion: that is, the conceptual division between the holy and the world, the excerpting of the Creator from the creation."

MF: Religion in the West has fallen into theism, just as science has. Theism is the belief that we're here and God's out there someplace. It's a very Newtonian idea, that God is behind the universe with an oilcan. And of course the next step after theism is atheism. It's very easy to reject a God who's way out in the sky. I don't know any other civilization that has invented atheism except the West. The word does not exist in indigenous languages. The spirit exists.

What I'm about theologically is the replacement of theism with panentheism, which is the idea that we're in God and God is in us. And by "we" I don't mean just humans, but all beings. The image I have is that the universe is the divine womb. We're all in here swimming together. It's an image of interconnectivity.

And it's a mystical image. By that I mean it isn't something conceptual; it's something experiential. People experience the divine in their lives. They always have.

The divine is not separate from anything in nature. Aquinas talked in the thirteenth century about the immanence of God in all beings. The mystery of existence, the goodness, the beauty—all of that is divine imagery, divine footsteps.

Last year in Seattle I saw a Native American teacher of mine, Buck Ghosthorse. He gets a lot of invitations to talk at public high schools, but he says there's one problem. He's told that in these schools he's not supposed to use the word *spirit*, because of the separation of church and state.

This is crazy, the idea that we can have a whole civilization that, misreading its own constitution, tells people they can't use the word *spirit* in front of young adults. We wonder why there's violence among the youth, and why there's a lot of teenage pregnancy.

No other civilization tells its young people not to use *spirit*. It's just the opposite: most civilizations have ways, practices, by which young people *experience spirit*. That's what sweat lodges are about, and sun dances, and the trance experiences that ancient peoples took for granted as necessary parts of human development.

We're part of something much bigger than ourselves. If we don't learn that, we're set up for greed, which is an effort to experience something bigger than ourselves. So are drugs, and so is alcohol. All addiction is.

If we can't do it in healthy ways—rites of passage, rituals—then the human species will find unhealthy ways, and that's what is happening.

DJ: Which ties in to the loneliness.

MF: A lot of drinking, drugs, shopping, and a lot of sex, is a covering up of the pain of loneliness.

DJ: The term *mysticism* is often used in a pejorative sense in our culture.

MF: Our cosmology has made us anti-mystical. In a machine universe— which for the last two hundred years we've been told we live in—there's no room for the mystic. You don't want mystics fouling up the machine. There's no room for artists, and there's not a lot of room for children. So the mystics have been hiding in closets for centuries.

But now all this is shifting. This is a sign of the end of the machine era.

Mysticism, etymologically, means to enter the mystery. And I maintain that the best, most profound mystical literature today is coming out of science. The new creation story is that everything—each of us—is mystery. What we're finding is that the smallest part of the atom is mystery. It's dancing. And then of course the macrocosm is a mystery.

In the previous scientific worldview, mystery was "just what we don't know yet. We'll solve it." It's not that way. Death is not something you solve. Love is not something you solve. A broken heart is not something you solve. It's something you experience.

It's Moses on the mountain. Moses had his experience with the burning bush. We're learning that every bush is a burning bush, burning with photons and photosynthesis and this amazing cosmic process that was invented a few billion years ago, a process that goes back to the original fireball.

Mysticism is awe. And I think any human being who's lost awe is really a lost person. A civilization that's lost awe, an educational system that can't teach awe and nurture it, a worship system that is devoid of awe because it is so full of human verbosity, is perverse. These systems are doing the opposite of what we have to do, which is to awaken the heart.

Mysticism is about heart-knowledge, heart-experience. It's a wonderful balance, a marriage between the left brain and the right. A brain researcher told me his twenty-one years of work on the right brain showed that our right brain is all about awe. So let's put our awe together with knowledge, and we're going to get some wisdom.

Currently we're running entirely on knowledge, and that's why we're running out of energy, money, time, land, beauty.

DJ: The denigration of mysticism relates to Einstein's question. If you feel the universe is unfriendly, it won't be possible to feel awe.

MF: Awe is a kind of terror. If you see the universe as unfriendly, that terror is converted into paranoia. That's what you have in fundamentalism and in fascism. Fundamentalism and fascist politics are the same thing. They're about fear and about scapegoating others.

But if the universe is friendly, that terror is contained within the boundaries of love and beauty. Because beauty also is about terror. That's why it awakens us. Rilke has this great line about how beauty "serenely disdains to destroy us."

In the presence of real beauty, we feel we're going to be destroyed. But it serenely disdains. Why? Because it loves us. There's that benignity that Rilke senses in the universe. That friendliness.

But if we don't have a cosmology, that cosmic fear turns over in our psyches into rancid political consciousness, into sentimentalism, and into violence, until the only ways you can mirror our culture are through things like professional football or wars. Those models won't do for survival, much less quality living. They lack the celebrative dimension of compassion.

And compassion itself has been sentimentalized. Webster's dictionary says the idea that compassion is a relationship between equals is obsolete. Compassion in the English language today means dropping crumbs from the table. It means pity.

That's not what it means traditionally, or in the Bible, or theologically. Both Eckhart and Aquinas say compassion means justice.

Compassion is about interdependence. That's why it's such an appropriate virtue for our new cosmology, because if there's any new habit of the universe that scientists agree on today it's interdependence. And how you translate interdependence into human behavior is compassion.

Compassion is about acting interdependently at two levels. One is regarding celebration. If we're interdependent in a beautiful and joyous universe, we can celebrate together.

Compassion is also about justice-making, because injustice is the rupture of relationships—the attempt to deny interdependence. And I'm not talking just about human relationships, but our relationships with the forests and the soil, the water and the air, the other animals and our children and the children to come, the future. All this is about interdependence.

So to be compassionate is an appropriate response to that reality of interdependence. And the two basic responses—celebration and justice-making—are the bottom line in all healing.

The word *justice* has also been anthropocentrized in the West. Justice is not a human moral category so much as a cosmic habit. It's that quest for homeostasis, for balance. We have it in our bodies. The body's wisdom, like the universe's wisdom, is a quest for balance. The ecosystem seeks balance, and therefore justice.

Children have justice inside. Just as we have a heart and lungs that work, we also have justice. And psyches have a quest for justice. That's where dreams come from. Many of our dreams when we're going through a crisis, not just individually but as a people, come to bring back the forgotten side of our psyche, personally or collectively.

This sense of justice can be destroyed, beaten out, and forgotten through bad education, but it's there. So justice is not this thing we get from Kant about a duty that humans have to perform. It's about joining the procession. It's joining the ongoing habits of the universe.

DJ: The different concepts of justice seem to spring from differing concepts of where and what God is.

MF: If God is up at the top, then God is wielding justice on people like a big judge, and compassion has to mediate and interfere. But if divinity is everywhere, including with the poor, you don't need all this mediation.

That is a very important image, because when people are in power they like to wield justice from above, make the laws, make people enforce the laws, and so on. It's a whole systematic co-optation of the real meaning of justice.

DJ: And it seems that much of religion has bought into that. You have written that Christianity has been a religion of empires.

MF: In the fourth century, the Roman Empire was collapsing and the Western church in Rome picked it up. Saint Augustine, who became the most influential Western theologian, lived at that time. One of his major works was called *City of God*, and it really set up a theology for running the empire.

We're still dealing with the wounds inflicted by Augustine's work. His theology is dualistic, and it's big on heaven and life after death instead of this life. Augustine was very patriarchal, sexist, and very much out of touch with his body. So sexuality got very badly treated in that context. There's a line from the ascetic philosopher Philo in the first century that is very revelatory. He said we must keep down our passions just as we keep down the lower classes.

DJ: Why is the dominant culture so afraid of the body? And so afraid of ecstasy? Why is this culture, as Erich Fromm asked, necrophiliac instead of biophiliac?

MF: That was Wendell Berry's point. You treat the body the way you treat the earth and the way you treat animals. Part of it is this theology that says heaven and God are out there somewhere. Patriarchy's number one problem is dualism. Separation—body from soul, spirit from matter, and nature from grace.

There are political reasons to keep people out of touch with their bodies. If people are out of touch with their bodies, with their own experience, empire builders can offer substitutes like consumer goods and military victories. Being out of touch with the body also means being out of touch with the *moral outrage* that we feel in the gut, where compassion is born.

DJ: But the oppressors are just as victimized as the oppressed.

MF: In some ways more and in some ways less. More oppressed because they remain stupid. They don't even know how unhappy they are. And less because in this life you might say they come out better. The way it's going now, with the ecological crisis, there's no winner.

DJ: Rollo May traced the evolution of Eros from early Greece, when Eros was the creator of the world, to later Greece, when Eros was a chubby little kid who never developed and ran around causing problems.

MF: We've devalued Eros, and we've divorced sexuality from cosmology in the West. We haven't taught the mystical dimension to sexuality. Instead we've made it just a moral issue.

Also, it's patriarchy. A big part of feminism is the celebration of eros as something positive. The Goddess religions clearly do that, within the context of the joy and ecstasy of creativity. Of course that's where sexuality belongs.

And I would come back to the idea of sexuality as playing in the universe. Sexuality as a mystical experience.

Sexuality is part of the creative invention of the universe. It upped the ante on evolution because it so shakes up DNA that all kinds of novelty is possible. So it's right at the heart of the creative. And of course it's also about creative relationships and children, all those things.

A society that devalues creativity, doesn't see creativity as part of the spiritual process, will always devalue sexuality. And misunderstand it. And a society that reduces sexuality to a strictly moral issue then runs from it, is without energy.

As Lester Brown says, the number one issue in the environmental revolution is inertia. What's the opposite of inertia? Zeal. Aquinas says zeal comes from the experience of the intense lovability of things. And of intense beauty.

I think frankly that our species is pansexual. I don't think we're heterosexual or homosexual or bisexual. You can have sexual experiences walking on the earth. But without a cosmology, without permission to be mystical with nature, we don't realize the whole matrix for our sexual being. Until we recover that, the environmental revolution is not going to go anyplace. It's going to be about duty and not about pleasure. And pleasure, or delight, is how you change people the most radically.

DJ: In the absence of a living cosmology, don't most people live lives, as Thoreau wrote, of quiet desperation? How do we reawaken pleasure in people?

MF: I would add that in our time not all desperation is quiet. There's a lot of loud despairing going on. The L.A. riots are an example. There are many examples, especially among the young. The young are screaming all over this planet.

The way you combat despair is with hope and joy and empowerment. First of all we need to redefine the idea of work, so the work that needs doing gets done. Also, we need to honor every person as a worker, because everyone has something to offer. We need everybody's work. Look around and see how much we need everybody's work.

And everybody needs work of some kind, because without it there is despair, self-hatred, and violence. Work is the way we give our blessing back to the community.

But we also need spiritual practices and ritual, because authentic work has to come from the inside out. You recover delight in life through the self-empowerment that comes through creativity, through art as meditation. And through ritual experiences, with which you can rediscover your child inside and that child's relationship to the universe and to a place. And through ritual we can nurture and heal this child.

I've read Al Gore's story about how he got soul. It was when he saw his son almost die in an auto accident. He felt a connection between his son's near-death and the fate of the earth. He was in his mid-forties at the time.

On the other hand, Tom Hayden got soul when he was nineteen and he fell in love. He followed his girlfriend to Texas, and lo and behold, the civil rights movement was happening. The whole world opened up, and Hayden got arrested twenty-two times.

So there are two ways to get soul. One is to have a broken heart, and the other is to fall in love. And they often go together.

We have to pay attention to both. Too much of our leftist ideology in this country wants to zero in on the suffering. Celebration is very important. Celebration—especially in a capitalist culture—is very radical, because capitalism by definition puts off pleasure. By "pleasure" I don't mean the goodies we buy. I mean *the art of savoring* being itself, relationship, health, color, sound—what is. Holy is-ness. Eckhart says "is-ness is God." We derive pleasure from all this—great delight—or at least we ought to.

So awakening eros, awakening celebration, is a very practical and necessary thing to do. And with the awakening of eros comes an increase in vulnerability. When you fall in love you're more conscious of death, because you don't want to lose your beloved.

DJ: Can art help to reawaken eros?

MF: Art is the only language we have for awe. I gave a talk at the Chicago Art Institute two weeks ago. It was a wonderful experience. I said three things to the artists. First, I said, Thank you. Second, I said, Welcome back, because you've been banished during the Newtonian era. Then third, I said, What you're here to do is teach us to behold being, to go into grief, and show us the intrinsic power of creativity. Art is not for art's sake, it's for creativity's sake, which is for evolution's sake.

DJ: What's your story? How did you get here?

MF: I had polio when I was twelve or thirteen. I lost my legs and doctors couldn't tell me if I'd ever walk again.

When I got my legs back, which surprised a lot of people, I was filled with gratitude to the universe, and I said to myself, I'm not going to take my legs for granted again.

The experience with polio was a kind of rite of passage. I really left my father at that time, as well as the archetypes of my culture in the fifties that said to grow up male you've got to be a football player.

And then reading Tolstoy's *War and Peace* when I was a junior in high school blew my soul wide open. Artists. Shakespeare. Beethoven. And experiences of nature. I felt my soul growing.

So I joined the Dominicans, because I was having spiritual experiences. I wanted to pursue this more.

Then of course the whole political thing blew wide open in the sixties, during my studies, with civil rights and Vietnam. So there they were, mysticism and justice. I asked, how do you bring these two together, or do you?

All my writings contain the question, "How do we relate the mystical and the justice-making, the mystical and the prophetic?"

I went to France, and when I came back, I taught at a women's college. Hearing women's stories, my feminism really took hold. In the seventies it was the gay and lesbian thing, and now of course the ecological thing has become important. It's really staring us in the face. And it's even bigger, because unlike other justice issues you can't do ecology without an aesthetic, without a sense of beauty. It's beauty, and being in love with forests, and with healthy soil, and healthy food, and healthy bodies that's going to give us the imagination and the courage to do something about it.

When you're in love, imagination works overtime. People who are in love find ways to find each other. That's another lesson from the universe. We have to fall in love. And we have to de-anthropocentrize this thing about falling in love, which our culture reduces to soap operas and finding a mate. We have to realize you fall in love with creation.

There's so much that's practical that comes out of healthy spiritual practice. Part of the bad rap mysticism has received during the Newtonian era is that it's ego-tripping or navel-gazing or something, but as Carl Jung says, "It's to the mystics we owe what is best in humanity."

We've all got a mystic inside, yearning to play in the universe. And that play is eros, it's erotic. Once we get that energy going, we'll have the political imagination and the moral imagination to change our ways. We'll have the *courage* (from two French words for a "large heart") to let go of lifestyles and attitudes that are contrary to our dreams for future generations on this planet.

And it's already happening. People committing their lives to something. That kind of commitment comes out of a love experience. And it's happening to a lot of people today. This little thing about Cupid shooting an arrow is very trivial compared to what's really happening to our hearts.

DAVID EHRENFELD

In The Arrogance of Humanism, *one of the most important books written in the past twenty years, David Ehrenfeld dismantles the fundamental assumptions of humanism: all problems are soluble by people, using either technology or social sciences; resources are either infinite or have infinite substitutes; human civilization will survive. He makes clear the costs of these assumptions, and points the way beyond humanism toward the human qualities we have forgotten in our quest for knowledge and power: simple pleasure, the abjuration of power, the capacity to acknowledge and cope with death, the capacity to love, and the capacity to stand alone. In his most recent book,* Beginning Again: People and Nature in the New Millennium, *David Ehrenfeld continues his exploration of the relationship between nature, society, and technology, offering many concrete suggestions for ways to build a sustainable life for ourselves in the new millennium.*

David Ehrenfeld, who holds degrees in history, medicine, and zoology, is a professor of biology at Rutgers University. He is also the author of Conserving Life on Earth. *In addition, he was the founding editor of the journal* Conservation Biology *and is a regular columnist for the quarterly magazine* Orion.

DAVID EHRENFELD: It's pretty clear that we have transferred to science and technology a lot of the mystical attributes people used to assign to supernatural forces such as God or the gods. And nobody is anxious to give up belief in a deity, even if it happens to be a false god.

Our false new god is the idea that we can order the future. It's a secular messianic view of a world in which there isn't any death, any sickness, any stupidity, a world we will have totally ordered by the force of our own intellect and technology.

Part of the problem is that this view keeps getting reinforced. Think of the false prophets who confronted Elijah, dancing around an altar and asking their false gods to supply them with fire. They danced around for hours, cut themselves, and did everything necessary, but of course no fire came down.

Unfortunately the false gods of technology occasionally strike a fire here and there. Minor miracles keep the myth going. We *can* do amazing things. I probably would be dead if it weren't for antibiotics. Maybe you would be, too. We have CAT scans. We have magnetic resonance imaging, which with very little invasive energy lets us see what's going on inside the body. These are miraculous kinds of things. We have computers that can perform inane operations at enormous speed, rather than our just doing them slowly as we had to in the past. They can even perform subtle, complicated, and not so inane tasks very quickly. We have things that buzz and whir and flash, and fire gets kindled when we press buttons. Many of these things *do* work, after a fashion. So the myth keeps getting reinforced.

The assumption is then made—a patently absurd assumption that has not the slightest shred of evidence in its favor—that because we can perform these minor miracles, we can perform major miracles. We assume that we can order our own destiny, make sense of our entire world, control nature, all of which we manifestly have not done and cannot do.

I think the computer is the best example. We've heard so much about the information revolution, artificial intelligence, the future of massive supercomputers, and so forth that we forget that computers can only do the things we give them to do, very fast. There's not the slightest evidence we can make the leap from doing things fast, as in the case of computers, to *really* understanding what's going to happen next on the basis of information we supply now. Nor do we know what to do to obtain desired results in manipulating our environment, which includes nature and ourselves.

Let's take the case of another area of strong belief—genetic engineering and molecular biology. There are many manipulations that can be done. We can move genes from one organism to another, often from organisms that are grossly dissimilar, simply because the genetic code is read in a similar way by the cellular mechanisms of different kinds of creatures. Because we can move genes around, does that mean we know what they will do? Do we know how they will act when they are in an alien genetic environment? Do we know what they will mean? Can we make superorganisms? Do we have the faintest clue as to how a set of genes might help regulate behavior? Altruism? Aggressiveness? Intelligence, in any of its many definitions? No, we don't. Is there any indication any of this is going to be discovered? No, there isn't.

I used to have a picture of the super-pig that was produced at Beltsville. They put genes for growth hormones from cows into it, I believe. The pig was propped against a fence. It was winter. You could see what looked like wire, and there was an arch over a gate, all looking very bleak. There was a man, a scientist, presumably, in an overcoat, standing next to this pitiful-looking creature that had swollen joints and couldn't walk. The pig was larger than it should have been, which is something. But the scene was so much like a scene out of hell that I penciled in on the picture the words *Arbeit Macht Frei*, which were the words written over the gate at Auschwitz—Work makes you free.

DERRICK JENSEN: You're suggesting limits to knowledge. I have a friend who went to an artificial intelligence conference and said the theme was that we don't quite know how the brain works yet.

DE: They always say *yet*. The assumption that, given the present evidence of neurological function, neurological organization, and neurological capability, we will be able to understand the brain in its totality is a view that has absolutely no support. The assumption that we will probably never be able to understand the brain in anything like its totality is, I think, a scientifically plausible view.

Even though scientific knowledge has increased vastly in the past, all the evidence we have indicates that we will never understand the human mind, we will never understand ecosystems, we will never totally understand physiological functioning of any reasonably complex organism, maybe any organism, we will never be able to totally manage environments, and certainly we will never be able to predict what happens.

DJ: What's the harm in trying?

DE: The harm in trying is that we waste time when we could be learning to cope with the horrendous problems that now face humanity; we dehumanize ourselves, because any kind of a life based on a lie ultimately dehumanizes; we do physical damage to the world around us; it costs a great deal of money we no longer have; and it's nasty. It makes an unpleasant, ugly environment.

There's plenty of evidence that we're not handling our affairs nearly as well as we could by using the sort of judgment one learns by being a mature and responsible human being with fidelity to a place and to a group of people.

The institutions that have power drive away exactly these people, the ones who are the most creative, most concerned, most qualified to help us out of the many crises we're in at the moment.

DJ: You mentioned minor miracles earlier. What's wrong with minor miracles? Antibiotics. Or, as you mention in *The Arrogance of Humanism*, the possibility of fusion power.

DE: The bottom line is really what we have to look at, and we've stopped looking at the bottom line. The bottom line with fusion is: What will happen if we have available to us a virtually inexhaustible source of energy?

We have to ask: How have we used energy in the past? The answer is, we haven't used it responsibly. Does anybody really want more neon signs? Do people really want more battery-operated snowmobiles destroying the environment of the north?

Having fusion power would be like having an unlimited supply of candy, and very few people have the willpower to resist this. Candy, too, is a source of energy. And we don't have any way physiologically to get rid of excess energy we take in. We just store it as fat, which isn't good for us. The same is true with energy. If we have too much we're going to get societally fat—and sick.

Also, energy destroys privacy. Do we really want to be able to go see anybody anytime we feel like it, without any thought to the cost of the fuel? The cost of fuel, although it's an annoyance, is a very useful thing.

There used to be a limit to how much you could run around seeing people and fragmenting your life. The limit was the distance you could walk conveniently. If you ever want to see how this functions, read Jane Austen's best book, *Emma*. In it she describes the functioning of what I would consider a healthy community, and it isn't till you finish the book that you realize that except for one fairly brief scene, all the action takes place within walking distance of the house of the central character. It's striking, when you see what kind of life this enforces.

There are very few mechanisms keeping us responsible. Ultimately there are many limits that prevent us from doing *anything* we feel like doing, and prevent us from damaging ourselves. We see these easily in our personal lives. For instance, the limits for children are the parents. Anybody who's had a one- or two-year-old knows that they have no sense about dealing with the world. And doing away with limits is like doing away with parents for a child.

DJ: Limits. The mere word is blasphemy. We always hear our economy has to grow, our population will grow.

DE: People are dimly beginning to perceive—although it probably won't be in time for most of them—that growth is horrendous. But whether people perceive it or not, growth can't go on forever.

A. A. Bartlett wrote a paper called "Forgotten Fundamentals of the Energy Crisis," which he published in the *American Journal of Physics* ten or fifteen years ago and which has now become quite popular. Bartlett shows mathematically—and it's easy to show—that with typical exponential growth we just can't keep growing for very long. He assumed, for example, that the entire volume of the earth is petroleum and that 100 percent of it is accessible. How long would it last? As I remember, it was four or five hundred years, at a 7 or 8 percent annual increase in the rate of use. When they discover a few billion barrels of oil somewhere in the Arctic or offshore, it sounds wonderful, but we're only talking about a supply for a few days or a few weeks or months or a year.

Now, Paul Ehrlich, who perceives this very well, made the mistake of betting with Julian Simon about what would happen to the price of metal resources in the future. Paul should not have made that bet, because the availability of any tangible resource is subject to market and economic forces that have nothing to do with the limits of its ultimate availability. There was a time, for example, when India was the major silver-producing nation of the world, even though there are no silver mines in India. The reason is that women in India have traditionally kept their wealth in the form of bracelets, and during hard times they sell their bracelets for silver. This is exactly what happened during the particular time that India was "producing" so much silver, and it has nothing to do with limits on the resources. What Paul Ehrlich should have done (and I should point out that he knows more about this than I do) is bet with Simon about crime, social disorder, transient famines, anomie—all the things that are caused by transcending the limit of population.

There are limits. Failure to recognize limits is the main proof that we are not capable of controlling our own destiny.

DJ: Through all this, are you saying it is impossible for us to cope with a complex system?

DE: No, there are many ways we can do that. One is to stand back and protect it and let it alone. And you have to be willing to accept certain things. You have to be willing to accept, for example, that every three or four hundred years you're going to get a monstrous fire in Yellowstone Park. You have to stop worrying about that. It isn't bad. It's just what happens. It's the way that system functions. It grows back, if you let it do it the way it has evolved. You have to be willing to accept the fact that changes in atmospheric gas composition and in climate—global warming for example—may make things happen you wish didn't happen.

But you can't always leave complex systems alone. It was George Marsh who, in his book *Man and Nature*, pointed out that when we have really altered the balance of nature by removing weights on one side of the pan, we have to, if we want to restore the balance, interfere on the other side. At the same time we have to understand the limits of what we can and can't fix, and this then should determine our actions.

For example, we can't replace old-growth forests. We suspect that old-growth forest is ecologically necessary for soil maintenance, species maintenance, and so on. And we know without any studies that it's necessary aesthetically. We also know without any studies that it's necessary for proper tourism, because nothing is duller than wandering around in an eighty-year-old planted forest. Anybody who has seen the slash pine plantations of Florida and Georgia knows you wouldn't go there on a bet as a tourist. So we know we need old-growth forest for various reasons, and we suspect we need it for others. We also know we can't make it.

There are some things we can't fool with, and if they have been fooled with we have to give up the idea we can fix them. There are some scars even plastic surgeons can't fix.

DJ: In the Northwest we always hear from timber companies, "We may have made mistakes in the past, but we've learned our lesson. We'll do better next time." We also hear the same thing with every oil spill and every leakage of toxic waste.

DE: There is no better next time for devastated watersheds and oiled beaches.

In addition, you can't learn something that is unlearnable. We finish with one massive threat to the earth and find ourselves confronted with the next one, which often is worse. We thought we had gotten rid of the idea of running the north-flowing rivers in Siberia south for the sake of irrigation, and now we hear Hydro-Quebec is going to destroy the entire environment around Hudson Bay with virtually no thought to either environmental concerns or the preservation of the life of the Cree Indians. I don't see any signs of learning.

I have seen individuals who have learned, who've had quasi-religious conversions. But people who learn also die. Many people don't learn, and there are always new people coming along and the lessons have to be learned all over again.

The idea of "now we know how to do it better" is wrong. When it comes to timber management, we don't really know what to do in most cases. We know in Oregon where we've clearcut, that after three plantings the trees aren't growing back. We do have some insight—maybe we should include mycorrhizal fungi when we plant a new little tree. But there are always lessons unlearned, and there are always lessons learned that have been learned incorrectly, even with the best of intentions. I'm not saying we aren't trying, or that we shouldn't try to do things in an intelligent way, or that we give up on education. What I'm saying is we have to drop the myth of thinking that even though we've never yet been able to run the show completely, we'll be able to learn enough to do it tomorrow.

DJ: Do you feel hope?

DE: I have a belief that if God is sustaining the world, which I think is the case, it is unlikely that all life will come to an end through our actions.

Also, and you'd never guess it from reading *The Arrogance of Humanism* or even *Beginning Again*, I am an optimist. Many of the changes in the future will be absolutely unexpected, and maybe not everybody will like what comes, but I think civilization can last.

Because we don't understand the way the world works, we also don't understand all of the sources and origins of goodness. Unexpectedly, good things happen. They happen fairly often. I think the Anita Hill/ Clarence Thomas hearings were an example of something very exciting happening. A whole country suddenly woke up to the idea of what sexual harassment is. The majority of people are resisting it, but it's out there in front of everybody.

We saw an election in which ten women were elected to the Senate. And although we're seeing terrible problems for minorities, we're seeing a constant awareness of these problems. This, ultimately, has got to have an effect. Just read popular literature from the 1920s and 1930s, and see the way black people are referred to. Then see what it's like in the 1950s and the 1970s and the 1990s. It's changing very dramatically.

Good things happen in the environment, too. Perception of the importance of wetlands is nice. Twenty-five years ago the only person talking about the importance of water was Ian McHarg of Pennsylvania. Now everybody's talking about it. Wetlands are protected by legislation, and although the president and vice-president of the United States wanted to get at these wetlands for commercial purposes, they were prevented simply by public opinion.

In twenty years we're going to see much more of an understanding of the importance of ecological systems, an understanding that doesn't depend just on charismatic megavertebrates such as the endangered rhinoceros or tiger, or beautiful creatures like endangered gazelles or antelopes, but the whole system. Soon, the public is going to understand the importance of conserving certain kinds of worms.

DJ: You've said you don't think we'll give up our humanism by choice, and that it may take an action like Gollum's, from Tolkien's *Lord of the Rings* trilogy, to help humanity give up this belief.

DE: One of the brilliant things about Tolkien's trilogy is that it mimics the relationship between God and humanity so beautifully. It's a parable about the relationship between God and people. The role of Gandalf is to warn Frodo and the group of nine, "Don't interfere too much with initial arrangements that are wisely made. And don't depart from your fundamental ethical principles by creating means that are wrong, because you don't know what the end is going to be." Gandalf may not foresee what's going to happen at the Crack of Doom, when Gollum in a frenzy bites off the Ring of Power that Frodo finds himself—at the final moment—unable to cast away. Then Gollum falls into the abyss, carrying the evil ring, which is destroyed along with him. Gandalf doesn't foresee this specific ending, but he does see that it would be wrong to behave unjustly and unethically toward Gollum. He also foresees that the proper course of behavior is more likely to result in good, even if this good comes out of something that is evil. That's a very powerful lesson, and one we should keep in mind.

John Keeble

In one sentence, John Keeble has described a clear and appropriate response to the natural world: "It occurred to me once again that the trick was to enter the chaos, not to control it, nor to wipe it out with one form of monomania or another, and yet at the same time to hold fast to a sense of right conduct, to keep looking outward, and not to get trapped inside an illusory net." He came to this understanding through studying the effects of the Exxon Valdez *oil spill on Prince William Sound, and through experiencing firsthand the power of huge corporations to destroy both human and other-than-human communities.*

Author of Yellowfish *and* Broken Ground, *John Keeble was mainly known as a novelist of the Pacific Northwest until he wrote* Out of the Channel: The Exxon Valdez Oil Spill in Prince William Sound. *More recently he has published short fiction, as well as essays on petroleum, ecology, community, and literature. He is now researching a nonfiction book on culture and the petroleum trade of North America.*

JOHN KEEBLE: One thing that struck me when I first went to study the Exxon *Valdez* oil spill was the paradoxicality of the whole situation. The oil spill was out of control. The physics of oil on water is quite extraordinary in any case, and all the more so in a place with the complexity of currents and winds of Prince William Sound. There was an ironic lag between oil being out of control and all the rationalizing talk about it by executives and government leaders. A great deal of talk was addressed to finding a systematic remedy to deal with an 11.2-million-gallon spill that was out of control and bound to take its own chaotic course. Between those two things lay a serious contradiction.

DERRICK JENSEN: The book that emerged from this, *Out of the Channel*, seems to be about systems, not only ocean channels but bureaucratic channels, too.

JK: Yes. Take for example VECO, the principal cleanup subcontracting company engaged by Exxon. VECO had two subsidiaries, one of which was union, the other nonunion. Neither would accept the other's recovered oil, even when there was no other storage facility readily available. That was the kind of absurdity of system encountered on a daily basis during the cleanup.

DJ: From the beginning everyone except the locals seemed to be more interested in setting up systems than in cleaning up Prince William Sound.

JK: It's true that to its detriment the cleanup rapidly became institution-alized. Exxon took charge and put in place an elaborate bureaucracy that slowed everything down, gave the paperwork Byzantine loops to run. Really, it was the Coast Guard's duty as an organ of the citizens to take charge, but it was seriously compromised by its own failures and willingly stepped aside. It's also true that there were a lot of scam artists and people otherwise delighted to make small fortunes from the cleanup. Never-theless, I don't think it's fair to say that most people weren't interested in accomplishing things. Many just had no idea how to do it, and they were woefully unprepared, even though Alyeska, the holding company owned by the petroleum majors, which operates the pipeline and ter-minal, had a legal mandate to be prepared. The executive types had to be browbeaten into listening to those who knew the sound intimately and who quickly set up their own volunteer response programs—the res-idents and fishermen.

Many of the Exxon employees were absolutely mortified by what hap-pened. Frank Iarossi (then head of Exxon Shipping) was probably one of them. One thing that separated him from some other executives was that he was there and made a point of getting out to see the damage. What I understand from people who worked closely with him is that this made a difference. Maybe the problem was not the employees of Exxon. Maybe they became scapegoats, just as Joe Hazelwood, captain of the *Valdez*, was a scapegoat.

So to get to the point, what we're really talking about is the failure of systems, and then of individuals who don't question the system they are operating within, even when it becomes apparent something is terribly wrong. The next problem is, how do you manage to shake people loose from these systems, or how do people manage to shake themselves loose? Much of the cleanup in Prince William Sound, you see, was a sham in-tended to quiet the American public, and some of it, the hot-water

washes and chemical treatments, for example, even deepened the damage to the environment.

DJ: Perhaps one way to shake yourself loose is to think of the Declaration
of Independence, where it states that when a government becomes destructive of "Life, Liberty, and the pursuit of Happiness . . . it is the
Right of the People to alter or to abolish it."

JK: On principle, of course it's the duty of the individual to fight an oppressive system. And the level of cooperation that exists between federal
and state governments and large private corporations amounts to an oppressive system. As the historian Daniel Sisson points out, Jefferson was
opposed to political parties, too, or to factions, and we can see what the
two-party system has led to. When corporations contribute to both candidates in an election, you have to ask yourself, is it really because they
just can't make up their minds? This says nothing of elections that corporations are openly trying to throw by spending millions on advertising
or other forms of influence peddling.

I think we need to remember that disinformation and propaganda,
and the fabrication of false mythologies (which advertising does in the
United States on a regular basis), genocide, and state-sponsored violence are the means by which fascism achieves its end—the conjoining
of government and industry in one totalitarian system. I find this very
troubling to think about, particularly when I consider how information
is handled in our country, the severe economic hardship in the cities and
the attendant day-to-day violence, the state-sponsored violence outside
our borders, and the violence regularly done to animals by industrialized
people. But it's really difficult for us as a people to take the effects of
oppression seriously, because we are living in a state of relative comfort.

DJ: What was the final death toll from the *Valdez*?

JK: The last official figure was as many as 580,000 birds, perhaps over
5,000 otters. The real figure for the birds will continue going up, particularly for species such as murres, 300,000 of which are thought to have
been killed by the spill itself. Since then, another 300,000 murre chicks
have been lost because of egg contamination and disrupted breeding
patterns. Some experts say it's seventy-five years to recovery for most
bird populations. Pink salmon fisheries have failed for three successive

years. The herring fishery failed in 1993 and was closed in 1994, because of a lack of fish. All of these results are probably due to what are called "sublethal effects" of oil. That's just a hint at an extraordinary set of figures, all of which contradict Exxon-funded science, the carefully orchestrated set of lies it has prepared for litigation and PR.

But few people are interested any longer, which is the American way. No memory. What distinguished the Exxon *Valdez* spill is that, though it was not the largest tanker spill in history, it was the largest ever in North America, and it was probably the most destructive anywhere in history because of where and when it occurred. It spread to eleven hundred miles of shoreline in the early spring in one of the most fecund marine habitats in the world. Also, unlike most events of human-caused destruction in North America, such as the pollution of Lake Michigan, Love Canal, the Hanford Nuclear Reservation, and the decimation of forests, this event happened suddenly in a pretty clean place and rapidly made its kill. So, it's like a parable in which the history of destruction is condensed and quite evident—the initial devastation, the cause, the continuing effects, the institutionalization of remedies, the denial, the propaganda, the forgetfulness. It's there for us to see and consider, and yet we choose not to.

Part of the problem is that death is not part of our daily life. We have a very curious, escapist attitude about death and have managed to distance it, too, through a bizarre form of institutionalization—mortuaries and heavy doses of sap. What is required is a change of heart, and in order to change our hearts we have to start seeing things differently. If death is a part of daily life, then one is much less likely to romanticize it and at the same time to deny it. The response among two very important groups in Alaska was one or the other. Because its primary consideration was public relations, Exxon was committed systemically to helping us to deny death.

Exxon issued a video in 1992 called "Science and the Spill," which argues that everything is finally OK, clean as a whistle. Not one image of an oiled or dead animal appears in the video. It's all sparkling landscape and cleaned-up animals. This video was distributed to public schools across the nation, and there's your denial and the government-enjoined disinformation campaign in one neat package. It's intended as an erasure of memory. To the same end, language is manipulated. What was known to scientists as the "hot-water wash," and which turned out to be a destructive remedy, is now referred to in Exxon material as the "warm-water wash." The word *pristine* is used a lot in the video . . . "restoring the sound to its pristine condition." That's a hollow myth. Nothing was ever pristine. The Exxon *Valdez's* name was changed to the *Mediterranean*. Now Exxon Shipping doesn't exist. It's been renamed SeaRiver Maritime. So the ship is called the SeaRiver *Mediterranean*. What ship?

Many environmentalists, on the other hand, were committed to romanticizing the death of animals. This invokes the sentimental, otherworldly system by which funds are raised. The truth in my view is that neither one of those views is honest or useful. It's more useful to begin by accepting death as a part of the grit of daily life. The effect of that would be to increase one's respect for it, and thus, one's respect for life.

DJ: Where are we headed?

JK: My answer to that comes in two parts. We're in a position where we're beginning to see quite clearly the warning signs of a world slipping away. The signs are becoming increasingly dramatic. Human beings are in all the nooks and crannies, and as a response, societies are falling into repressive systems as an attempt at control. But the world is still slipping away, in terms of pollution and animal extinctions on the one hand and devastation of peoples and cultures by war on the other hand.

DJ: And the devastation of individual psyches.

JK: On a massive scale. These are the early warning signs of a system that is starting to slip away. We are losing our ability—I almost said grip, but that's not the word I want to use—our ability to hold our balance. All you have to do is look at the Persian Gulf, Somalia, Haiti, Serbo-Croatia, or Palestine.

DJ: So we're in for more of the same.

JK: Until either a new balance is found or an old balance is restored. I would prefer the old balance with every bone in my body, but there's a part of my brain that tells me that won't happen. Part two, then, is how do we conduct ourselves. There are a number of stages one can go through. The first stage is to try to be like some of the people I observed in Alaska, people who were faced with what they thought might be the end of their life as they knew it. They had the capacity to contain the horrifying contrarities, or the paradoxes they were presented with, yet to continue to conduct themselves in positive ways toward restoring health and effecting change. They found that they could be empowered, that they could walk into a legislative session or public forum and be empowered by their honest concern and outrage. Now, because of public pressure from Alaskans and savvy politics, much of the settlement money is being used to buy up and set aside threatened timberlands along Prince William Sound as a means of securing the entire habitat.

What some of us need to do, who aren't faced directly with crisis, is to conduct ourselves as if we were faced with it. From there you go on to community action, so long as you can continue to act with some kind of hope.

DJ: It seems easier to conduct yourself in a positive way when you're not associated with a system.

JK: Systems tend to create routines. By creating routines, they reduce the fluidity with which one can interact with the world. Ken Adams, a vice-president of Cordova District Fishermen United, asked: "When do the oil companies become accountable, and when do companies undergo a change of heart?" When they do, then the number of spills will be drastically reduced. No amount of Coast Guard regulation, no number of double-hulled ships will matter until the oil companies have a change of heart.

DJ: But within a market framework, if a company does have a change of heart, won't it become economically inefficient and be replaced by one whose heart is still bad?

JK: What we could have done in the case of the Exxon *Valdez* is very clear. We could have said we're not going to buy Exxon fuel until Exxon becomes accountable as a company. Then when we had an agreement with Exxon, and we were convinced they would follow it, we could have moved on to Texaco and Chevron. The strategies for doing something about the situation are very simple. The problem is not figuring out how to do something, but getting enough people to have a change of heart themselves to do something and to have enough heart to stick with it. We'd probably have to be prepared to do without oil for a while, which would be interesting in itself. Riki Ott, a fishing person and scientist based in Cordova, said, "We're evolving. Evolution is revolution." What she implies is that if we pay attention to necessary evolutions, we might find ourselves in the midst of a revolution.

DJ: What response would you hope for from readers of this interview?

JK: That they would be conscious of the incompleteness of the information they receive through normal channels. Behind the information about all manner of things is a great deal more complexity than they are led to believe. It is very likely that there is a great deal of heavy-duty political and economic maneuvering going on behind the scenes that they're not going to be aware of unless they look closely into the story. I came into writing the story of the spill as a literary person, I should say, with a literary person's admiration for the richness of language and human conduct.

Language is a natural resource, or maybe I should say natural wonder, born of the air we've taken into our lungs from the atmosphere, loaded with the detritus of the air, and shaped by bone and cartilage and flesh as it comes out in words. It's a way we have of keeping contact with each other and of giving form to our dreams. Language is extraordinarily diverse. It should be treated with respect and not just thinned out into uniformity for the sake of making a buck.

One of the things I'm really trying to communicate is the necessity of rejecting oversimplified versions of complex problems. We have political campaigns based upon the American flag and the perverse use of unfortunate people, like the criminal Willie Horton—or the hypocritical populism of Ross Perot. Those kinds of symbols are used to replace information.

In some ways, particularly as it applies to information, our society is totalitarian. There is, as Milan Kundera says, a lightness of being. The flag, Willie Horton, and Perot's country twang, those symbols are all very lightweight. Exxon is being sued in federal court by its insurers on the grounds that the cleanup was a public relations exercise and therefore not insurable as a loss to damages. Exxon's response has been to supply the court with five million pages of documents. Five million pages! Who's to read it? This is the oppressive hand of industry and the court system making an overwhelming, false answer from which we are compelled to turn away, and this, too, makes us light. Whereas to try to take in the sometimes contradictory, sometimes unsettling and difficult-to-comprehend reality makes one heavy. We have to accept some of the burden, including the pain of bearing witness to animals suffocated in oil, as did many Alaskans.

I would hope readers would think about how to address the problem of information. And how they can conduct their lives in ways that will be effective. One of the most compelling things in Prince William Sound was the seeming powerlessness of communities. And yet set against that is the fact that the Native people and fishing people are very self-reliant and very willing to do things, both mechanically in terms of the oil spill and also politically in terms of changing public policy and of trying to inform the public of what was actually going on. In the face of the economic power of Exxon, and the ties that the petroleum industry has with government, the communities are at an incredible disadvantage. That's one of the major problems that we need to deal with, how to find a way for communities to claim their rightful power.

DJ: Do you see any way to do that?

JK: I see a couple of ways, but they both would require a tremendous amount of work and a serious change in our way of thinking. The quickest way to accomplish this change is to have a national catastrophe. It sounds terrible, but as long as people who managed to stay alive through it stayed alert and of good heart, that would be the quickest way. The other way is to try to reform the system. I suppose we could have a series of setbacks that are not on the level of a national catastrophe. We've seen intimations of the power of communities to mobilize with the California earthquakes.

DJ: Let's return again to the problem of superficial information. Tell me your ideas on sound bites and the medium of television.

JK: When I was researching *Out of the Channel*, I traveled between Alaska and my home outside Spokane. As a result, I would see what the media was covering up there, then come home and see the results of their coverage. Frequently, there seemed to be very little connection between what I had seen and what was being presented on television. The print journalists were in general more accurate. The network TV presence in Alaska was abrasive, aggressive, and destructive—shining their lights on dying otters and the like. Then I came down here and saw the sound bites, which were so fragmentary in their presentation that they were untrue.

That's more of Kundera's "unbearable lightness." We have to hope that the thinness of information that people receive, the thinness of entertainment that people indulge themselves in, the thinness of so much of our so-called literature, and the superficialities of human relations will take us to a point of exhaustion, and that we will then turn to something else.

There's a relationship between capitalism of the sort we have developed and the way in which information is handled. It's exploitative, particularly when there are capitalist institutions with tremendous power. Any information that comes under their purview is going to have a spin to it. It swerves lightly in the air. In the publishing industry, there are now a very small number of very large companies.

When we get to the point where the industrial and economic monoliths have either direct or indirect control over information, then our society will have locked up. Maybe the Information Superhighway will finish that job off for us. It may be a good thing when the superhighway arrives and the five hundred channels complete the parody of diversity, because our seriousness needs to be called into being. In the same way that it took an environmental catastrophe to bring the Alaskan people outside of themselves, it may take a catastrophe of the word to do the same for those of us who care about language.

DJ: So what can we do? In your book you mention people blockading oil tankers. Is that OK?

JK: Yes. At the start, Ken Adams said, "Exxon is not accountable." We can conclude from that that we must find a way to make these companies accountable. And it may take blockading the channel, which has happened, incidentally, or tying a fishing boat to the anchor of a tanker, which means the tanker cannot move without capsizing the boat. Of course, if the tanker decides to go ahead and move, the people on the fishing boat are all dead. Then we're on the other side of the veil. It would be interesting to see what would happen if we moved to the other side of the veil and took stock of ourselves from that vantage point—the world of the dead.

DJ: Would it be acceptable to go beyond blockading a ship in?

JK: You're asking me to advocate a revolution. I'm not sure I'm going to do that in public. Besides, I'm not by nature a violent person.

DJ: I'm asking what *you* think is acceptable.

JK: Blockading the channel would be acceptable. In Cordova, especially, which is a very politically active town, they were very close to doing that in 1989. In 1993, the Prince William Sound seine fleet, which is mainly based in Cordova, did blockade the channel. They were frustrated by the failed pink salmon fishery, enraged by what they called Exxon's "media blitz," and tired of seeing the settlement money wasted. A lot of them were also close to bankruptcy. For a period of several hours the sound had no oil tankers in it, for the first time since the opening of the pipeline. The channel into Valdez was blockaded for three days. When they pulled out, the storage tanks at the oil terminal were two days away from capacity, which if reached, would have created havoc all up and down the West Coast.

DJ: What held them back?

JK: In 1989 I think they hoped that things could be corrected. That and the obvious hazard to one's life that such an action carries with it. Some, I'm sure, were prepared to take action and would have, had there been more people to act with them. By 1993 the frustration caused by the failed fisheries, their fear of permanent damage to the sound, and Exxon's lies reached critical mass. So they blockaded and faced down the first tanker to come in on them, and did so at tremendous risk to their safety and livelihood. They pulled out because the Interior Secretary, Bruce Babbitt, met with them in Valdez and convinced them they "had reached the top of their curve" so far as effect was concerned. He promised to help them, but whether or not he has remains to be seen.

Personally, I think Exxon's North Slope oil leases should have been lifted at the outset. With the billion dollar out-of-court settlement for damages reached between Exxon, the federal government, and the Alaskan government, Exxon will end up paying a total of between 3 and 4 billion. I don't think it's sufficient, because ultimately it's their responsibility to make things right. But of course they can't make things right—not even if they paid the latest estimate of 20 to 25 billion in damages to Prince William Sound. Exxon should have been shut down on the North Slope. If I rob a bank, I'm probably going to be sent to jail as an example to my peers.

All across the country, plant after plant is dumping toxic materials into our waterways. My view is that those places should be shut down. It's that simple. Pretty soon the rest would get the message. As a culture we're not the least bit serious about implementing the remedies available to us. And if it takes action to make it clear that those remedies are necessary, I'm in support of it. Am I going to do something like blow the pipeline? No. Would I have tied onto the anchor of a tanker? Maybe, if I had a boat. Would I participate in a blockade of the tanker channel? Yes. But mainly what I'm trying to say is that you've got to begin with the conduct of your own life.

DJ: Are you hopeful?

JK: I'm fighting, I'm writing. That's got to be an indication of hope.

DJ: What is the source of this hope?

JK: I believe in the human spirit as it is bound to the world.

DJ: Where does capitalism fit into all this?

JK: What is capitalism? Do you mean the international superproprietors? What I witnessed in Alaska was the tremendous gap between hardworking, ambitious people and the power of monopoly. The operation of the pipeline is a history of graft, mechanical failure, environmental violations, and tax evasion, and this when the combined profits from the North Slope alone by the three principal leaseholders—BP, Exxon, and Arco—would make a company that would be in the top five of the Fortune 500. Such abuses by monopoly have an incredibly devastating effect, not only economically but also spiritually, on energetic people. What we're seeing in this fifty-year microstep of our Holocene epoch is that we've lost our capacity to keep big corporations accountable. To insist on their accountability.

Since we do still have the vestiges of a democracy, people need to start demanding accountability on the part of their elected officials, probably starting with voting for someone else. We're at the point where we could use a good third political party. And we have to change our hearts . . . allow them to become heavy.

It's a question of what kind of a shift you can make. It's also a question of whether we are going to make the necessary shifts now or later. We tend to forget how fragile our so-called infrastructure is, and how close we are at all times to a complete breakdown, whether by natural or human causes. When this happens elsewhere, as with the Kurds, or in Yugoslavia, or even in California, we're inclined to look at the these people through news accounts and photos as though they were monkeys in a zoo and we the privileged onlookers, like we're watching the Civil War from wicker chairs on an out-of-range hilltop. But we have to remember the Alaska pipeline is extremely vulnerable. The oil delivery system and Grand Coulee Dam are vulnerable. Our food supply system is vulnerable. The California aqueduct system is vulnerable. We could all be on the other side of the veil in an instant. When you have monolithic systems, your vulnerability increases. When you live in the midst of diversity, you're strong. The rule works in biology and community, as well as in economics. If we don't make the shifts now, we will have to make them later. We need to turn off the TV and start trusting our native abilities.

We have to continue to fight. For writers, our job is to hang on as tightly as we can to the power and grit and invocatory powers of language and to mean every word we say.

Jerry Mander

Many people view technology as neutral, and believe that many of the horrors we've seen during this century—Hitler's Final Solution, Hiroshima, Three Mile Island, ozone depletion—are a result of technology's misuse. These horrors continue to happen, they say, because the wrong people control the technology. Jerry Mander, probably the world's most articulate and clear critic of technology, disagrees. During our conversation, he said that "the very idea of technology being neutral is itself not neutral, as it produces a passivity about our role in technological evolution." It is possible that there is no more important question facing us today than how to deal with the massive web of technologies with which we have surrounded ourselves.

Author of Four Arguments for the Elimination of Television *and* In the Absence of the Sacred: The Failure of Technology and the Survival of the Indian Nations, *Jerry Mander was president of Freeman, Mander & Gossage advertising until he quit in the 1970s to devote himself to public interest campaigns. He is now a Senior Fellow at the country's only nonprofit ad agency, Public Media Center in San Francisco, and a director of the Berkeley ecological think tank, the Elmwood Institute.*

DERRICK JENSEN: Is megatechnology—the web of technologies that surround and inform our everyday living—compatible with democracy? Is megatechnology even compatible with survival?

JERRY MANDER: When I use the term *megatechnology*, I am trying to describe something entirely new on the political, social, and environmental scene; a condition only recently made possible by the global interlock among new technological forms.

As recently as two decades ago, it was possible to speak about different parts of the planet as distinct places, separate from one another, with distinct cultures, living habits, conceptual frameworks, behaviors and power arrangements, and it was possible to speak of distinctly different geographies as well. One could also sensibly speak about individual technologies as if they were separate from one another; television from computers, the laser from the satellite.

However, technological evolution has brought us to the point where such distinctions among cultures, places and systems of organization, as well as technological forms, are being wiped out under the homogenization drives of a much larger technical juggernaut that seeks to encompass everything. All rights that have been presumed for cultural or national self-determination, and separate identities among peoples and nations, as well as diversity of landscape, of biological form, culture, perception, and so on, are under fierce assault these days by a new web of technical forces, of which transnational corporations are a key example, that operate on a global scale and are unified in their purpose and form.

Telecommunications, high-speed computer technology, satellite systems, robotics, lasers, among other new technologies, have made possible, practical, and inevitable an interlocked global communication system that enables corporate actors to perform on the global scene with a speed and efficiency not possible only a few years ago.

Critical to understanding this issue you raise, of democracy, is the realization that the corporations themselves must be understood as an intrinsic part of the technical machine. In fact, they are technical forms themselves, inventing the machines that operate on this global scale, and in turn being spawned by them, in an accelerating symbiotic cycle. The megatechnological web that has now been put into place around the world makes possible the instantaneous transfer of corporate capital anywhere on the globe, while simultaneously accelerating the corporate invasion of the natural world and of any resistant nations and indigenous peoples. *Corporate power on the present scale simply could not exist without the benefit of such new technologies.*

There is one more technical form that completes the picture. That is the recently restructured global economic system, designed to overcome or circumvent resistance to the megatechnological homogenization drive. I speak of course of the new supranational economic bodies, like the General Agreement on Tariffs and Trade (GATT), the North American Free Trade Agreement (NAFTA), the World Trade Organization, and the other planned regional trading agreements. Through the new powerful international bureaucracies they create, they are gaining real power to overrule many major decisions formerly reserved to national governments, state governments, and other sovereign entities, including local communities and Native nations. These unelected un-democratic bureaucracies have effectively assumed power in a new world government, as they have enforcement capabilities that require the conformity of all sovereign entities, thus affecting each of us in everyday life—and yet they remain opaque to all democratic processes.

By the time this book is published, I hope there will be far greater awareness among environmentalists, human rights activists, and all people interested in democracy that the main purpose of these supra-national agreements is not to improve life for people, as claimed (and there's little pretense about protecting environment or culture), but actually to bulldoze all resistance to transnational corporate sovereignty over lands, resources, and governments. In this way, the agreements reproduce and become the fuel for the megatech machine. And the police power for it too. The trade agreements, combined with the intrusive powers of the World Bank and the International Monetary Fund, have sufficient veto power over domestic laws that it will soon be impossible for any community to: prevent the exploitation and export of local resources, control the driving downward of wages, restrict the movement of toxic or hazardous materials, protect wildlife habitat or biodiversity, control pesticide use, create standards for human rights, workers' rights, or healthful products, or maintain cultures rooted in small-scale indigenous activities like family or communal farming. Any and all efforts like these can and will be deemed efforts to restrict the free movement of corporate capital and prerogatives, or to restrict access to resources, workers, or markets, and will therefore be subject to serious challenge.

So these agreements must also be understood as an intrinsic part of the web of technical structures; in fact they are the "consciousness" of the megadevelopment, megatechnological, monocultural model that will soon encircle the globe and our lives.

In such a context, to speak of the survival of democracy is preposterous. Democracy is having its greatest setback globally, and it's a direct result of this effective conspiracy of technical structures, technologies themselves, and corporate purposes, all within the Western technological paradigm, that combine to lead us to a grave outcome. Understanding of that entire set of forces and the global web of connections that I mean by *megatechnology* must be grasped quickly. Otherwise this new world order is sure to lead to a scale of destruction of nature, culture, and diversity beyond anything that has preceded it. It will bring homogenization of consciousness, homogenization of cultures, suppression of diversity in every form, including the land itself.

Individual technologies have specific roles to play. Television serves as the worldwide delivery system for the new global corporate vision, homogenizing and implanting imagery. Computers are the nervous system that makes possible these new global organizations. Trade agreements wipe out resistance. Telecommunications provide instant capital and resource transfer. Genetics and space technologies expand the world market into the new wilderness areas: the internal cell structure of living creatures and the far reaches of untrammeled space. Together, these and other technologies combine to form that new technosphere, that megatechnological structure that is anathema to democracy and diversity.

The answer to this trend is, of course, to work to reverse it, and bring real power back to the local community, while supporting communities and cultures or nations that are attempting to stand in the way of the juggernaut.

DJ: So, you see the whole evolution of technology as having gone too far?

JM: It has, yes. But this has been inevitable in a society that was never trained to think about technology in systemic terms. Quite the opposite. We've been told that new technology equals progress and that progress in invariably beneficial. Even critics of technology have tended to critique technology in terms of who gets the most access to it, or who controls it, or the choices that they make for its use. The usual perception is that technology is merely a "neutral" tool that can be used well or badly, depending on who controls it. But it's my opinion—and I am joined in this by a growing number of technology doubters—that the very idea of technology being neutral is itself not neutral, as it produces a passivity about our role in technological evolution. We never ask the most radical questions: Is a technology good or bad? What are the full dimensions of its effects? Can it be reformed? Are we better off with it or without it? We are not given a chance to say no to any technology. Well, we can say no in personal terms, but the technology can still utterly reshape society. There are no national referenda, no national debates, no media debates about the basic forms or effects of technology, since all technologies are assumed to be basically neutral. So the goal becomes how to get our hands on the controls. It becomes a mad race to see who can control which technologies for their own ends. That race is usually won by the right wing and the forces of expanding development, since their goals suit the technologies best and they have the financial resources to utilize these machines. And then it's only years later that some of the downside effects begin to be visible, but by then we are surrounded by the technologies and it is far more difficult to get rid of them.

The great tragedy is that technology is one of the few subjects that the left and the right, and the environmentalists and the corporations, all tend to view in the same way. And yet technology is certainly not neutral, and we need to understand this.

Langdon Winner wrote that "all artifacts have politics," meaning that every technology has predictable social, political, and environmental outcomes. And McLuhan said "the medium is the message," that is, that the important point about a technology is not what it delivers in its apparent content (for example, the tv program) but what the technology causes to change in society: how it alters knowledge, thought, experience, participation, power.

Let me offer an example in the energy field. Nuclear power and solar power will both light the lamps in your house. But to have nuclear power requires that society provide huge financial resources from central sources, apply fabulously high technology skills, and employ a military capacity to protect poisonous materials from terrorism and from accidental release, for all the 250,000 years that it remains highly dangerous. So society is essentially committed to a centralized technical military and financial mode of organization for a quarter of a million years. On the other hand, solar energy, which also lights your lamps, could be built by you and me and my sons, paid for by us, and it would not require support from any central system, whether technical, military, or financial. At least not from now on, since the technical base has been achieved. So it would be fair to say that nuclear power is intrinsically geared toward sustaining a society that is centralized and that maintains huge financial and military capabilities. Solar power, on the other hand, fits very well into a more decentralized, community-based arrangement that does not require centralized capabilities and doesn't want them. Now, these qualities of each of these technologies are *intrinsic* to them. It doesn't matter whether good people or bad are put in charge of them, they maintain their basic form. If you and I controlled nuclear power plants in the United States, we'd find ourselves managing them more or less the way people presently do, albeit with perhaps more caution. But all of the problems I described above would remain, and these are as much political problems—centralized military and finance is surely political—as they are environmental. So it's not correct to say these technologies are "neutral," as certain elements within them require certain outcomes.

It's a major survival skill of our times that we begin to look at all technologies in similarly systemic terms, ferreting out their intrinsic systemic outcomes, so we can grasp where they will lead us. But instead, we interpret technology the way we are trained to, in strictly personal terms. The tv entertains us. The computer helps edit our copy and permits us to work with like-minded people. These attributes are useful, of course, but we never learn to ask the more important question about technology, which is not if the technology is useful to us—they always have some aspect that is useful—but to whom is it most useful. Not who benefits, but who benefits most. Only at that point are we capable of understanding the full systemic effect and impact of any technology and of making a judgment about whether a line of technical evolution has gone too far.

The next question becomes how we can gain the social and political power to get rid of it. If that turns out to be the wisest course.

Of course these have been difficult points for people to accept, since our society is so immersed in the basic paradigm that declares all technical evolution good and equates it with progress. This is virtually the religion of Western society.

Making matters even more difficult is that we, as a society, now live so far within technological forms that we can barely see around them or outside them. Not very long ago, we had a direct connection with the earth, which gave us our basic information and knowledge, and kept us sane, with a sense of our appropriate place in the natural scheme of things. This is what I meant by the retention of a "sense of the sacred," in my recent book; a sense of the natural order of things that informs us as to what kinds of behavior are sane and what kinds are crazy. But now that virtually all of us live inside an entirely homocentric reality—in artificial environments, interacting at all times with objects, rhythms, and environments that are completely the product of the human mind—you could say that we're living inside our own brains. Our evolution is now a kind of intraspecies incest, and we're coevolving only with artifacts and environments created by our own minds. This expresses a kind of insanity and leads to destruction in the end.

Military and corporate systems of evaluation, for example, are abstract, designed to create a complete separation from a sense of consequences to one's actions. Look at the Iraq war. It was reported in such a way that there were no human beings there. Two hundred thousand people were killed, and yet that information just barely made the news. And think of the emphasis on precision bombing, as though there's nobody inside the buildings that are getting blown up. Or the separation of pilots from the consequences of their acts. Warfare has become a computer game; wars are now fought between software programs. The effect has been to accelerate the separation of people from the consequences of what they're doing, an expression of alienation.

DJ: If you strangled someone, you would be forced to feel their life go out. If you stabbed someone you would still have to feel their blood. And now, somebody can push a button . . .

JM: And somewhere else something happens. There's no awareness of it at all. That's a major effect of technology.

DJ: And it applies not only to war. Flying gives an unreal sense of geography. Buying a steak wrapped in plastic gives no sense that this thing once lived.

JM: Think about the media for a moment and about what we're asked to relate to as reality. When we watch television we see very edited, speeded-up versions of reality that are also heavily intermixed. You watch the so-called news, which is supposed to be real but might have been filmed earlier, or might be descriptions of things you can't actually see, or descriptions of things that actually are not the same as those being described. And then you watch fictional programs that move you forward and backward in time and also condense time. This is mixed up with commercials, and sports, and also docudramas, which are re-created, fictional versions of former reality. All of it is cut and edited and very hyperactivated. The camera is over here, the camera is over there, then you're out on the street, then there are two images on the screen, and then there are cartoons on the screen.

Remember, we are creatures not very far away from when we depended entirely on our senses for concrete reality. It used to be that one of the ways we survived was to look at the sky and say, "I see birds and they are flying south. I know that is happening."

I could rely on that being a real thing, with a real meaning. By your senses you make your judgments, and you make your experience, and you make your decisions about how to live your life.

In the case of media, however, we are relating to a world that is absolutely re-created. Still, as the phrase goes, "Seeing is believing." We have not been trained to mistrust the information from our senses. We can therefore be led around by the nose by advertisers, presidents, corporations, and everybody else, because we can no longer rely on the information from our senses as being concretely true and guaranteed to be the way things actually are.

People who watch television a lot will say they understand what's real and what's not, but that's of course not possible. Two hundred and fifty thousand people wrote to Marcus Welby asking for medical advice.

People like to believe that intelligence and experience and knowledge will keep them from being impacted by, for example, advertising. This is another complete misunderstanding of the way the technology operates. We think if we watch a commercial we can say, "This is not real. We're not going to be influenced by it." This is preposterous, because advertisers spend fortunes creating images that do not have logical content to them. Ninety percent of advertising makes no statement. It's just people on beaches smiling and laughing and having a good time. There's nothing you can look at and say, "This is true. This is not true. I understand that."

And even if there were, that's not the point. Because whatever you say about it, the image is in your head. If you've *ever* watched television and I say to you, Colgate toothpaste, or McDonald's, or Ford Taurus, or Michelob, the images pop up, however intelligent you are. *You* think the images don't affect you, but the image is in your brain, which is the

· whole goal of the advertiser. The advertiser knows if they put that image in your brain often enough, you will walk around the world with that image like a neuronal billboard, and when you're in a market and see the product, the billboard lights up.

DJ: The argument has been made that television viewing creates a more violent society.

JM: People complain about the number of violent images on television. Are they stimulating violence? Definitely, absolutely, undoubtedly, yes. It's clearly a case where people imitate the images they see. It's part of the way human beings have always learned to behave.

The Goodman/Gross study at the University of Pennsylvania looked at heavy television viewers in terms of how they viewed the world. The researchers found that those who watched a lot of television lived in a more violent universe. We live in a violent culture, but you can go a whole day or week and not see somebody murdered. On television you see it five or eight or ten times an hour. So that world enters people's minds, and that's the world they carry around.

But even if there were no violence on television, heavy television viewing would still cause violence, because when you watch television you see action on the screen. You have an impulse to react to what's happening, but since it's on television, and so is not reality, you suppress the reaction. And then it happens again and again and again, with all of the reactions expressed silently, internally.

In addition, there is a rapid speedup of the perceptual systems. When you watch television, the experience is that of never getting down to organic natural time. That is to say, you're moving inside a perceptual universe which is hyperactivated—you're watching an informational field that is very very speedy. This means that while your nervous system has to go through the process of containing itself, your perceptual system is also being sped up to meet the rapid flow of images.

Then the set goes off, and the room's not whirling around, nor is it leaping around in time. You go out in nature, and it's hard to see anything happening, other than breezes blowing or a river running. To really tune in to nature requires great slowness and calm. One of the things that's happening because of television and computers and fax machines and high-speed travel and city life and automobiles and Walkmans and the pace of life that technology induces is that people are being sped up to where they can no longer relate to slower systems.

People are now faster than the natural world, literally. That's not just an intellectual separation. It's a real separation. A concrete separation. A physical separation. It's a separation of the body and the nervous system from their former relationship to the natural world into a dimension that moves faster and is tenser and therefore more prone to react speedily and violently to circumstances. This new dimension is not conducive to pleasure, or calm, or contemplation, or understanding, or depth.

Television has had a big role in causing people to become techno-humans. It moves them to become machine-compatible. In the same way that computers are compatible with each other, people are made more compatible to the machine world, to the technological world, and therefore, I think, inherently more simple in form and tending toward more violence.

DJ: A lot of environmental activists talk about doing some sort of jiujitsu with technology. We're all pretty torn. I use a computer to write, and I flew here for this interview.

JM: This is a very big problem, and each person has to make his or her own engagement with the subject.

The thing we must learn is to view all technology not from where it benefits us but in terms of the totality of its impact on the planet. As I started to say before, I understand the benefits of using a computer. It can help you write, and hook you into E-mail and help you network with compatriots. But the fact of the matter is that computers have far more benefit for the military and for corporations. Computers make possible that systematic reorganization without which the current voracious scale of development is impossible. They've made possible transnational corporate activity at a much more hyperactivated rate. They make possible genetics and robotics and space travel and nanotechnology, and all the other horrors that could not exist without computers.

I fully recognize that your computer helps you edit your copy, but you should be aware every day as you sit down at that computer that developers and so on have a lot more access to those computers than you do, and they're using them with greater force than you are, and that the existence of computers is a net loss in terms of environmental protection.

Of course, if you stop using your computer, that doesn't mean they'll stop using their computers, so it's a dilemma. Everybody has to make their own decisions about it. I don't use a computer—I feel it would change me in a way I don't want to change. Also, I refuse all interview offers from television, and I won't make television, although there are people here at Public Media Center who do. Even though television is biased in the direction of the major corporations, you can occasionally still get your message on there. Should you not take advantage of that opportunity? I see the value of that as well, obviously, but it's not for me.

I also live quite simply. I'm not much of a consumer. All the things I have are old. But I do have a car. I fly in airplanes when it's necessary for the work I do. I talk on the phone. I make use of a lot of technologies to do my work, and I think it's hypocritical that I do, but I feel I have something to contribute. The question for me is always this: What is the minimum level of technology I can use and still get the thing done? That's an unsatisfactory answer, but it's an impossible dilemma.

Withdrawing to the farm and raising your own vegetables is an acceptable statement to make and an OK thing to do. Right at this time, though, with things advancing at the rate they are, and forces gathering for this leap into a horrific future, I think it's important for those of us who are aware of it all to stay in there a while longer to see if anything can be done about it. And actually I think quite a bit can be done about it.

DJ: What can be done about it?

JM: I used to be in commercial advertising, and now I spend most of my days at the Public Media Center, trying to construct arguments in media against some of the tendencies I also write about in books.

Most people don't have that opportunity, but I think everybody has the opportunity to do something. This is a time when the old dictum "Think globally and act locally" is especially valid. GATT, for example, may be a gigantic international trade agreement, but it affects every person in their job, in their home, everywhere.

These days we're finding that acting locally is just as efficient as acting globally. It's really important to try to take charge of your local situation. Something's happening right where you live that you can affect in some way.

You can get involved with national activities as well. I'm a strong believer in joining such organizations as the Sierra Club and whoever is out there doing good work. It's not a question of who's got exactly the right philosophy. You won't agree with every stance. But get hooked up with somebody who's going in the right direction. You'll get educated from it and learn about what the pivotal points are and where power lies. If you stick at it you'll find many things that are possible to do.

DJ: Where do you think we're headed? Whenever I made an offhand comment to my college students about this country being a democracy, they laughed.

JM: That's progress. Ten years ago students wouldn't have laughed at that. But the fact is, we really have a democracy. It's not a pure democracy, but you can still get organized and do something. You can make things happen, especially on a local level. We've seen it here, with all the campaigns at the Public Media Center. Many bad things have not happened because we and others have gotten engaged on these subjects.

The way to be absolutely certain that change is impossible is to assume it's impossible. Pessimism gets you nowhere, and in any case is inaccurate, because we are seeing tremendous opportunities now.

There are many examples around the world of people protesting against trends that they have begun to recognize as dangerous to their community, their environment, their culture, or to sanity and survivability. We have seen a million farmers in India protest against Cargill Corporation's stealing of native seeds and a similar number in the streets against GATT. We have seen almost the same kinds of protest in several countries in Europe, in a few cases aimed at Disney and McDonald's. We have seen indigenous peoples all over the world—from Irian Jaya to the Amazon to North America—expressing their outrage and resistance to the Western development juggernaut being imposed on them and the destruction of both their environment and their sovereignty. We have seen whole communities rise in protest against the entry of corporate giants like Wal-Mart, as they drive out small businesses and local economy. We are now seeing unusual coalitions of workers, consumers, family farmers, native peoples, environmentalists, advocates of sustainable communities and traditional democracy beginning to see their causes in common. The question is only whether the growing awareness of the present danger will advance faster than the juggernaut, and whether it can possibly gain real power to cut it off. But it is definitely not impossible, and not too late. And in any case, it's a far more worthy activity to engage in these issues than be simply depressed and paralyzed by their apparent power. Eventually, the unsustainability of present trends will be visible in a highly disturbing way. It's obvious that no society that feeds on itself can live for very long. We need to be fully awake to the emerging opportunities and help, as best we can, to steer society toward the kind of alternative visions described in books like this one.

NEIL EVERNDEN

*R. D. Laing has written that "our behaviour is a function of our experience.
We act according to the way we see things." Neil Evernden's work has been
primarily concerned with making explicit the connection between the way we
as a culture see the world and the fact that we are destroying our own habitat.
His book* The Natural Alien *has been called "a brilliant, difficult, passionate assault on the dominance of economic—in fact of western—thinking."
It is also, in Evernden's words, "a defense of wonder," that is, a defense of
the assumption that all beings have intrinsic value, that human beings are not
the sole bearers and dispensers of value.*

*Neil Evernden was born in Vancouver, Canada, and was educated at the
University of Alberta, where he did research in mammalian ecology and in
ecological aesthetics. Since joining the Environmental Studies faculty at York
University, he has concentrated on "environmental thought" in general, and
more specifically on the human apprehension of the wild "other" and on the
social constitution of natural entities. He is the author of* The Natural Alien:
Humankind and Environment *and* The Social Creation of Nature.

NEIL EVERNDEN: Nature is a dangerous word. It's never exactly what you
think it is. People conventionally talk about nature as a collection of
trees and rabbits and so forth, as opposed to the treatment of Nature as
a system of regularities bound by "scientific" law. The Renaissance is the
period in which you first see this conception, one that isn't so concerned
with a direct encounter or a sympathetic response to the world but to the
hard-nosed discernment of that which lies beneath the surface.

It's a rather awkward distinction to have to make. So, for want of a
better way of doing it, I decided that when I was speaking in a colloquial
sense I would use nature with a small *n*. When I was talking about what
came to be after the Renaissance, I would use the term Nature with a
capital *N*. There has to be some distinction, and short of inventing a
new word I couldn't think how else to do it.

DERRICK JENSEN: Where does one's individual experience fit into this?

NE: We're dealing on three levels. One is the individual experience,
which can be quite chaotic. The second includes the colloquial con-

ventions of the time, which are constrained by what other people see. The third is more formal, more "scientific," rationalistic, and more highly structured, that is, the way Nature *must* behave.

DJ: How would these three approaches differ in response to the colors of fall?

NE: The "Nature" response entails chlorophyll being dispersed after the cold weather comes. Red is caused by cold, which is a logical connection, a necessary connection, but not an obvious one. I think the colloquial expression would be much the same, because we're so prone to pick up scientific terms—not necessarily the meaning, but the words. The individual explanation is the one the Dutch psychologist J. H. van den Berg was talking about. The reason the leaves are red, he said, was "because it is so beautiful. Don't you see how beautiful it is, all these autumn colors?" How else could it be?

DJ: I've never before been in a deciduous forest in the fall. This may seem a bit fuzzy-headed, but I'd swear the trees are showboating.

NE: Yes, but this *is* our earthly experience. It's a human interpretation. So what? I happen to be human. It's a funny situation to try to deny that, to say, "Oh, that's what you experience, but that's not really there. What's really there is a molecular interaction."

The legitimacy of your own experience can be undermined if people can convince you it is "only" subjective. What authority do you credit? What constitutes real knowledge, or "factual" information about the world? Undermining subjectivity by denying the merit of your experience leaves you open to the acceptance of somebody else's idea of the system of Nature.

What I'm really saying is that there is no such thing as Nature. There are simply other entities. We say the Native Americans and other indigenous peoples had a nice relationship with nature, but I suspect the reason they did is because they never had any "Nature." They had a cosmos, full of other beings, entities, others. But not Nature.

The belief in Nature becomes a danger when you begin to mistake your own abstract conceptions for *things*. You make these ideas up, but then you forget they're concepts. That's why it's tricky to talk about concepts of Nature, because that's all they are—concepts of Nature.

I'm not quite happy saying this. It sounds a bit precious to make these kinds of distinctions. There's something I want to say, and there are no easy words for saying it. A lot of the time you have to use metaphorical language to talk about these things. I suspect that's because only logical and descriptive language is normally used to talk about Nature.

I notice it with my students, who may have a very good idea why something needs to be changed, or why they need to advocate a certain position, but who also feel their views must be legitimated by the language of science, by some piece of quantification, which as a rule proves nothing. It simply allows them to say what they wanted to say in the first place, but apparently with authority.

It's really a dilemma. I don't know what the solution is, other than to refuse to speak the other language. But once you're in court, you've got no choice but to use the language of the court.

John Livingston did an odd thing years ago. There was a proposal to put a huge pipeline down from the Arctic Ocean, and there was an inquiry called the Berger Commission. It was supposed to be just another commission to get the public off the politicians' backs, but they gave it to a judge who had much wider interests. He allowed *any* kind of testimony from *everybody*. So, many people, including Inuit grandmothers, testified, and of course their language was different from the lawyers' language. The commission was loosened up enough that a lot of so-called emotional things got mixed into it, which would never happen in a regular, constrained, preplanned, "expert" kind of inquiry. When John Livingston was sworn in as an expert witness, they asked him to promise to tell the truth. He said, "No." The judge bristled, and John said, "I don't know the truth, but I'll give you my opinion." The whole thing was like that.

DJ: Why the cultural imperative against emotion?

NE: It's a contamination of objective knowledge. With the capital N Nature idea, any human property, such as emotion, that you claim to find in nature, or anything that colors your perception of nature, is a contaminant. The moment one of them shows up, it stains the entire testimony and allows it to be dismissed.

It strikes me as a bit hopeful that feminists have been partly successful in changing language use. It means you can no longer take certain things for granted. I hope the same might be true for environmental writing.

The philosopher Richard Rorty talks about the idea of not worrying whether something is true, and instead just worrying whether or not it's accepted at the time. What's important, then, is not who can prove a new reality, but who can utter a new reality. The person who can say something differently, shock, and unsettle the conventions is the one who in the long run may have the greater effect. That seems to me to be a hopeful hypothesis.

There are other people who tie into that, too. One of them is Uwe Pörksen, who has a book that is not formally into English yet, called *Plastic Words: The Language of an International Dictatorship*. He defines a plastic word as one that has been used in science, given authority by virtue of its use there, and then relocated back into the vernacular, where it sounds important but doesn't really mean anything. He listed a whole series of important-sounding words like *development* and *sexuality* and *resource*. You can put them in any combination in any sentence and appear to be saying something when you're not.

This whole package of things—the feminists, Rorty, Pörksen— makes me think there's something about to emerge that's going to entail a different way of talking, a reconsideration of that stereotyped language that doesn't permit anything but a certain kind of posturing without very much content or analysis.

DJ: In *The Social Creation of Nature* you write, "As members of twentieth-century industrial societies, and as functionaries of technological thought, what we fear most is the loss of control (or at least the illusion of control)."

NE: The idea of control is an obsession with us. If we're going to approach problems at root level, we've got to get over the idea of universal control, and we've got to get over resisting the concept of limits on ourselves.

DJ: What is the root of our culture's obsession with control?

NE: It has to do with the modern conception of Nature, or perhaps more accurately, with our preferred form of achieving knowledge of Nature. Francis Bacon's insight was that we could question nature in such a way as to understand how to control it. Consequently, the notions of "knowledge" and "control" have become subtly intermingled. In fact, Hans Jonas explicitly contrasts Bacon's form of knowledge with the kind sought by earlier thinkers, such as Thomas Aquinas. People like Aquinas assumed an unchangeable and eternal nature of the cosmos, which implies that the cosmos can be contemplated endlessly and, in some measure, understood *in theory*. On the other hand, they assumed that *practical* knowledge should derive from experience, and that theory should inform the practitioner of the wisdom of choosing one form of action over another. In contrast, Bacon begins with the assumption that practice comes first, that humans must inevitably intervene and control, that is, conquer "necessity," and that theory must be the handmaiden to such pursuits. One does not "know" and then seek the means to act properly, one acts and seeks knowledge to facilitate such action. Bacon's science helps command nature in action, and its method is therefore to catch nature at work, as Jonas says—to ask questions that illuminate the "how" rather than the "why."

The pre-Renaissance person tended to expect to find *meaning* in the world—nature was a repository of messages from God, which, when correctly discerned and interpreted, could guide one's actions. Yet it was just such "anthropomorphic projections"—that is, the assumption of such human artifacts as meaning in nature—that were dismissed, even forbidden, by the Renaissance revolutionaries who sought to redefine nature and knowledge. Once nature is stripped of such supposedly human characteristics as meaning and purpose, it becomes simply a material object whose form is determined by the forces of necessity, and an entity which can be, so to speak, strapped down and cross-examined until it is forced to reveal its secrets—that is, its necessities, its regularities, its properties, which once discerned will facilitate the prediction and control of Nature.

DJ: You quote Rilke that "Men only began to understand nature when they no longer understood it."

NE: Once you've declared there's nothing human in nature, that it is an alien force that has to be known by separating yourself entirely from it, then you begin looking for those rational understructures, the mathematical or geometrical properties that you can then claim are Nature.

This is also a statement about what constitutes real knowledge, of course.

DJ: How does the scientific worldview relate to a feeling of aliveness?

NE: It denies it. The idea that materials are made up of particles that are subject to discernible rules certainly doesn't give you the idea of the self-willed unpredictability of life. The most exciting thing about wild animals is that they're wild animals. Not that they're animals, not that they're behaving matter, but that they're wild. We don't know what they're going to do, much as we like to think we do.

DJ: In *The Social Creation of Nature*, you refer to Dennis Lee's remarks on neurobiology and to the fact that when we scientifically study the brain we find synapses but no trace of anything we could call consciousness. You say, "This is a dilemma: we cannot mistrust science, even when it proves we do not exist."

NE: It's the snake eating its tail—you can't quite grasp what's going to happen. On the one hand, we like to think of ourselves as qualitatively distinct from nature, presumably because as hyperconscious beings we are able to direct our own destinies and be freed from the so-called tyranny of nature. For example, we become very nervous, if not actually violent, when someone asserts that we are "nothing but" animals—that our behavior is in some way delimited by our genes, for instance. Yet on the other hand, we are also highly respectful of the very philosophy that *assumes* an underlying likeness between ourselves and other organic beings—that is the basis of biomedical research on animals. The difficulty is that we seem to have two separate and contradictory views of ourselves, one as a suprabiological being, the other as a material body discernible through normal scientific procedures. The occasional glimpse we get of this deeply held contradiction usually arises as a consequence of either a direct nerve-tingling assault by a sociobiologist who dares to treat us as mere animals, or an epistemological failure, such as a biologist failing to discern the seat of consciousness (or the soul) in the course of an expert postmortem. The two contrasting understandings, and the expectations that follow, are unsettling whenever they present themselves in tandem: we can comfortably accommodate one or the other, but not both.

DJ: Which makes our man/nature dualism very fragile.

NE: The dualism is fragile because we've put our faith in reason, and then this reason has studied humans and found that they are *not* different; reason legitimated the establishment of the dualism, and then reason went and outreasoned the dualism, so to speak.

DJ: Which leaves us confused.

NE: And paranoid. The knee-jerk reaction to sociobiology is indicative of that. Someone actually dares to make deterministic statements about humanity. It's OK for us to say that everything else is rigidly determined, bound by Nature's laws of necessity. It's very amusing when scientists suddenly find themselves in trouble because they said something which is perfectly in keeping with all the work they do and the examples they have, and all the things society admires them for doing. For merely applying it to humans they suddenly get in terrible, terrible trouble. That shows me they've touched a nerve.

DJ: Where does God fit into this picture?

NE: I've noticed a lot of interest in "something else." I don't think anyone knows where it's going to go, and I don't much trust the people who think they know. There's a great deal of "nouveau Christianity" stuff out there, which is very well meaning and may be very good. I don't know. Some of it is definitely just trying to say you can't get by without some form of spirituality. You can't explain everything any other way.

The opening up to the nonrational, I suppose, derails the requirement that nature can only be reasonable. If your definition of nature is not "that which is bound by reason," then you open the possibility of things that are "not reason." You've opened the door to something beyond "Nature." And what is it? So far as I know, the only two categories now are human and nonhuman. I guess you're reopening the door to what was once God, but which today is perhaps only the "wonderful" or even the "miraculous"—that is, the experience of the world which transcends rational explanation. One can imagine all kinds of reasons that people might be induced to look for something in the world beyond explanation, but it is rather surprising to find such a search initiated by people who do not seem inclined to be religious in any traditional sense. I can't explain it, but I do observe it, frequently.

DJ: *The Natural Alien* seems to be about relation.

NE: There's a slight contradiction between the two books in that, in the first one, I was more willing to think of the virtues of the "extended self," particularly of regarding the self as part of nature. But I think we will always see it objectified in some cases and personified in other instances. Recently I haven't emphasized that extension of self so much and instead have tried to get at something else: the shock of the other.

In some of John Livingston's writing, for instance, there is a consideration of childhood experiences, the shock of encountering a frog or a cat or just listening at a frog pond. Those are the kinds of things you find in people who are strongly motivated to speak in defense of the nonhuman. They don't usually know why they're motivated. They just know it's there.

It's something that gets lost in talking. It's a very emotional thing. I view it as not an expansion of self but a loss of self.

John mentions an example in which he sat listening to his lovely frog pond and reached for his coffee, only to find that it was stone cold. This means that in the interim he wasn't aware of time at all. He was totally lost.

Northrop Frye claims that in what he calls the primitive language, the poetic language, duality disappears. That's one of the reasons it's so awkward when people try to describe these events. You can't talk about them in anything short of metaphorical language. If your experience is loss of self, or of one's identity with the other, it makes no sense in a logical sentence.

But metaphor gets over that, allowing you to mix subject and object together. I think that's one of the reasons we're lucky to be able to hear about it from nature writers, the Barry Lopezes and Annie Dillards, who don't tell you how nature works, but instead tell you about the experience of it.

DJ: The dance.

NE: Yes. It's experiential, and it's looking for a theme, a metaphor, to convey the experience, the sensation. They're not trying to *explain* anything.

I heard someone say once that they tended to write through images and aphorisms rather than through logical argument. I think this is what

I tend to do, too, partly because I don't think a logical argument would do the job as well. It's got to be an emotional affect; I don't think argument alone changes much.

DJ: Near the end of *The Natural Alien* you say, "But environmentalism, in its deepest sense, is *not* about environment. It is not about things but relationships, not about beings but Being, not about world but the inseparability of self and circumstance."

NE: An illustration I've used is the idea that we think you can take an animal, put it in the zoo, and have the animal exclusive of the habitat it belongs in. Charles Bergman, in *Wild Echoes*, talks about a lot of things being done as attempts to save endangered species, almost all of which involve intensive management and captivity and so on. I like the way he talked about the last California condor being caught and caged/ saved. Saved in a cage.

The gist of it was that it was only saved if you define a California condor as a feather-crusted bundle of meat. But if your concept of Condor includes the animal's context, then it hasn't been saved at all. All you've done is accepted the primary destruction of the creature's habitat, the creature's place. And once the place is gone, of course there is no animal, in a contextual sense. So what you've done is redefined what the bird is, or as he says, you've allowed biology to define what a bird is. Just this creature with feathers, this expression of DNA, rather than a creature in its place.

DJ: If, as our culture teaches, we're simply an ego in a bag of skin, how do I account for the pain I would feel if my brother were to die?

NE: Many people have had the idea that a person does not die as long as the memory survives in those who were part of him or her. As long as you don't think a person is just the body, the person is the event that carries on.

J. H. van den Berg, in *The Changing Nature of Man*, wrote about Jean Cocteau going back to his childhood home and trying to re-create the impression of childhood. He couldn't quite get the feelings, so he crouched as low as he would have been as a child, and pulled a stick along a picket fence. Then all the memories came back. Van den Berg asked, "Where was the memory? Was it in an engram in the brain? If so, why wasn't it there all the time?" He says, "It was in the fence." It's all around. The self is in the place.

DJ: In *The Natural Alien*, you wrote that environmentalists are protesting not only the stripping away of natural resources but of meaning. In *The Social Creation of Nature*, you come across very strongly at the end saying that the world *is*, and we need to release nature from our meaning.

NE: Well, the kind of meaning I was talking about freeing nature from was the idea of trapping it in "Nature." The belief that our role is to describe and explain, and thereby contain.

The other one, the meaning environmentalists are defending, is the idea of living in a world that makes sense—that we should belong in a place that seems to have significance, that speaks to us. I don't think we experience ourselves as walking through empty sets of atoms that have no significance, nonliving sets of behaving particles. The world is experienced as something that we do belong in. It is a home. Someone lives there. I think the meaning I'm talking about is this place being the home of us all, human and nonhuman alike.

Linda Hogan

Linda Hogan has written that "our renewal often flows from loss, pain, ashes. We are like giant redwood trees, with new life springing from our fallen selves." Every person who cares about the earth is intimately familiar with loss, pain, ashes. Much of Linda Hogan's work is about having the strength to accept that loss and pain, and through that to be transformed. She has also written, "We are in the middle of overthrowing an internal dictatorship that has been forced on us, and in that revolution we are becoming whole."

Linda Hogan is a Chickasaw poet, novelist, and essayist of international recognition. She is the author of several books of poetry, a collection of short fiction, and the novel Mean Spirit, which is about the exploitation of the Osage people and land at the hands of oil-seeking white Americans. Her book Seeing through the Sun received an American Book Award from the Before Columbus Foundation. The Book of Medicines was a finalist for the National Book Critics Circle Award. She is a professor at the University of Colorado.

DERRICK JENSEN: What's the connection between language and the healing of the earth?

LINDA HOGAN: Language is. It has force. Someone like N. Scott Momaday would say language is an entity, a living being. Perhaps all language is a song or a prayer. Octavio Paz wrote that when you go to more primary ways of thinking, the word and the subject are the same thing. There is no abyss between the word and what it speaks.

Seen in this way, words have a great potential for healing, in all respects. And we have a need to learn them, to find a way to speak first the problem, the truth, against destruction, then to find a way to use language to put things back together, to live respectfully, to praise and celebrate earth, to love.

However, English seems to be a language that has more to do with economics than emotion. We do not have words in English for our strongest feelings. It's not a language that can touch the depths of our passion, of our pain.

English also has trouble with the idea of wilderness. I've gone to wildlife conferences and found that we do not have the language to talk about what wilderness is. If we have a language that can't even express all our human emotions, how can we expect to be able to talk about wilderness? And in this lack, English has little to express about reverence for the land or the human need for wilderness.

It's no coincidence that Indian people are under the Department of the Interior along with forests and wildlife. Indians have been called "wild" and seem to represent an unfathomable mystery to Christians and to European colonists. This is because of the connection to land, the recognition that life resides in everything, the understanding indigenous people have of how the forces and cycles of nature work. The fear of wilderness, the fear of indigenous people, and the fear of not having control are all the same fear.

The psychologist C. A. Meyer's work appears in a book called *Testament to the Wilderness*. He says that as the wilderness outside ourselves decreases, the wilderness inside ourselves increases. Of course, his idea is that wilderness is overwhelming and that the wild—nature—is necessarily violent, which isn't always the case. But the point he makes is a strong one.

What's "wild" is something we haven't yet been able to define. I'm not sure we can preserve it until we find the language for it. We have to work very hard and try with all our energy to find a way to speak what wilderness is. Yes, wilderness is the place where violence happens, but it's more than that, and it's deeper than that. It's the place of creations.

DJ: How does this fit with your work as a writer?

LH: My main work has been to find a language that expresses a care for the land and its creatures, that bypasses the mind. When words go straight into the body, the inexplicable happens to a person. You know those moments you have when you enter a silence that's still and complete and peaceful? That's the source, the place where everything comes from. In that space, you know everything is connected, that there's an ecology of everything. In that place it is possible for people to have a change of heart, a change of thinking, a change in their way of being and living in the world. What I want my work to do is show possibility, to show another way of being in the world where there is relationship and a recognition of that relatedness. It is about a community larger than human. It is about our bond with other animals, with creation itself.

DJ: And story?

LH: Story is the most essential thing we have. In some ways it's the *only* thing we have. Some people who want healing go to a therapist and tell the stories of their lives. Then they see the story differently, shift the pattern, and that is healing for them. In stories you have a shortcut to the world of emotion, a direct path to the mythic and unconscious, to meaning.

We all have our own stories we live in, and changing the American story, showing people another story, is a worthy thing to do. I'm working on an essay about the Gaia hypothesis and other contemporary physical theories, all of which return to what Indian people have always said— that the earth is alive. And look how long it took for the new people to discover this ancient knowledge.

There is a language beyond human language, an elemental language, one that rises from the land itself. I remember Dan Rather saying about Chernobyl, "If it weren't for the wind, nobody would know this story." The wind was the person that told the story. Left to humans, it would have remained secret and hidden.

Barbara McClintock won a Nobel Prize for the discovery of gene transposition in corn plants, and the way she did her research was by listening to the corn. It turned the scientific community on its "ear" when it found she did research by, in her own words, intimately getting to know each plant of corn, the "story," she called it, of each plant. She found what the other members of the scientific community wanted to know but couldn't discover through their learned methodologies.

There is a way that nature speaks, that land speaks. Most of the time we are simply not patient enough, quiet enough, to pay attention to the story, to be attentive.

DJ: Early in *Mean Spirit* you write, "Second sight, it was a known fact, was easy to lose when new shiny cars honked in the dirt roads, and fine china plates were being thrown up in the air and shot down like clay pigeons."

LH: A belief system is like food in that it sustains people. One of the things that happened even before Wounded Knee and some of the other massacres was the attempted, sometimes successful assassination of belief.

Actually it was the assassination of more than belief, because traditional religions are land based. They stemmed from centuries and centuries of knowledge about how the land works and about its processes—intimacy with the land. So it was the severing of the sustaining connection with the land.

Even the traditional belief in the reverence of life was quickly destroyed because here were people—new people who came to the continent—who did not have that reverence and who would kill and mutilate men, women, and children.

By the 1920s, when the novel takes place, aggression and violence composed the American way of life. Everything that had been accomplished on and against the whole land had been accomplished through aggression. No matter what Indians did to survive and keep communities and ways of life intact, it was a nearly impossible situation, because the plan was to exterminate us and take the land. Even for those people who did survive, there was then a policy of extermination of their being, the very essence of what it was to be that person. A tribal person. The time of assimilation, when it was thought that "to kill the Indian was to save the man," was a time of war against the hearts of people.

I was at a conference for tribal wisdom keepers, writers, and artists, and Susan Harjo said, "When you people came here, it was like you threw a blanket over our heads. We've been in darkness all these years, and only now are we starting to lift it up and see who we are."

It's essential the blanket come off now, not only as we reclaim and strengthen ourselves and our ecosystem but also because of the genocide that's going on to the south of us. People here need to insist that there is a halt to the genocide that is continuing there.

DJ: What is the mean spirit that throws the blanket?

LH: John Hay has mentioned he used to think people were governed by rationality and logic, but now after seventy years he knows they're ruled by fear and rage. I also think a money economy is the source of much devastation, as well as the greed that accompanies it. In Mean Spirit, for instance, one of the things I wanted clear was that "nice" people do commit crimes. The real-life person on whom I based the character John Hale, for instance, was known as a friend to the Indians. The Osage people loved him. He gave them jobs, he went over and did things for them, and then he plotted murders on the side. To people like Hale, Indian people stood in the way of progress, and progress is a sort of madness that is a god to people. Decent people commit horrible crimes that are acceptable because of progress. And because of money, or land.

Money is a very abstract thing, and it's very symbolic. Look at the history of coinage, and its symbolism. You have a coin with a buffalo on it at the same time buffalo were being exterminated, and the face of an Indian person at the same time there was a policy of genocide against Indians. What does this say? Abstraction takes the place of matter; idea becomes as important as life. As the wilderness is destroyed, audiotapes of endangered animals are being sold. This way they are safe. Wilderness on television replaces the real thing.

The money economy itself is totally abstract. I don't know how to remedy that. I just know almost all the sins I can think of have been committed in the name of a money economy. Money justifies any kind of behavior.

And this behavior often yields absolutely unforeseen consequences. We need to learn how to be conscious in our actions and in ourselves. We don't think enough about what could happen. We don't even really think enough about what *does* happen.

DJ: Is the Forest Service intentionally destroying this country's forests, just as the federal government intentionally destroyed the herds of buffalo? The destruction of forests eradicates any chance for us to listen to the forests and learn the lessons they have to offer us.

LH: Yes, there is an antilife force at work in that. I think of it as evil and a power hard to reckon with.

I didn't know until recently that there was a nineteenth-century policy to actually starve people into submission, but there was. In the novel I'm working on, there's a scene, which really did take place, where a tribe was so hungry they ate carcasses of animals they had found, not knowing they were laced with strychnine to kill the local wildlife, wolves, bears.

As mentioned before, people do these things in the name of progress and money. And they put a veneer over it. That's what Manifest Destiny was. There was a document called the *Requerimiento* that was to be read, in Latin, to indigenous people. If they didn't agree with it, they could be killed, because that meant they were not Christian and did not deserve to live. This just places a framework, a belief system, to allow them to take what they want, to make it right, make it legal. People do this all the time. Now it's often called denial. Sometimes it's called law.

DJ: You wrote in *Mean Spirit* that right and wrong are very simple . . .

LH: But the legal system makes it very complicated. I'm not the first to mention that the legal system has more to do with property than it does with individual rights or justice. And the legal system rarely considers community rights, nor does it consider the nonhuman community, extended community rights, the sovereignty of all species.

The American Indian Religious Freedom Act was passed in 1978. It was one of the wonderful things that happened when Indians went to law school. All indigenous religions on this continent were banned in the 1890s, and this new act was supposedly going to help tribes have religious freedom again. So far, though, it hasn't been a viable act because it deals with land issues—sacred sites, access to sacred sites—and it has conflicted with the economic interests of the dominant culture. The two cultures are very different.

DJ: That reminds me of something you wrote, interestingly enough, about tadpoles and frogs, "Wouldn't you want to wake up as one of them someday and be able to live in both worlds."

LH: I think most Indian people are amphibious, because we have to live in those two different worlds.

When you're living in the dominating culture, things are done differently, things are taken care of differently, and you live at a different pace, with a different mind-set.

I get very tired when I work at the university. One day the reason for this occurred to me. I always have several processes going on at the same time, while the white men who work there only have one. They just do their job. I have to do the job, and at the same time I'm aware of the racism, the classism. And of how different this life is from *mine*, the one of my birth.

Because I'm Indian and I live in another world the rest of the time, or when I'm fortunate enough, I have another process, and I have to translate between the two. It's like doing double time.

It seems to me now that the two cultures are irreconcilable. I'm trying to see if there is a way to mesh them, sew them, weave them together. I used to think it was possible, and I constantly tried to do this, but the older I get the more impossible I think the task is. For me, at least, the difference is too great for people to endure.

Also, the older I get the more I feel *not* a part of the white world. Other people I know feel the same way, and go home. They joke about being like elephants going to their own grounds to die, but there *is* a magnetic pull of place, of people, land, home, for indigenous people.

People who come here from different immigrant backgrounds don't usually have that. It's possible to have the connectedness to the land, but it's not the land all your stories took place on, the land all the myths come from, your ancestors.

Five hundred years is not very long to live here. Compare that to people who've been here ten thousand or thirty thousand years.

DJ: Let's go back to the idea of the cultures being irreconcilable.

LH: At this point I feel like those in the dominant culture cannot even imagine indigenous thinking. Every action they make is different from every action indigenous people make. I'm sure you know about anthropologists who stay with a tribe to learn about their spiritual traditions, and then go home and write about it. That means they didn't get it.

DJ: Can the cultures be synthesized?

LH: Synthesis is thought of as positive, but that's not necessarily the case. There is also the possibility of separate cultures living side by side, cooperating with each other without being synthesized. Shared, perhaps, but not enmeshed. They don't have to integrate in that deep structured way. What's wrong with a love of difference?

DJ: Haven't there been attempts at coexistence?

LH: You can't coexist with someone when they want what you've got. And now of course people want not only the Indian land base but also the Indian soul. They want the spirituality. They want to learn the belief system. But the belief system at the very base is about respect for the land and reverence for life. That's the basic thing people need to have in common. That's where it all begins to heal.

DJ: In your essay from *The Stories We Hold Secret*, you write about growth being a process that can't be hurried. You call it a ripening.

LH: People become impatient. If they pay $125 to take an overnight vision quest with somebody from southern California, they want results. We've become accustomed to instant gratification. Sometimes people do feel better after such a weekend, just from the time away, time off, but it is temporary. Growing is something we do in our own time, not by schedule.

DJ: You write in that essay, "Growth does not come from putting on any spiritual clothing. Growth comes from removing and removing, ceasing, undoing, and letting ourselves drop down or even fall into the core of our living being."

LH: That's the silent place we talked about earlier. You have to have time, and you have to have quiet. We don't take that often enough. I like to take a day off every week not to do anything. Not take off work to do other work, or chores, but take a day off. It's an incredible experience. Magic happens.

DJ: When I'm done with this project, I'm going to sit for a long while listening to my bees.

LH: And they'll tell you what to do next. That's very hard for my writing students to get. They think you have to keep driving and thinking and working really hard, but actually you have to stop all that. We all keep forgetting this.

DJ: Which goes back to second sight disappearing in a world of honking automobiles.

LH: It's hard to keep integrity of selfhood—the spirit and emotions and body and everything working together—when you have noise around you and things happening and people honking at you and flipping you off. One of my friends says, "Nobody wants to go through the American experience. It's toxic. If you go through it, you get toxic along with it. You have to participate." Maybe she's right.

DJ: Are you angry?

LH: You cannot go through even the experience of our lifetimes and not be angry, because there is so much injustice. Anger can be a wonderful thing, and probably if I didn't have anger I would never have written the novel.

But I also think it's really important not to be controlled by that anger and not to spend all our time fuming and acting it out, destroying other things and ourselves. That's not the way things happen or changes are made. And all the people I know who write, write because they feel it's important to do so, and that it contributes to some kind of change.

But I notice when people do that in an angry way, the response they get is angry, resistant. You almost have to think of it as being a spy. You're infiltrating, and you don't infiltrate a place wearing a weird outfit—you try to blend in. And you don't go in with your hackles up, because people are not going to listen to you. They'll match your hackles with their own.

DJ: You've written that during the forced march by your people during the nineteenth century, when a woman fell to weep over a child the white soldiers had killed, the others would say to her, "Come on, sister. Walk with us a while." Because some of us have to survive.

Aren't we on a forced march today, watching and having to walk on as our children are killed by the side of the road?

LH: It's a different walk, with a different historical source. But our futures are being killed. Our futures are being killed.

WILLIAM R. CATTON JR.

*The earth cannot permanently support the current human population. It fol-
lows that someday there will be fewer humans than there are now; how the
population will decrease is an open question. William R. Catton Jr. begins
his book* Overshoot: The Ecological Basis of Revolutionary Change *with
the statement, "In a future that is as unavoidable as it will be unwelcome,
survival and sanity may depend upon our ability to cherish rather than to dis-
parage the concept of human dignity. My purpose in writing this book has
been to enhance that ability by providing a clear understanding of the ecological context of human life."*

*William R. Catton Jr. has taught at Reed College, University of North
Carolina, University of Washington, University of Canterbury (in New
Zealand), and Washington State University. He won the Pacific Sociological
Association's 1985 Distinguished Scholarship Award for articles in its jour-
nal expanding on themes from* Overshoot. *Vine Deloria called* Overshoot
*"one of the most important books I have read in my lifetime," and Dave
Foreman called it the most important book published in the last forty years.*

WILLIAM R. CATTON JR.: Anthropogenic ecosystem breakdown is the
specter haunting the world today. We have to learn to recognize the effects of ecosystem overload. Our cities are running out of disposal sites
for wastes. More and more, our need to draw potable water from rivers
and aquifers is in conflict with the disposal of our effluents and other end-
products of our industrial mode of life.

We need to recognize that the rising levels of greenhouse gases, the
widening hole in the ozone, the drawdown of aquifers, the depletion of
mineral deposits and fossil fuel stocks, the deforestation of vast land
areas, the loss of topsoil, the spreading of deserts, and the accelerating
decline of species diversity around the world are all signs we are seriously
overloading our planet.

Every environment can support only a certain level of load placed
upon it by its inhabitants. The load consists of the resources the inhabitants consume as well as the wastes they expel. When the load exceeds

what the environment can tolerate, the environment begins to break down.

This environmental tolerance is called carrying capacity. Technically, an environment's carrying capacity for a given kind of creature is the number of individuals living in a given manner which that environment can support *indefinitely*. Indefinitely is the key word, because it means that carrying capacity is *not* an impenetrable ceiling. There is an important difference between the maximum load that can be imposed briefly versus the load that can be supported indefinitely. Unless the other components of that ecosystem can continually supply us—or whatever creature we're talking about—with what we need to live, and unless the ecosystem can absorb and recycle our wastes, the system will begin to break down, to our own ultimate detriment. This is exactly what we're seeing in the world today.

The natural consequence to carrying capacity overload is population crash. Perhaps the clearest example of this process is the introduction of yeast cells into a wine vat. The yeast find their habitat abundantly endowed with moist, sugar-laden fruit mash, exactly the resource they need for explosive population growth. As their population increases, though, the accumulation of their own fermentation products makes life increasingly difficult, until eventually the microscopic inhabitants of this artificial ecosystem die. The cause of their death is self-inflicted pollution—the fermentation products.

Another example that I cite in *Overshoot* is the introduction of twenty-nine reindeer to Saint Matthew Island in the Bering Sea in the 1940s. By 1963 the herd had increased to six thousand, on an island with a carrying capacity for about two thousand reindeer. Since overshoot leads to habitat damage—it is in essence stealing from one's own posterity—the crash brought the population far below what could have been previously sustained. By 1966 there were just forty-two reindeer left on the island.

Not all of the mortality in a crash is due to actual starvation. This is very important. During a die-off of introduced sika deer on James Island in Maryland, the deer were well nourished and parasite free at the time of die-off. Their growth, however, had been inhibited by physiological disturbances caused by behavioral stress associated with high population density.

Overshoot and die-off happen to people as well. After overshooting Easter Island's capacity to support human beings, the Polynesian inhabitants began their own crash by commencing genocidal conflict between two factions, the "long ears" and the "short ears," followed by malicious disruption of food production that caused many survivors of the battles to starve.

DERRICK JENSEN: How serious is our current predicament?

WRC: I feel less certain now than I did twenty years ago that outright extinction of the human species is an imminent prospect. We are, however, beginning to see the processes of crash. So far, the places in which that is resulting in increased death rates are more than offset by the natural increase going on in other parts of the world. It will be some time before enhanced world death rates exceed worldwide birth rates and global population begins to decline.

But I think we will see the cessation of growth in a lot less time than many demographers are predicting. They still make projections that extend for a couple more doublings. I don't think we'll actually have even one more doubling. Life will become sufficiently disorganized before then. The estimated population of the planet now is 5.5 billion. I doubt we're going to reach 10 billion. I even doubt we will reach 8 billion, and I'm somewhat skeptical we'll reach 7 billion.

Look around today. The violence happening in the Middle East, in Central America, in the former Yugoslavia—the fact that these human societies are coming apart and that various ethnically distinct categories of populations are having at each other—is the sort of thing that seems to be expectable when you talk about overshoot and crash.

DJ: Why?

WRC: Increased population pressure intensifies competition. And the greater the competitive pressure, the greater the tendency for each person to see his or her neighbor as a threat to his or her access to resources.

In an age of overpopulation each person is in as much danger of being considered superfluous as the next. We each want to be reassured that it is the *other* person who is redundant. Thus we vilify our competitors, portraying our "enemies" as so malevolent that preemptive aggression is acceptable.

Unfortunately, we're not seeing very many people interpret this violence ecologically. We're still seeing it interpreted almost entirely politically and economically. People compare what is being called ethnic cleansing to the Nazi holocaust. That comparison is realistic, but you can't fully understand it unless you see it as another instance where surplus people want to declare others, not themselves, to be the surplus.

The truth is, we're far beyond an age of exuberance, and the expectations that the future should be brighter than the past have broken down. That makes it possible for people to be receptive of the idea that it's because of "those guys." The Serbs think the Bosnian Muslims are the cause of their woes, and the Bosnian Muslims think it's the Serbs.

But all 5.5 billion of us are the cause of woes for all of us. That's too many. And it's especially too many if we want to live by the ravenous methods modern technology has accustomed us to.

DJ: You said that we're far beyond an age of exuberance.

WRC: An age of exuberance is a period in which there is so much carrying capacity surplus that the natural response is to expand exuberantly.

When Europeans encountered America they thought of it as the land of opportunity. They were right—it *was* the land of opportunity. Here was a continent being used as habitat for hunting and gathering peoples, with some also practicing forms of horticulture. To Europeans it seemed like an empty continent. There were millions of people here, but they didn't count because they weren't using it the way Europeans were familiar with. The resource base was available for a much more lavish style of exploitation.

So to Europeans it was the land of opportunity, meaning there was an opportunity for them to indulge in the intrinsic rate of increase of our species—to double their numbers every generation.

For a while they were not only doubling by natural increase, but by migration from Europe, which took some population pressure off that region. And then people started shipping goods from America to Europe, which further took the pressure off back there. So Europe experienced a great exuberance too, even though it had been, as of the New World's discovery in 1492, essentially a filled-up continent.

Because of the growth of human numbers and technological progress, we have since ceased to have a surplus of carrying capacity. Now America is more densely populated than Europe was then, and we're in an age where exuberant expansion just isn't the order of the day.

DJ: But doesn't technology increase carrying capacity? There are certainly more people living now than before.

WRC: There is a difference between a temporary load and one that can be sustained indefinitely.

At present, technology has the effect of increasing per capita resource and energy consumption.

But life has always depended on the existence of an outside, a place from which we obtain resources and to which we expel our wastes. And human reproductive and technological "success" has put a large proportion of the planet within our human/technological system. When we learn to see the air intakes and exhaust pipes of our millions of internal combustion engines as the nostrils of what I call *Homo colossus*, and realize how much more oxygen per capita we require than our ancestors consumed, and how much more we can now contaminate our surroundings by our normal activities than they could by theirs, it becomes evident that these mechanical servants have become our ecological competitors. We and our engines breathe and transform the same air, and compete for the same space, the same water, and so on. Technology, then, while originally a means of increasing human carrying capacity per acre, has become a means of increasing the space, energy, and material required per human occupant. To put some numbers to that, primitive hunter-gatherers use 2500 to 3000 kilocalories per day, whereas modern Americans use about 200,000 kilocalories per day.

DJ: Why isn't this on the front page of every paper every day?

WRC: Cultural lag. Different parts of a culture change at different speeds. Sometimes tensions arise when two previously synchronous parts of a culture get out of adjustment. One part changes and another doesn't. Some people still consider the world a cornucopia. With the European settlement of the Americas, all of Western civilization experienced about four centuries of exuberant growth, and we haven't yet gotten over the idea that that's the natural order of things.

The cultural lag becomes apparent when our political leaders still talk as if we can and should stimulate economic growth further. Responses based on the idea that the country needs growth lag way behind actual conditions confronting the country and world.

And so we still proliferate and keep on inventing more ways to use more resources per capita. This has the effect of digging ourselves in deeper and deeper.

DJ: Where does petroleum fit into this?

WRC: Ever since we began burning fossil fuels, we have been supplementing human carrying capacity by using some of the solar energy that was captured by plants during the Carboniferous period and stored underground millions of years ago. Since this energy is prehistoric, it is not renewable in human terms. The use of it results in a *temporary* augmentation of carrying capacity. I call it phantom carrying capacity. It won't last.

This temporary extension is significant in size. More than nine-tenths of the energy used by *Homo sapiens* is now derived from sources other than each year's crop of vegetation. To live sustainably with current population and per capita energy consumption, modern man would require an increase in carrying capacity equivalent to ten earths, each of whose surfaces was used to the extent we are currently overusing this one.

Our reliance on petroleum really took hold in the 1920s. Starting then we began doubling our use of petroleum every decade, and although we've slightly reduced our rate of increase in the past twenty years, our use is still increasing. Obviously this increase can't go on forever. Even if the entire planet were petroleum, in about three hundred years we would have burned up the whole planet with that sort of doubling of consumption each decade. Nowhere near the entire planet is petroleum, so that three-hundred-year estimate is absurdly optimistic.

All of this of course raises the question: What's going to happen when we no longer have prehistoric energy to subsidize our population and patterns of consumption?

DJ: I've read that by 2005 or 2010 it will take more energy to find new reserves of oil in the United States than the reserves will produce.

WRC: By that point we will have effectively used it up. There might be billions and billions of barrels of petroleum inside the planet, but if drilling and pumping use more energy than the energy content of the petroleum, there's no point.

DJ: Does this speed up the crash you envision?

WRC: It would, except that economists favor a ploy called resource substitution. Just as we stopped using so much coal when we shifted to oil, there already is a shift underway to the use of more natural gas. But that again is a finite resource. The more conversions we can do to natural gas, the more we postpone the day of reckoning. That's all we do, though, is postpone it. We don't escape it.

In the meantime, we continue to pump carbon dioxide into the atmosphere when we burn any fossil fuels. So even if there is still plenty of fuel available, that will produce a day of reckoning, when the level of the oceans starts to rise as a result of global warming.

There's just no escaping the fact that we are now changing the planet in ways that are adverse to the future of our species, ways we need to be taking into account.

DJ: What about nuclear power? Hydroelectric? What about massive solar? Won't these keep our age of exuberance alive just a little bit longer? How about going back to coal?

WRC: We could go back to coal, but that would just increase the pollution problem, which is already severe in many localities. I think there will be more use of solar energy in the decades ahead. That will help somewhat. But I don't think the exuberant way in which we have been increasing our per capita use of energy for the last several lifetimes can be projected much into the future just by those technologies.

Nuclear energy seemed like it promised that after World War II. Some of us immediately began envisioning owning a nuclear-powered automobile. That's been the American habit, to have an excessively optimistic projection of technological progress. But in the past few decades we've been shutting down nuclear power plants. It's been more than a decade since the last one was opened, and it's been two decades since the last authorization to start building one was either sought or attained. With Chernobyl I think the Europeans are looking askance at nuclear power now too.

There was a little flurry of hope when those people in Utah claimed they had achieved cold fusion. That turned out to be at least a false alarm. And I think the prospects of actually generating usable energy from high-temperature fusion are getting dimmer and dimmer. It's useful as a bomb, but it's not useful for turning on the lights.

So I think we're approaching the point where the per capita availability of energy is going to level off and possibly begin to decline, from the depletion of fossil fuels.

One of the problems we've created for ourselves is that all the machinery driven by fossil fuels has made it possible to harvest timber faster than ever, and made it possible to increase agricultural yields per acre and per man-hour of farm labor. The upshot of all this is that we've gotten into the habit of using even renewable resources in nonrenewable ways. The lush wheat fields of the Palouse with their yields of a hundred bushels per acre are dependent not just on the local soil but on the anhydrous ammonia farmers pump into the soil, anhydrous ammonia which is based on the use of natural gas as a feedstock. So we are in essence farming nonrenewable resources—not to mention the several tons of topsoil lost to erosion for each ton of grain harvested.

Our population is also dependent upon petroleum-based transportation. By joining together different areas through trade, the composite carrying capacity can exceed the sum of the carrying capacities of the separate regions. This happens because people living where carrying capacity is limited by a shortage of one essential resource can trade with the residents of another region that have an abundance of that resource while being limited by a different scarce one. Another way of interpreting this, though, is that if the populations of the regions have expanded to fill the composite carrying capacity, and then either the transportation system breaks down or the political atmosphere changes so you don't have the exchange going on, you've got an excess population load. And people will feel it.

DJ: So are NAFTA and GATT then attempts to extend the age of exuberance?

WRC: Precisely. But you never see the media pundits defining them that way.

DJ: A moment ago you mentioned the reliance of farmers on fossil fuels for their yields. That reminds me of something you've written about farming. You've said that farms stop the natural process of succession.

WRC: A farm, or even a garden, is a contrived ecosystem; it requires continuous attention to keep it in its desired state. Efforts must be directed toward compensating for the soil changes caused by its occupants, and toward preventing the invasion of unwanted plants, or weeds. Thus, a farm is an engineered effort to stop nature's process of succession. If you abandon a farm, succession takes over and a couple of centuries later it becomes something very different from a farm, perhaps a woodland. The conversion of forests to tree farms is an example of the same kind of effort. Second-growth forests are noticeably different from climax forests.

In order to support even a lesser human load than we've got now, there's no doubt we have to hold back succession in some places. But we can't try to convert the whole world into one big farm, much less one big city. Still, so much social history in the last couple of centuries since the industrial revolution has seemed an attempt to convert the world into the contrived kind of ecosystem that a farm, a garden, a city, constitutes, with the failure to recognize that the city is utterly dependent on the hinterland. Imagining that the destiny of rural places is in due time to become urban has really been heading us for trouble. We've defined progress as antisuccession, and that just can't go on forever.

DJ: And by the same token, aren't attempts to extend the age of exuberance also antisuccessional? You've written that it's almost impossible for the ecological dominance of any species to be permanent.

WRC: Yes, except in climax communities, where things have come into such a balance that the environmental impacts of the several member species are mutually offsetting. Or, you might say, dominance is less specific to one species and is more shared in a climax community.

In most other circumstances, dominance tends to be ultimately self-destructive. In the case of modern human beings, human dominance is flagrantly self-destructive.

DJ: Thomas Berry has written that a species is well adapted to its community if both it and its community benefit from its presence.

WRC: Our aggravation of the rate of extinction of other species is a manifestation of our dysfunctional dominance. Since some of those species have turned out to be necessary for serving some of our special purposes, the harmfulness to ourselves has become evident.

DJ: How did writing *Overshoot* change you?

WRC: Most of my publication since this book came out has been on topics pertaining to overshoot. Increasingly I've been trying to get my fellow sociologists to see that sociology needs to become an ecological discipline. We need to stop thinking of human ecology as simply a small specialty within sociology; sociology is instead a small specialty within general ecology. A few of my colleagues have caught on to that, but not many.

And since writing the book, I became convinced we were not really facing imminent extinction of the human species or even its northern hemisphere branch. Some fraction of it, I am now inclined to think, will survive. When I was writing *Overshoot*, we still had years of the cold war ahead of us, but gradually it began to feel as if we were over that hump.

I continue to be an optimist, even though, facing reality, I don't think you can be too confident about the future of the human species.

Let me add that one of the tragedies of our time is that when we needed to be taking this kind of analysis of our situation to heart—for the whole twelve years Reagan and Bush were in office—we wasted our time, instead of coming to grips with the real situation of humankind.

Actually, it would have been nice if we had begun to face this at least a century ago. If a century ago we had caught on to the fact that we have to cut off population growth, we could have leveled it off by now at a level lower than our present population, and things would be a lot brighter.

Still, I guess it's better late than never, except if you're *too* late, then it is tantamount to never.

DJ: You've written that in a postexuberant age, it is important to ask, "What must we avoid doing to keep from making a bad situation worse?"

WRC: There are proposed solutions that may do more harm than good. I commented earlier that the present administration still wants to get

America moving again, still wants to increase the GNP and so on. That is going to do harm.

It's a little like getting your car stuck in a muddy place; the temptation is to bear down on the accelerator. Often all you accomplish by spinning your wheels is to dig yourself in deeper. A lot of the proposed solutions to some of the aspects of our global ecological problem are like those wheels spinning, digging in deeper. The perceptive driver doesn't do that—he or she tries to rock the thing by intermittent little surges of power. So the more knowledgeable we are about how ecosystems really work, the more likely we are to avoid digging ourselves in deeper, and the more likely we are to find something at least mildly beneficial to do.

We have to remember that being human doesn't exempt us from ecological principles. We're not just involved in humanity, but in ecosystems—in associations of many species of organisms. We need to remember that what we do to an ecosystem, we do to ourselves.

ROBERT JAY LIFTON

When I asked Robert Jay Lifton the first question of our conversation, "How is it that ordinary people participate in horrifically destructive acts?" he paused a moment before responding, "That could not only be the first question we talk about but also the last, because it is such a big subject." It is the subject with which almost all of his work has been concerned; he has written about Hiroshima, Chinese Communist thought reform, Nazi genocide, Vietnam, and nuclearism. His observations in all these cases are in the direction of hope—that human beings needn't participate in such acts of destruction.

Robert Jay Lifton, M.D., has been named Distinguished Professor of Psychiatry and Psychology by the City University of New York, and teaches at CUNY's John Jay College, the Graduate Center, as well as at the Mount Sinai School of Medicine. He is also director of the Center on Violence and Human Survival. Lifton is the author of numerous books, including Indefensible Weapons: The Political and Psychological Case Against Nuclearism *(with Richard Falk),* Death in Life: Survivors of Hiroshima *(winner of the National Book Award),* The Nazi Doctors: Medical Killing and the Psychology of Genocide, *and* The Protean Self: Human Resilience in an Age of Fragmentation.

DERRICK JENSEN: How is it that ordinary people participate in horrifically destructive acts?

ROBERT LIFTON: Most evil—or destructiveness, which is almost the same thing—emerges from shared ideology and practice that tend to be unquestioned. In the extreme, a culture can develop an ideology that drives its people to destroy all Jews, Gypsies, Slavs, or whomever, for some claimed higher good. Or an ideology can declare that a higher good demands you build and be prepared to use limitless nuclear stockpiles. Most of the participants within these potentially destructive projects are quite ordinary. These ordinary people engage in profoundly immoral acts through ideology, group process, unquestioned personal decisions, and the group, national, or corporate behavior and policies they become part of.

DJ: Does this mean people give up their moral autonomy when they participate in a group?

RL: Since there is no such thing as completely isolated individual moral behavior, what we like to see as individual moral autonomy always depends to some degree on relations and shared assumptions with others. That inevitable connection with others, morally as well as psychologically, is part of being human.

What we give up, then, is an awareness of the consequences of our actions and commitments. By and large, when we act in direct individual ways—one person engaging another—we have some sense of responsibility for what we do. But when we move away from one-to-one interactions, the clarity of moral cause and effect diminishes. It can be easy to become part of something without considering the consequences of that project. For example, if we are part of a corporation that cuts down trees, we are engaged in helping that corporation to succeed in its goal of making money, and we block out the effects of destroying forests.

I've worked extensively with psychic numbing, an idea I first described in *Death in Life: Survivors of Hiroshima*. For the survivors of Hiroshima, numbing was a life-enhancing mechanism—by an almost automatic shutting off of feelings one could survive. But in groups involved in destructive behavior, psychic numbing is dangerous. Think about Nazi technicians working the gas chambers and SS troops shooting Jews face-to-face as part of the genocidal project. They had very extreme and gross forms of psychic numbing.

The psychic numbing is less dramatic in people who work for that company cutting down forests, and it's even less visible in the rest of us who fend off impulses and images from the environment so we can get through the day. Within this culture you could call the numbing of everyday life a necessary defensive maneuver.

DJ: Does technology exacerbate psychic numbing?

RL: Technology exacerbates everything. Technology has come on with tremendous force and has generated revolutionary change, rapid variation, alteration, and expansion. It has been unmanageable. It intensifies every form of dissociation. Where it is a technology of destruction, the ways in which it does that are quite obvious. But even where it is a technology that is allegedly for peaceful and life-enhancing purposes, it can always help the dissociation by distancing decisions not only from the consequences themselves but also from awareness, psychological perception, and psychological response to the consequences.

DJ: How does numbing tie to what you call doubling? You wrote in *The Nazi Doctors* that this is the century of doubling.

RL: Doubling in Auschwitz was almost always involved with violence, both on the part of the person committing it and on the part of the victims. In that book I investigated Nazi doctors who doubled in connection with their activities in Auschwitz. Their function as Auschwitz doctors was to supervise the killing process. But they would also go back to their families every month and be more or less ordinary fathers and husbands. They were functioning as if there were two separate selves.

Of course at Auschwitz they numbed themselves not only to the violence but as a way to adapt to the whole Auschwitz environment, creating a whole different self-structure. This led me to think about all brutal treatment as being accompanied by doubling. My criterion for calling something doubling was the formation of a second self-structure that was morally at odds with the prior self-structure. You could say I'm a different person when teaching a class than when I'm at home, but is there a significant moral difference in the self-structure?

Contrast that with Mafia leaders, who may be pillars of their communities and give to their churches while at the same time ordering people's deaths. The same is true for terrorists or members of death squads. A doubling process occurred, also, among the nuclear physicists and strategists I interviewed for the book *The Genocidal Mentality*. This doubling process was not as intense as with the Nazis, because they weren't directly killing anybody. But the doubling process did occur. One part of them would be a very decent, likable, attractive human being, but in the laboratory they would shut out the outside world, forming another self, a nuclear-weapons self.

A major point to make about doubling is that it's an adaptive mechanism. It was a way in which the Nazi doctors adapted themselves to the Auschwitz environment and a way in which weapons designers and strategists adapt themselves to their professional environments. The extreme irony is that this is an example of the exquisite human talent for adaptation, which is our genius as a species. But presently that very talent for adaptation to genocidal environments can do us in, in terms of ending *all* adaptation as a species. And doubling is a key to this, because it's one of the most extreme forms of dissociative adaptation, as well as one of the most widespread.

DJ: People double within corporations as well. The CEOs of Union Carbide offered victims of Bhopal five dollars each in disaster relief, Armand Hammer poisoned the residents of Love Canal, Richard Bressler of Burlington Resources decided to simultaneously lay off workers and liquidate the forests in the Northwest . . .

RL: There is a consistent sequence of corporate response. First there is a denial that they did it. When it's quite clear they *did* do it, the next step is, "It isn't real damage. It won't hurt people." When it's clear it will hurt people, they claim, "The alleged victims show signs of chemical poisoning, or whatever, because they have a predisposing tendency."

I could well imagine that within the minds of corporate heads there is the need to convince themselves they are decent human beings. They struggle to realize their moral values by attempting to convince themselves they are acting on behalf of the victims. But this is of course a form of doubling insofar as they carry through, vigorously and uncompromisingly, policies that try to avoid restitution, while at the same time attempting to be decent family members.

DJ: How does group behavior come to manifest values that disallow life? I'm thinking of Manifest Destiny and the continuing genocide of indigenous peoples, the Third Reich's policies, Mutually Assured Destruction, the valuing of corporate bottom lines over life.

RL: Perhaps the most troubling principle is that there is always a claim to virtue. You cannot kill very large numbers of people without a claim to virtue. The Nazis saw themselves as not only getting rid of an undesirable population group but as performing a service for humankind by eliminating Jews. This is because the Jews were, at the extreme end of this ideology, a culture-destroying force. If this culture-destroying force were eliminated, the Nordic race, which was the only culture-creating "race," could once more thrive. The element of virtue and service to humankind, or the larger good, was crucial to the carrying out of that ideology. Even people who didn't fully believe in that ideology could believe the Nazis functioned as a revitalizing force. This was the case for most of the Nazi doctors I interviewed. They believed the Nazis had value for Germany in that they made the Germans feel strong again, powerful, a force in the world.

This claim to virtue is true as well for the more subtle processes of numbing involved in the destruction of the natural world. This *must* be understood if one is to get at what is happening with some depth. Under a capitalist system, making money and "developing natural resources" are considered good and necessary activities. If one is part of such an enterprise, one will internalize that claim of virtue. In that way ideologies influence the function of organizations like corporations, and then internal dynamics of corporations—the pressure to influence the bottom line—can absorb everybody associated with that organization. What we call socialization to bureaucracies and organizations can be a profound process by which you step-by-step come to offer your intellectual talents and capacities as a human being to the project of that corporation, military group, laboratory, or other group.

A good example of this is the role of chaplains and psychiatrists in Vietnam. Sometimes when young GIs wanted out or were terrified or broke down, they were sent to these people, who then helped the GIs be strong enough to return to duty and to the committing of daily atrocities. These chaplains and shrinks, as the men called them, were very decent human beings for the most part—no different from you or me, presumably, in their ethics or in their moral behavior ordinarily. But they were part of a project that called for them to keep people at duty. This underscores that it's not enough to be individually ethical; one has to examine ways in which one's ethical standards are realized or violated in group behavior.

DJ: What would you have done had you been drafted during the Vietnam War?

RL: If I had full awareness of the filthy nature of the war, and of the relationship of the individual to immoral projects, I would have refused. I would have struggled against being drafted, and would have declared myself a conscientious objector, even as a psychiatrist.

DJ: That sort of awareness seems difficult to attain.

RL: We spend most of our lives either seeking awareness or avoiding it,

or some combination thereof. That's because there is something terri-
fying about absolute adherence to moral principles. A person seeking
uncompromising moral consistency is uncomfortable all the time, because of threats to that consistency. Each of us makes compromises, and
for most of us such compromises are probably necessary. But what form,
what kind, and with what awareness?

The issue of moral consistency arises more and more in relation to the
environment. What one does individually as well as collectively is very
much at issue in the kind of probing you're doing. Also at issue is the
question of awareness of the consequences of one's behavior, and therefore awareness of one's moral consistency in advocating a life-enhancing
environment and what one does in relationship to that advocacy.

DJ: Perhaps it's not so important to be consistent as to act flexibly from
one's center. Whenever I cling to dogma, I stop listening and thinking.

RL: When one contemplates the threats we face, which involve apocalyptic dimensions of killing or destroying, one is likely to call forth
dogma. This longstanding dogma doesn't seem adequate to these
threats, at least in part because the historical context that created the
dogma has changed.

My argument in *The Protean Self* is that we have of necessity formed
a more flexible sense of self, because the traditional symbol systems
which sustained us are no longer there or at least no longer fully believ-
able. That protean openness on a large scale, which is with us at least as
a potential, is a hopeful development. In other words, much of our hope
lies with a more flexible approach in which we pull together a sense of
self and a sense of shared behavior—shared commitments—through
bits and pieces. This requires a center, a core of stability or principles
larger than the self. Any believer in spiritual principles knows that, but
no matter how secular one may be it applies equally.

DJ: How can this help us develop a culture that values life?

RL: I'm interested in the revolutions in Central and Eastern Europe in
1989 and 1990, and have interviewed people in Prague about their experiences. These people had of course been socialized to the communist
regime, but there was also a socialization to the oppositional movement,
which had developed its own press, ways of disseminating information,
and code of behavior. This was a socialization process you could describe

as being in the service of freedom. And this wasn't just a movement toward political freedom, but also toward truth, and toward more desirable or noble human values. The dissidents were constantly aware of this long before they achieved political power. Achieving political power came suddenly, and as a surprise.

The general point is that there *is* a possibility of socialization to life-enhancing processes. There is simply no getting away from values in collective enterprises. That becomes a crucial vantage point from which to look at the kinds of problems we face today.

DJ: Let's talk again about genocide. Genocide forms a theme in Western history. What function does it serve?

RL: A consistent set of motivating emotions with genocide and mass violence is the sense of threat to one's own group and an impulse toward violent resolution of that threat. This impulse is toward what Richard Slotkin used as the title of a book describing the emergence of the American nation, *Regeneration through Violence*. That's very true of the Nazis, and it's true in a different way of the potential nuclear genocide toward which we and the Soviet Union had been building and of which we are now by no means free.

Bosnia is another example. There, particular groups have been threatened or assaulted in the recent past. These groups are now revitalizing themselves with an extreme nationalism that sees a higher good in greater Serbia in a way that can block out the unspeakable brutality and pain caused in others.

DJ: How are victims chosen?

RL: The designated victim must be seen as simultaneously powerful and vulnerable. They must be powerful enough, at least in one's own perception, to serve the psychological function of allowing the victimizing group the revitalization it seeks. At the same time it must be vulnerable enough that it can be destroyed or at least treated brutally. The Native Americans were the designated victims early on in this country's history. Their victimization has not stopped, but their role as primary designated victim has been displaced, from the time of slavery to the present, onto the blacks.

An additional requirement for designated victims is that they must be seen as death-tainted. I first noticed this in regard to my work in Hiroshima. There, the survivors met a second wave of discrimination because of their association with death. Other examples include Japanese outcast groups, so-called *burakomin*, and the untouchables in India, who were relegated to handling feces or dead bodies. If potential victims can be seen as death-tainted, they are, so to speak, OK to kill, because they are perceived as in some sense already dead. That psychological stance becomes very important. Through it those perpetrating genocide can reinforce what they perceive as their own life power, what I speak of as their sense of immortality. They do this by denying life power and symbolic immortality—the continuity of a people—to a designated victim. This is the crux of revitalization through violence.

DJ: The world's population will decrease with what anthropologist Marvin Harris calls the bursting of the technological bubble. What lessons do the survivors of genocide or other catastrophic collapses of population have to teach us?

RL: Survivors of catastrophes can, as a result of what they have been through, either open out or close down, or sometimes do both. If they open out, there is a process I speak of as survivor illumination. These survivors, having encountered death, having witnessed deaths, having felt themselves very close to death or as if dead, can bring a certain quality of awareness back into the world. This is a knowledge of death and of the possibility of large-scale killing or large-scale dying.

It's terribly difficult to achieve and maintain awareness of large-scale killing and dying. An Auschwitz survivor and valued international colleague once said to me, "Robert, you know I've done nothing but think about and be involved with survivors for forty years, and I still can't believe it really happened." Of course he knew it happened, but there was a real side of him that almost disbelieved it. In a sense he was saying, "There still isn't quite a place in my mind for the kind of event that I actually witnessed."

That's a revealing story, because there is hardly a place in our minds for human life being threatened because of nuclear holocaust, or because of the various other means we have of destroying the environment. If my friend the Auschwitz survivor had difficulty convincing himself that the Nazi genocide occurred, think of the difficulty for the rest of us, from the president to the environmental activist. That in itself is a major stumbling block, a major difficulty with coping with nuclear weapons, environmental destruction, and genocide.

This is reflected in our response to what is happening in Bosnia. Any television viewer can say, "Yes, I saw those things. They are terrible." Yet we simply turn off our television, feeling a mixture of anger and guilt and general discomfort. At least for periods of time we deny to ourselves what we see, and at a certain point one turns off one's awareness of what actually is happening—one's full awareness of what this really is and what it signifies.

There are different psychological terms for this—denial, disavowal, psychic numbing—and there are many reasons why one turns off that awareness. The awareness is very uncomfortable, and one doesn't like to have to confront it, especially when one is uncertain about what to do, and one sees one's own group or one's own country doing nothing. But an additional reason one turns off the awareness is that there's no preexisting place in the mind for it. We don't grow up with a concept of people on a massive scale destroying another people. We may hear about it, dip into some historical description of it, or even study its occurrence in history. But we may not take it in fully and humanly, that is, in relation to the consequences or the suffering that is involved.

Survivors, more than most of us, have from their experience a palpable knowledge of our capacity to impose mass death, to engage in genocide or mass killing. The rest of us require that knowledge, that level of consciousness, that survivors can bring. And we require ways of applying that consciousness in life-enhancing directions.

DJ: How does one fight evil without taking on the tools of evil oneself?

RL: It's easy to justify to one's self and to one's group the necessity of draconian methods to fight what is perceived as extreme evil. This leads to exactly the danger you are asking about.

A beginning answer lies in being aware of that danger and searching rigorously for alternatives. A very good example of this kind of problem is the situation in Bosnia now. You do want to fight the evil of genocide being committed mostly by the Serbs and Croats against Bosnians or Bosnian Muslims. If you provide more arms to the people being attacked, are you expanding the war making and the killing? Yes, there is that danger. Yet inaction in the face of genocide is an expression of immoral or even evil behavior. A group of us have responded by advocating what we call Assertive Safe Havens. That is, UN military controlled forces could protect populations and also go out to disarm anyone who attacks any population. That might be a way to stop evil using only enough force to do what needs to be done.

Fighting evil without becoming evil oneself entails thinking about new, relatively nonviolent, ways to combat violence.

DJ: Do you have hope?

RL: Almost all of my work has been concerned with highly destructive events—Hiroshima, Chinese Communist thought reform, Nazi geno-cide, Vietnam, and other disasters. But my observations in all these cases are not in the direction of us being doomed to a hopeless chain of destruction and self-destruction. Although that kind of chain is very possible, there is always the assumption in my work—in the very act of studying or confronting this possibility—that there are alternatives.

Recently I've been working with the idea of species consciousness. This is a sense of self that is not abstract and idealized, but that is grounded in a psychological and personal sense of being a human being. This means that all other identities, such as physicist or teacher or en-vironmentalist or businessman, are subsumed to one's sense of being a human being. The more I work with this idea, the more I see that at the same time the destruction has accelerated, so has our sense of the po-tential alternatives. I see the situation as in many ways dire and danger-ous in the extreme. At the same time I am hopeful. I don't see the possibility of humankind suddenly emerging with full sweetness and light to renounce war and to do what is best for life-enhancement in re-lation to the environment, but I do think we have the possibility of at least bungling through, of taking certain life-enhancing steps. All of the opinions I've offered, and all the conclusions that others within your study have come to, should be seen and used as efforts in furthering that hope.

If one only stresses the genocide and its inevitability, one is contrib-uting to the massive destruction or the apocalyptic end result. If one probes the dimensions of hope, one is contributing to an alternative possibility.

There is another way to look at this. If one does not look into the abyss, one is being wishful by simply not confronting the truth about our time. One is not, to use Martin Buber's term, imagining the real. On the other hand, it is imperative that one not get stuck in the abyss. With the knowledge from the abyss one looks toward alternatives, toward the transformation that we desperately require.

WARD CHURCHILL

Prior to the arrival of Europeans, an estimated 12 million human beings lived within the present borders of the United States. In 1890, when the federal government declared the "Indian wars" to be officially over, the native population was less than 250,000—a little over 2 percent of what it had been four hundred years earlier. And the genocide against indigenous peoples continues unabated to this day.

One author who has explored the genocide extensively is Ward Churchill. In his work, Churchill makes the connections between the direct destruction of a people, the appropriation of their land, and the more insidious roles played by literature and other forms of culture in the committing of genocide. How does genocide continue to this day, both in the United States and across the world? How do assimilation, ideology, and even such seemingly harmless actions as the dominant culture's appropriation of Indian spirituality relate to questions of Indian identity and, ultimately, existence?

Churchill's numerous books include Fantasies of the Master Race: Essays on Literature, Cinema, and the Colonization of American Indians; Struggle for the Land: Indigenous Resistance to Genocide, Ecocide and Expropriation in Contemporary America; *and* Indians R Us?: Culture and Genocide in Native North America.

DERRICK JENSEN: You're the first person I've seen make the explicit connection between Manifest Destiny and the lebensraum policy of the Third Reich.

WARD CHURCHILL: Actually, the first person I'm aware of to make that connection was Adolf Hitler. He stated clearly in *Mein Kampf* that he did not take any of the old empires of Europe as the model for what he saw as the destiny of the German people. Rather he took the Nordic population, as he called it, of North America, who had had the "strength of will" to exterminate an "inferior" people and put their land to its own use, making of itself in fairly short order a continental power capable of projecting a global influence on the course of events.

The only way for the German people to fulfill what he saw as their destiny was to expand into areas occupied by inferior peoples. With the exception of the Jewish and Gypsy populations, which were not partic-ularly endowed with landholdings at the time, the most inferior group in sight, in his estimation, were the Slavic peoples. He therefore artic-ulated a drive by Germany from west to east in direct correspondence to what he perceived as the history of the Nordic drive in North America from east to west. The nazis were pushing in the opposite direction but for the same purposes, from the same philosophical perspective—a mat-ter Hitler made quite clear—and utilizing much the same methods that he discerned as having been employed in North America.

This is about the notion of a given people defining itself as being in-vested with a superior right to the use of land belonging to people they concomitantly define as inferior. In part this second group is considered inferior because it uses or relates to the land in ways considered inappro-priate by the expanding group. The designated inferior group is to be completely displaced from the land, which will be put to "better" use by the self-defined superior group. If there is nowhere to displace the infe-rior group, then it will be eradicated altogether.

Both dislocation and extermination are present in the American expression of this. Dislocation was manifested perhaps most clearly in the pre-1850 drive to take those peoples resident to localities east of the Mississippi River and remove them physically and forcibly to localities west of it. These new localities happened to be somebody else's territory, but it was all "Indian Country," and Indians were interchangeable in the minds of the American master race.

After 1850, when the United States decided this "permanent Indian Country" west of the Mississippi might also be useful, a shift occurred from this policy of dislocation to one of outright extermination. This shift begot what David Savaldi has described quite properly as a "rhet-oric of extermination," which was evident at every level: popular media, scholarly forums, and official policy articulations. It was quite literally an expression of a willingness, even a desire, to liquidate inferior beings who were cluttering up the landscape with their existence. They had to be removed to make way for progress and civilization, meaning to make way for members of a superior race, a superior culture, which held a su-perior destiny—a manifest destiny, if you will—to utilize the land in ways it deemed to be a culmination of a civilizing impulse on the part of humanity, of which it proclaimed itself the representative.

Take the whole sweep of Manifest Destiny in the United States, which reduced the Native population by some 98 percent, and the lebensraum impulse in Germany, place them side by side, and both practically and philosophically you've got a direct correspondence. Distinctions between the two can be readily accounted for by evolutions occurring subsequent to what happened in North America, in terms of technological capacity to eradicate or displace populations and further refinement in terms of social/military organization.

DJ: Is genocide a thing of the past in the United States?

WC: There seems to be a popularly held notion that while genocide "may" have occurred, it's something that ended with the Wounded Knee massacre of 1890. This stems more than anything—aside from the emotional desire of people who are now benefiting from the legacy of genocidal policies to set themselves apart from it—from a very profound misunderstanding of the meaning of the term itself. This confusion has been inculcated in U.S. society, rather officially, through the posture of the United States government in refusing to endorse, and effectively refusing to comply with, the requirements of the United Nations Convention on Punishment and Prevention of the Crime of Genocide from 1948 onward. Popular misperceptions go with the notion that in order to be perpetrating genocide against a people you must engage in the outright killing of the members of those societies targeted for elimination.

Let's be clear on this. While killing large numbers of a group is mass murder, it may or may not be genocidal. Genocide is by definition the elimination of identifiable and targeted human groups *as such*, and you can eliminate a group—cause it to go out of existence in identifiable terms—even if every member constituting that group survives as an individual.

In the genocide convention framed by the United Nations in 1948 there are five classifications of action that constitute genocide. The first of these has to do with killing members of a group with intent to bring about the disappearance of the group. The remaining four—80 percent of the definition—involve means *other than* killing to bring about the desired result.

Those perpetrating genocide can, for example, create conditions that bring about the forcible dismemberment, destruction, or dispersal of the group, so that the group is ultimately dissolved.

They can intentionally visit acute psychological or physical discomfort upon the group, so that group members "voluntarily" separate themselves and bring about the group's dissolution in order to spare themselves the individual discomfort.

They can force the transfer of the children of the group to another group at an early age and train them to see themselves as something other than a part of that cultural context into which they were born. If that happens, the culture cannot perpetuate itself and goes out of existence. That's understood to be a mechanism of genocide. It is genocidal conduct under the law.

And finally, those perpetrating genocide can prevent births within the group through involuntary sterilization or abortion. The word "involuntary" is what is at issue here. When the *state* imposes birth control as a matter of policy on targeted groups so they cannot conceive and/or reproduce themselves, with the ultimate intent that the group disappear, that is genocide.

Now, particularly with the forced transfer of children—the boarding school process, blind and other adoptions—which was imposed throughout Indian Country during most of the late-nineteenth and twentieth centuries, you have genocidal conduct on the part of the federal government toward Indians. This was continued—and arguably it hasn't really ended—in full force at least into the last generation, which is well *after* the atrocities visited upon the Jews, the Gypsies, the Slavs, the Poles, and everyone else considered to be *untermensch* (subhuman) by the nazis.

In a couple of those generations, upwards of 80 percent of Indian children were compulsorily removed from their family and community contexts, taken to boarding schools, and trained to see things in terms of their oppressors' value structures and priorities. These children were denied the right to speak their language, to practice their religion, to dress in a manner allowing them to visually present themselves as being who they were. They were forcibly shorn of their hair, which has a spiritual significance in most native societies. They were raised to see themselves as integral parts of the culture—the society—that had conquered and dominated their parents. The idea was that you would have a bunch of brown-skinned, black-haired, dark-eyed people wandering around who felt and thought and considered themselves to be a part of the European tradition, having no particular knowledge or cognizance of their own tradition, and that on that basis they'd systematically intermarry with whites and eventually be absorbed into the dominant population. That's a pretty quick, relatively sophisticated, effective means of getting to a genocidal result, and it was part and parcel of a formally pronounced and undertaken U.S. policy that was maintained for at least four consecutive generations.

It's what they called "assimilation." Assimilation in this sense is essentially the *digestion* of conquered peoples; when it was completed, the idea was that Indian societies would no longer exist in any coherent form at all. The perpetrators were very out front about this. The articulation of this concept, interestingly enough, came mainly from a group calling itself "The Friends of the Indian."

Assimilation was the "friendly" alternative to more immediate and direct forms of extermination—"be assimilated and you can continue to live." That was the choice presented to Indians by the United States, once they'd been decimated by military action, overwhelmed and subordinated. You just have to become that which you are not and abandon that which you are, altogether, forever, permanently, irrevocably. In the alternative, "hard-liners" will finish the job of physical liquidation. So you get a choice between cultural genocide and physical genocide. But it's genocide either way.

DJ: Recently I heard Russell Means talking about the horrible conditions on reservations, and someone asked him, "Why can't Indians just move to a city and get a job?"

WC: That's classic assimilationist thinking.

The reason things are bad on reservations is because the assets of the people there have been stripped away and put to the use of the dominant society. Not lawfully, not ethically, not morally; the resources have been taken through a combination of fraud, deception, and force. The "solution" implied by the questioner to the miserable conditions on the reservations is to finish the job: all the Indians need to do is go out of existence, as Indians, and they won't suffer any more.

Well, that is true, no doubt. But if you don't see anything wrong with this solution, then ipso facto you must not see anything wrong with genocide.

People try to displace responsibility for victimization onto the victims. When confronted with the facts, people in the dominant society all of a sudden can't understand the relationship between what their grandfathers did and the fact that they are now benefiting from those deeds at the direct expense of the victimized groups. They say, "We got your land, we got your resources, we got your identity, we got everything, we even want your spirituality at this point. Now, with all that said and done, let's pretend it's a 'level playing field.' Come on and get in the game with us. If you don't, then whatever happens to you is your own fault. You're just 'lazy' or 'shiftless' or otherwise 'inferior' and are therefore deserving of your fate."

Were all of this to happen to Euro-Americans, they would be every bit as bad off as Indians. In some areas, like Appalachia, they happen to be.

DJ: The American Indian Movement has taken some flak for not professing nonviolence.

WC: Indians are the most peaceful people, traditionally, you would ever wish to encounter. But if you tell any people—to their perpetual suffering, agony, disenfranchisement, dispossession, disallowal of hope— that they are irrelevant long enough, they may just prove to you, in desperation, their relevance by utilizing violence. It's a natural response. If they blow your brains out, you see, there's no question they're relevant. This applies to Indians, Palestinians, people of the inner cities, anyone who is oppressed.

So if you don't like the possibility that we will resort to armed struggle to defend ourselves and our future generations from what is being done to us, change what is being done to us. Do that in the most nonviolent possible manner, with my blessing. But if you don't actively pursue an alteration of the context of pervasive violence to which Indians are subjected, you are in a poor position to complain if some of the violence eventually comes back at you, don't you think?

DJ: Earlier you said members of the dominant culture have taken Indian land and now want even Indian spirituality. How can someone steal spirituality?

WC: Let's take this step by step. First the land. It's gone. Native people within the contiguous forty-eight states have residual, nominal rights over about 2.5 percent of their original land base. I say nominal because it's all held in trust by the federal government, with Indians having occupancy rights allowed them by the dominators. Important decision-making capacities in regard to that land are in the hands of the dominators, not the occupants. But being as charitable as possible, 2.5 percent of the land base remains in Indian hands. That means 97.5 percent has been taken outright.

Even by the government's own legal definition quite a lot of that was illegal. If you stretch U.S. law and its predications in English law to the absolute maximum, you still can't cover about 35 percent of the land transfers. That's the federal government's Indian Claims Commission talking there, not Indian radicals; the commission admitted flat out it could find no basis for U.S. title to about a third of the forty-eight contiguous states, even in the most polite of interpretations.

OK, the land's gone, the resources are gone, and even our identity is controlled by federal statute. You've got to meet blood quantum criteria before you can be federally recognized as an Indian. The feds claim they're "protecting the sanctity" of indigenous nations through the imposition of race codes. Ask yourself: What's a nation in terms of a racial code? There is no genetic structure that is Lakota, for example; Lakota is a political and cultural designation. But that's how they've indoctrinated Indians to think. We no longer have control over, or even common sense about, our own identity, not in terms of how our peoples always understood themselves in relation to their own society, that society in relation to other societies, and all of those societies in relation to nature. That understanding of ourselves has been obliterated for the most part and needs to be reconstructed.

So identity has been taken, along with our land and resources.

What's left? Well, there's the intellectual property of the few people who didn't get totally screwed up and "deculturated" in the other three processes of expropriation. This is a fairly thin repository of something truly Indian, and now we've got every yuppie New Ager in the universe deciding they have an inalienable right to take that, too, and use it for whatever purposes they see fit.

We can cut through this real fast with a statement that Onondaga Fire Keeper Oren Lyons has made. He said, "I'm a spiritual leader among my people, and I don't understand what you're talking about with respect to rights to our religion. We have no rights in this regard. We have *responsibilities*, and it seems to me that's one thing you're trying to avoid."

Couched in those terms, there would be very few New Agers who'd queue up to learn about indigenous traditions, because these people are attempting to avoid responsibility, to sidestep the heritage they're a part of. Rather than rectifying it, putting it right, putting it back in balance, they want to step out of it and appropriate something else from somebody else so they can pretend to be other than who and what they are.

This is not helpful to us, to them, or to the cosmos in general. People within a tradition that has created any sort of imbalance need to recognize that, and do what is necessary to rebalance the situation. That can only be done from within their own tradition. It cannot be done by them opting out and "becoming Indians."

Within certain parameters, nobody really cares if you want to talk about Indian religion. There are spheres that are public domain, and there are spheres that are not. That's true of indigenous spiritual traditions, and it's true of other forms of spiritual traditions. There are of course differing extents of public domain, depending on the tradition.

Christianity, for example, is a proselytizing religion, so it's got a very wide window of public exposure. But by and large, when you're talking about indigenous traditions, you're not talking about proselytizing traditions. Instead of trying to recruit and convert, they're trying to sustain a given balance *within* their social orders. That cannot be done when their prime symbols become the common property of anyone who wants to walk in and play with them.

Even with Christianity, as Wendy Rose has pointed out, Catholics would resent her, an Indian, impersonating a priest. If she delivered communion in serious fashion to the faithful, you would hear an uproar among Catholics about it. Compare her hypothesis of impersonating a priest on one hand to Harley "Swift-Deer" Reagan's *actual* impersonation of a native spiritual leader on the other hand. Hers in a context that is relatively open to outside participation, his transgressing against traditions that are in fact not open at all. Now conceive even further that in her impersonation of a priest she mixed in a little Islamic, Buddhist, and Hindu ritual tradition as well, as if these were actually Catholic. You can amplify the shrieks and screams you're going to hear from people who believe in Catholicism. Her performance has gone beyond mere heresy into blasphemy, even obscenity. But that's what ersatz "medicine men" do as a matter of course. They mix a little Lakota, a little Diné, maybe some Shoshone with the medicine wheels, some Cherokee herbal stuff, and just a little bit of snake oil hucksterism. They stir that up and call it "indigenous spirituality" and sell it to whatever suckers are willing to buy.

In that process, they undercut the integrity, the sanctity, of the real traditions from which they draw. Undermine them enough and they'll disappear. So the whole thing we're talking about is *not* harmless. It's part and parcel of the overall process of genocide we've been discussing.

DJ: What can I do to rebalance my own tradition?

WC: The easy answer is look around you and figure out what's going wrong. In a way that's an overwhelming task, because so much is going wrong. But on the other hand, it's easy because so much is going wrong that *everyone* can find something and go after it. Oppose. Don't go along. Resist in terms you can understand, in the context you're in, from where you are. Do *not* try to sidestep. Take it head on. Move on it. Force change from *within* the particular reality you confront now. That, in one immediate sense, causes the system to break down. It can only happen through opposition, so many forms of opposition I couldn't enumerate them all. You can be rich, poor, black, white, green, polka dot, male, female, young, old, all of it; you know there is an overwhelming mass of things you're uncomfortable with, that you *know* are wrong. *Do* something about setting one of them, or five of them, right.

But there's another thing, I think, that fits for Euro-Americans in particular. What we have to understand is that in order for Europeans to do what they have done to virtually all non-Europeans, all non-Westerners on the planet, they had to colonize themselves. These colonizers are colonized.

They too are indigenous people. Not here. But *somewhere* they are indigenous people, with indigenous traditions and understandings of the land, and all the things we counterpoise to the predator reality that engulfs us now. They need to get back in touch with that, you see. They must recover that which was taken from them in the process of colonization, taken in the same fashion that things are being taken from us, now.

Euro-Americans have got to psychologically and intellectually reverse the process of colonization, to find out what went wrong for them clear back in the beginning. And then they can begin to recover knowledge of those traditions, to bring about the decolonization of Europe itself, most of all the European mind.

And it may be that we can be helpful to them in that regard, once they have recognized the need for that to occur, to get back to what it meant to be Gaelic or Celtic, to find out what Anglo-Saxon really meant before the synthesis of "Europe" was effected.

When that occurs there is no more European mind, there's the human mind. I can talk to Basques and Celts. I can't talk to Europeans. Not in the sense of people who come from a given piece of geography or a people who occupy a certain mental space.

It's getting back in touch with your self, your origins, your continuity, your sense of balance in this universe. These people could never be indigenous here. It doesn't mean they can't be here. It just means they can't be indigenous here. There is a set of consequences and relations that stem from that. We can deal with that if we can properly understand it.

I talk about the landing at Jamestown, and about the pilgrim fathers coming over in 1620. I talk about what the dominant culture has done, and all of a sudden I get a bunch of red-faced, uncomfortable people talking about "white-bashing": "What? Are you talking about me?"

I reply, "Not unless you're old enough to have been around in 1620. I'm not white-bashing. I'm just recounting what happened. But you're really uncomfortable with what happened, aren't you? You're identifying with something here, and I didn't identify you with it. You did."

The lightbulb goes on now. You think you're "white"—whatever that is, that's an invented term, too—and since I'm talking about white people, you feel some need to identify with them, with the perpetrators of the massacre. That's exactly the psychology that perpetuates the legacy of it. *You* didn't do it, so why are you defending it? You don't have to, because you can oppose it just as easily as you can embrace it. But you can't do both at once. You *can* separate yourself from what has been done—and what's *being* done. But first you have to be willing to call what's being done by its right name.

The dominant culture—the colonized mind—is at war with nature, and so by definition is at war with all peoples of nature. The more natural the people, the greater the degree of hostility the dominant culture manifests toward them.

This is an alienation from nature so profound and so virulent that no one in the dominant flow of things wants to acknowledge that it even exists. Theirs is the normal and correct ordering of consciousness to relate to the world, they say, they assert, they insist. So long as they look at it that way, there can be no admission of pathology. It follows that, absent an acknowledgment of the pathology, there can be no cure.

What's necessary is for people to come to grips with the fact that there is something radically wrong with the tradition into which they've been conditioned, and for these people to want to get out of that.

This may seem unlikely, but I want to stress that it is possible. Nothing human is impossible, at least in terms of human interactions and relations. There's nothing preordained or "immutable." We're not dealing with glaciation or some other geologic process here. What's at issue is the result of choices, often conscious choices, made by human beings.

So it's all possible. None of it is—as the dominant culture contends—"unrealistic." If it's possible it's also realistic. If you let that which oppresses you define what's real, you will always be oppressed. Define a different reality, one which makes more sense, and go after it.

FREDERICK TURNER

The anthropologist Stanley Diamond began his book In Search of the Primitive *with the observation, "Civilization originates in conquest abroad and repression at home." Why have all encounters between Europeans and indigenous cultures resulted in the decimation or destruction of the indigenous populations and cultures?*

Frederick Turner explores questions such as this in his book Beyond Geography: The Western Spirit Against the Wilderness. *Charles Bowden wrote of* Beyond Geography, *"If you wonder how we lost our souls, destroyed the standing of women, polluted our sexual feelings, and gained the sheer insanity necessary for us to be able to loot a hemisphere in the name of God and machines and greed,* Beyond Geography *will explain the answer to you."*

Frederick Turner is the author of six books, including a biography of John Muir titled Rediscovering America *and* Spirit of Place: The Making of an American Literary Landscape. *His essays have appeared in such publications as* Wilderness, Smithsonian, American Heritage, Orion, *the* New York Times, *and the* International Herald Tribune.

DERRICK JENSEN: You've written that the conquest of North America was "the tragedy of a failure of vision and of that missed opportunity for spiritual growth and renewal that comes but once to a civilization." How did this happen, and why have the Europeans and now Americans committed genocide against the original inhabitants of this continent?

FREDERICK TURNER: In *Beyond Geography* I tried to account for the conquest of the New World in terms of the development of Christianity from a mythological cult to a state religion that was essentially historical and nonmythological in nature.

A mythology, as I see it, is essentially cyclical in nature. To use Mircea Eliade's phrase, it is an effort through ritual enactments and ritualized retellings to ensure the eternal return. Things don't roll forward toward some apocalyptic future, but move in cycles based on the rhythms of nature: the seasons, the tides, day and night, the mating, molting, and migrations of animals.

The evidence suggests to me that Christianity began as just such a mythology and that it was only after the death of Jesus, probably some time during the ministry of Paul, that Jesus began to be transmogrified from a mythological figure into a historical one. As a result, the emphasis in the religious practices changed from expecting a renewal of the spirit and a renewal of the mythological, spiritual insights of the leader to an absolute, hysterical insistence that the phenomenon of Jesus happened in history. The purpose of Jesus came to be that of redeeming human beings from a cycle of error and putting them on the path of a history, which would eventually end with Christ's return. The historical progress of Christianity in effect signed the death warrants of any mythological cultures that this particular messianic historical religion encountered in spreading its orthodoxy.

To me, one of the critical distinctions between mythologies and historical religions is that mythologies not only allow for the possibility of individual enlightenment and revelation, but actually expect it. The whole idea of the vision quest, for example, is founded on the idea of revelation. But Christianity sealed that off and said, "All the revelation we need was had in the time of the apostles." Because of this distinction, even into the midst of the twentieth century you find mythological religions sometimes characterized in sober anthropological literature as unorganized. By that is meant, among other things, that their canon of saints, their dogma, and so forth, is not fixed. Revelation is a returning and recurrent possibility. Therefore from the point of view of an "organized" religion, which has fixed things by canon and in scripture, they appear to be unorganized—which is about the same as "untrue."

By the time the Christian West blundered into the New World, the West had to account for that New World in terms of Christianity's own predilections, perceptions, and psychological prisms. This was not easy, because the New World was so various and because its peoples were living in a mythological past the West had gone beyond.

It wasn't quite so difficult in the beginning, when the Spaniards encountered the Aztecs and subsequently the Incas. After all, these were civilizations which, however barbaric they seemed, could at least be accounted for in a roughly analogous kind of way. They had cities, a monarchy, a class system, slaves, dependencies, mediums of barter, and so on. But after that the analogies, which were only of limited use to begin with, didn't work. It's one thing to encounter the Aztecs and Incas, and another to encounter the tribes of the eastern seaboard or Northwest Coast in North America, to say nothing of the tribes along the Amazon.

There was something that both profoundly frightened and angered the Europeans about their inability to account for these tribal cultures, especially because something about these mythologically based cultures provided vague and unpleasant echoes of where the Europeans themselves had once been. Worse yet, these peoples seemed to be, at least to an uneducated European mind, more contented in their existence, even as primitive as that existence may have seemed to sixteenth- and seventeenth-century Europeans.

I think this inability to account for these cultures reached its apogee in the very last stages of the North American conquest with the Plains wars, which are for various (mainly technological) reasons the best known of the wars. To the whites there seemed to be an element of ritual play about the way these tribes made war. I'm not so sure it seemed that way to the Lakota, the Cheyenne, the Arapahoe, the Crow, and so on. But to whites, who had already enslaved themselves to the machine and to an enormously proliferating technology, the fact that these people spent a hell of a lot of time dressing up and putting on finery, even in the deadly serious business of warfare, was an affront of a profound nature.

I'm interested in the Plains wars because they bring into sharpest possible focus the antagonisms at work, and, as it must seem to us now, the inevitability of the genocide. One would have thought even a rapacious hell-bent civilization such as we had developed would have thought, "Enough is enough. We've conquered west to the Mississippi and east from California to the Great Basin; maybe we ought to just leave these folks alone." But the people who did say this, such as George Catlin and Henry Thoreau, were mere squeaks amid the roar of progress and the absolute refusal of our civilization to tolerate the kinds of differences that had really been at issue ever since Cortez landed on the shores of Mexico at Vera Cruz.

DJ: Why the refusal to tolerate the differences?

FT: The insistence that revelation happened only once upon a time and that Jesus intervened in historical time to save humans from eternal damnation leads to the notion that your mission is to convert. You cannot be content with having the good news and the light within; you have to share it. Christians are of course still absolutely determined to do this; witness Pope John Paul's missions to the Americas.

Wherever that restless civilization goes, it's going to encounter mythological peoples. This will necessarily lead to conflict, because the mythological peoples are not going to readily assent to their own error. This conflict leads to the Christians saying, as they did in the days of Renaissance exploration, "Christianity or death."

DJ: What is the connection between this restless civilization and its need to possess lands without being possessed by them? How does this manifest itself on a personal level?

FT: A major part of early Christianity's charge, as it moved away from its mythological base, was to distinguish itself from competing cults in the declining years of the Roman Empire. One of the most dramatic ways to do this was to adopt the attitude of the Old Testament that peoples who worshiped the earth and any of its phenomena were doomed to perish like the phenomena themselves. True, God had created the earth and its creatures, but natural phenomena were not therefore sacred. Man was the apex of God's creation, not subject to it. To pray to the earth, to be possessed by its mystery and power and beauty was therefore to make a terrible, a blasphemous mistake. The obligation of humans was rather to possess the earth and use it to their benefit—not be possessed by it like a child might be by sunlight on sparkling water. The many contests of the Old Testament pitting the Israelites versus nature-based peoples chillingly prefigure later contests enacted in the New World.

DJ: Isn't the same thing happening today, in North America, South America, Indonesia, and in the forests of the Northwest?

FT: Everywhere. Everywhere.

DJ: Where do you see it going?

FT: There is a countermovement now in Christianity trying to reformulate the missionary aspect of the religion and trying at the same time to reestablish the religion's connections with the mythological roots. But the world is now so densely populated and the islands of intact aboriginal culture are so small and so completely surrounded, it's difficult to see how they can persist intact. They'll have to make accommodations of varying degrees of severity.

What the long view will disclose of the history of the Navajo culture, for example, remains to be seen. The Navajo have been very resistant to Christian missionizing, although Christians have been at it for a long time. While the Christians have not succeeded in weaning the Navajo away from their religion or their language, they *have* succeeded in destroying much of the material base of the Navajo culture. What you have now is a terribly impoverished and imperiled culture riddled with alcoholism, welfare dependency, and a certain amount of incest—all the kinds of aberrations that would have been unthinkable in precontact times. I am not prepared to say we are witnessing the slow strangulation of Navajo culture. It's *possible* this is a part of a long continuum, a long process, that will eventuate in the Navajo reestablishing a material basis for their culture that will allow them to survive within the dominant culture. Not as they were and not as they are, but as they will be. And they will still be Navajo, in some sense.

That seems to be essentially what the Iroquois did. In the eighteenth century they found themselves surrounded, and densely so, by the dominant culture. Threatened with cultural extinction, the Iroquois reformulated their mythology to take into account this alien force that was pressing in on them and that had been successful, in some unaccountable and bizarre way, in defeating their power, their Orenda. The resulting religion of Handsome Lake was a brilliant combination of traditional Iroquois/Seneca mythology, combined with certain aspects of white Christianity, which in effect saved the Iroquois from killing themselves. One wouldn't say the nations of the Iroquois are rolling in opulence now, but they have been able to survive as intact peoples to some extent.

DJ: What about us? How can we recover our balance?

FT: I find the American environmental movement, which has been gaining in scope and momentum since the 1890s, an enormous source of optimism. The environmental consciousness of the average American has come a hell of a long way since that time. Of course the destruction has proceeded much more rapidly than environmental consciousness, because the means of technology have become so much greater, which means the destruction can be accomplished much more quickly.

It has also proceeded more rapidly because most of us are not brought up to express or expect a primal connection with the natural world. Having been brought up in Chicago, I include myself in this.

All of us, though, *do* have some kind of species knowledge of what it once meant to be so connected. This knowledge is in our archaic brain stem and can never be expunged. It can be covered over, and *is* covered over, with layers and layers of cultural appliqué, and maybe with the development of the cerebral cortex, but it can never be erased. Wherever we come in contact with the natural world, it is awakened.

As a kid I went to northern Wisconsin in the summers, and although I never thought about such things as environmentalism, I always felt something in the woods. I felt something about the lakes and ponds that my brother and I would watch for reasons that were obscure to us. Now we have with us people like Barry Lopez, Gary Nabhan, Gretel Ehrlich, Terry Tempest Williams, John Hay, and Peter Matthiessen, exemplars who by their words meet our internal promptings with external confirmation. There hasn't been a time anywhere in the history of humanity where there have been more, and more brilliant, natural history writers practicing than there are right here and now in America. Never. And I can only anticipate this will continue, because these people serve as guides for further naturalists and for students coming up. But more than that, they serve as confirmations of what every kid knows is true.

DJ: How did you disentangle yourself from the Christian culture?

FT: I was raised by parents who were occasional Sunday Christians, but at the same time I had daily contact with two women who were Christians of a strong fundamentalist persuasion. They tried their damnedest to save me but only succeeded in scaring me. The effect of this juxtaposition of occasional Sunday church attendance versus Pentecostal religion was to make me feel very uneasy about what the truth of this whole business was.

I did a lot of soul-searching as an undergraduate, and after college I consigned Christianity to the dustbin of history. I became a card-carrying atheist and then a humanist. Then when I was working on my Ph.D., my path crossed that of Anthony F. C. Wallace, a specialist in

Iroquois religion. In taking his course and also reading in Native American tribal mythologies I became aware once again of the spiritual dimension to life. I realized that not subscribing to Christianity was no good reason to become an atheist, and that atheism was kind of a childish, sophomoric rejection.

The more I studied Native American tribal religions and then began to visit reservations, the better I felt about my own spiritual basis. I like to feel that in the time left to me I will become more and more spiritually active and spiritually consistent. And I would like to be able to suggest to my own children something of that.

DJ: How do we change our basic way of knowing, when everything we see every day all day points us in a different direction?

FT: My wife is a profound skeptic about everything she sees, and especially everything she sees on television, which is by far the most effective brainwashing enculturation technique yet devised. It's such a bombardment that it's very difficult, especially for a kid, to filter out these things. It doesn't seem so much a matter of saying, "I don't believe that if I buy a Buick Skylark my life will be better or brighter" or the rejection of any discrete pitch of that nature. It's a matter of rejecting the whole cultural thrust of advertising and consumer-based culture, which is awfully difficult. The easy pitfall I see with kids is bringing up a generation of naysayers who for every affirmation return a negative and who will grow up with a kind of cynicism. We're already in danger of that, because we've been lied to so much in everything from White House press statements to advertising jingles.

Here again I turn to people like John Hay, Barry Lopez, and others, whose approach to life is *positive* as opposed to negative. It's not enough to say no; you've got to have a countervailing force. That's where examples play a critically important role.

DJ: You mentioned earlier that Christian culture has enslaved itself to the machine. What do you mean by that?

FT: Technological inventions have at their very basis the raison d'être of making life a little easier. As such the technological impulse in human beings is just as natural as the religious one. But it seems to me that what happened, probably beginning with the Neolithic revolution, was that the technology began to create a distance between the humans and their environment. With that distance humans began to imagine they were omnipotent. So while each invention, whether it was a hand ax, a jar, or a system of transportation, made life just a little bit easier, in the main it began to substitute for Neolithic people's connection to the source, for their religious impulse. The great statement of this recognition for our time was by Henry Adams, who after looking at a dynamo at the Chicago World's Fair in the 1890s said something like, "This is what we now pray to, this humming machine, which seems the objectification of the harnessing of those powers which primitive peoples once ascribed to rocks and winds."

This brings us back to that connection to the natural world we were talking about earlier. There *is* power in the rocks and winds. John Muir said that even rocks have their history and their life. This is true. Ditto for trees, and for everything else. Each child setting out into the world, whether it's in Chicago or Larned, Kansas, or Malaysia, carries within him- or herself a foreknowledge that there is a mysterious and undoubted connection between them and this world, and also the foreknowledge that all of this world is animate. I have to think that's the basis of what optimism we can have.

DJ: It seems the worship of the machine is ultimately narcissistic, because the machine is a part of us, as opposed to "the other."

FT: I've always liked dogs, and never understood exactly why. But when you look into their eyes, even into the eyes of some pedigreed designer dog like my own, you see the other. Much of what one was told thirty years ago about the life of dogs is merest bullshit, about how stupid they are, how they can't think. The same with birds. Of course they can think, and of course they have souls, as Saint Francis said they did. I think one of my earlier misgivings about Christianity was being told that animals have no place in heaven. What kind of a heaven would it be that was reserved only for the Lord and Apex of animate creation?

I find it immensely comforting to not only know but to *feel* I don't have a destiny separate from everything else. Maybe that was one of the things that bothered me about Christianity—it seemed such a lonely thing. Here you are going toward some apocalyptic moment, whenever that might be, and meanwhile the trees and grasses and birds and your animal friends share a different destiny—dust. Something's going to happen to them, but ultimately they don't have anything to do with you.

DJ: What is the religious impulse about? What does it mean to be fully a human being?

FT: To be aware. To be aware of the moment and everything that's in the moment, and to be aware that everything that is in that moment is everything that ever was and ever will be. To know you are connected, whether you want to be or not, to the enormous force of Life. The extent to which you can maintain that kind of awareness in your daily life, which is the most difficult of all existential exercises, is the extent to which you are really living. Of course that's the idea of Taoism, and particularly of Zen, but really the religious impulse in its truest sense seems to me to be about that awareness of how extraordinary everything is. Everything.

Starhawk

A feminist and peace activist, Starhawk is one of the foremost voices of eco-feminism and practitioners of what she calls "native European spirituality," a return to the spiritual roots of indigenous or pre-Christian Europe. She travels widely in North America and Europe giving lectures and workshops. She holds an M.A. in psychology from Antioch West University and since 1983 has been a lecturer at the Institute in Culture and Creation Spirituality at Holy Names College in Oakland, California.

Starhawk is the author of The Spiral Dance: A Rebirth of the Ancient Religion of the Great Goddess, Dreaming the Dark: Magic, Sex, and Politics, *and* Truth or Dare: Encounters with Power, Authority and Mystery. *She consulted on the films* Goddess Remembered *and* The Burning Times, *directed by Donna Reed and produced by the National Film Board of Canada, and cowrote the commentary for* Full Circle, *a third film in the same Women's Spirituality series. Her first novel,* The Fifth Sacred Thing, *was published in 1993.*

She lives in San Francisco, where she works with the Reclaiming collective, which offers classes, workshops and public rituals in earth-based spirituality.

DERRICK JENSEN: You've written, "How we see God literally shapes and limits what we can become."

STARHAWK: Our models of God are ultimately our models of what is sacred. And what is sacred tells us our most important values—what we're supposed to work for, not compromise, take a stand for.

It's important for each of us to think about what is sacred to us, in the sense of what it is we most value. And then we have to ask, "Is my life in alignment with that? Do my relationships, my work, my celebrations, the ways I spend my time, further that? Or do they work against it? What kind of support do I need to continue what I'm doing, and what kind of support do I need to change?"

I make a declaration at the beginning of my new book, *The Fifth Sacred Thing*: "The earth is a living conscious being. In company with cultures of many different times and places, we name these things as sacred:

air, fire, water, and earth. Whether we see them as the breath, energy, blood, and body of the mother, or as the blessed gifts of a creator, or as symbols of the interconnected systems that sustain life, we know that nothing can live without them. To call these things sacred is to say that they have a value beyond their usefulness for human ends, that they themselves become the standards by which our acts, our economics, our laws, and our purposes must be judged. No one has the right to appropriate them or profit from them at the expense of others. Any government that fails to protect them forfeits its legitimacy.

"All people, all living things, are part of the Earth life and so sacred. No one of us stands higher or lower than any other. Only justice can assure balance. Only ecological balance can sustain freedom. Only in freedom can that fifth sacred thing we call spirit flourish in its full diversity. To honor the sacred is to create conditions in which nourishment, sustenance, habitat, knowledge, freedom, and beauty can thrive. To honor the sacred is to make love possible. To this we dedicate our curiosity, our will, our courage, our silences, and our voices. To this we dedicate our lives."

That was my idea for a manifesto for the twenty-first century that people from a wide variety of religions and political traditions could agree on.

DJ: Where does God fit into this?

S: If you see God as something outside the world, the world becomes subtly and not-so-subtly devalued. But if you see God—or Goddess, or whatever you want to call it—as embodied in human beings, in trees, in plants, in rocks, in animals—in the living world itself—then all those things, and particularly the interconnections between them, have that kind of deep intensive value.

That changes the way we see ourselves. The sense of personal authority we have to direct our own lives, to make choices about our own bodies, our own selves, who we are, changes very much if we see ourselves as embodiments of the sacred, as literally *being* the Goddess. It's a very different feeling from being a poor miserable sinner.

When we talk about the Goddess we're not talking about an abstraction. We're talking about rocks, about digging up the plants in your garden and moving them from place to place, and about stomping on the snails. She's a Goddess of many aspects—there's growth and there's death.

To me when we refer to the Goddess, or use the plural—gods or goddesses—we are simply using different names to acknowledge the cycle of birth and growth and death and rebirth that happens in nature and culture and human beings and every other aspect of the physical world.

We are also describing doorways—sets of symbols—that open up particular sets of experiences to you. If you meditate on Aphrodite, for example, who is the goddess of love, and all the symbols associated with her, you're going to have a very different experience than if you meditate on Hecate, who is the goddess of death and the goddess of the crossroads, the hag, and the crone. You're going to open your life to different sets of challenges, and you're going to call in particular kinds of strength to meet those challenges.

I like to call the Goddess tradition native European spirituality. It's very important for those of us who have European or Middle Eastern ancestry to look to those roots and understand the kind of traditions and the richness they offer. Only in that way can we approach any learning we might receive from Native Americans in some kind of clearheaded spirit. Otherwise too often people are *so* hungry for something spiritual and something earth-based they don't have much sense of boundaries about what they can use and what they can take.

And the Native American traditions often have very strict boundaries about things. If you don't know where they are, you're going to cross them a lot. And there's no need to, because you can go into the European traditions and find things that are very free and open for anyone of any ancestry to use and take and change and develop in whatever way they want.

DJ: And they're *ours*.

S: They're ours. And nobody who is practicing the Goddess tradition now would say we're practicing exactly what they did two thousand years ago. It's not the same kind of unbroken chain of tradition some indigenous peoples have. Anything we do is in a way being created anew.

For us that's very positive. We believe inspiration never went out of the world. There's no reason why you or I shouldn't have as much of it as somebody two thousand years ago who was probably struggling with a different set of problems anyway.

DJ: What God does the dominant culture worship?

S: What is the thing we most value? What's the thing by which all our other laws and economics and purposes are judged?

DJ: Not life.

S: It's definitely not life. I would say the defining criteria for almost every decision have been profits, as well as growth and a certain idea of progress, the idea that everything is getting bigger and better and newer and brighter and will continue to do so.

None of this deals well with limitations. That's one reason why I think it's healthy to be a polytheistic culture. One god is all very well if you're talking about the underlying oneness of the universe, but mostly what we're talking about is one particular set of symbols or names—one particular metavalue. If you have multiple values you can trade them off against each other.

DJ: Like stability in an ecosystem.

S: The more diversity the more stability and the more resilience.

DJ: If life is not sacred to this culture, how do individuals gain self-value?

S: The major value of this culture—which is more accurately termed a war-archy than a patriarchy—is war and the ability to wage war, the ability to defend and to conquer.

To get to that point required, historically, a psychic shift inside every human being. For men it required the shift from seeing their value as individuals who are free and self-actualizing, and who have long, happy, and possibly creative and inventive lives ahead of them, to seeing themselves as soldiers who are valued for how they perform in a particular kind of life-and-death situation, for how much obedience they are able to give superiors and how much loyalty they are able to give fellow soldiers—essentially how they are able to function as cogs in a machine.

For women, as women became more and more the prizes of war, and also in another way the field on which battle is waged—like we see right now in Bosnia, with the mass rapes of women as a particularly gruesome tactic of war—it required the devaluing of women, and particularly women's autonomy, women's sexual autonomy, and women's sexuality in general. Once devalued, women could breed up future soldiers, and also could be used as rewards for this particular kind of male behavior, male behavior that actually goes very much against the grain, I think.

Men had to become so frightened of being seen as women—less than men—that it became more important to them to act in a certain way, even if they were killed doing it, than to look out for their own survival instincts and to make their own decisions about right and wrong. We still see that.

DJ: Why do this? How does it serve the individual's best interest?

S: Once societies around you get involved in warfare, it's very difficult to maintain a peaceful culture. Many different societies have tried many different strategies—some were conquered, some migrated elsewhere, some adapted, and some turned themselves into mirrors of the other war cultures in order to survive.

The challenge we face today is that the culture of war has come to its ultimate conclusion. Nuclear weapons are so powerful we can't use them.

We've also seen in the last few years that although these cultures of power-over seem invincible, they have a self-limiting quality to them. As they get too big and top-heavy, they crumble from below. That happened with the Soviet Union, and we're seeing signs of it here in the United States. If you put all your resources into war, you impoverish yourself, because war is waste, and resources are finite, no matter how infinite they seem. You can't waste enormous amounts of them without creating a wasteland.

DJ: Within as well as without?

S: People internalize the models of power in their society. Each of us has within us the conqueror and the judge—the self-hater in its various aspects. We all have to struggle with this, and many people in this culture are defeated by it. They end up in emotional pain their entire lives.

DJ: How did you work past the internal self-hater?

S: The work I've done for years in my covens and circles has focused a lot on that. Therapy was helpful. Twelve-step programs. Writing *Truth or Dare* was helpful. When I wrote it, I could formulate the ideas beyond where I could apply them to my life.

It's also very helpful to have other images or models of power. It's not enough just to uproot an image. You've got to replace it with something.

In *Truth or Dare* I talk about three types of power. There's power-over—which is the most common form we all recognize—where one person or group can control the resources of another, determine their choices or lack of choices, and impose sanctions or punishments on other people. We are all in systems of power-over, everywhere from the schools we go to as kids to the jobs most of us have when we grow up.

Then there's what I call power-from-within, which is akin to spiritual power or empowerment. The Latin root of power is "to be able"—ability. Power-from-within is our ability to realize who we are meant to be and what we're meant to do.

There's a third kind of power—power-with, or influence. Even in nonhierarchical groups, certain people's ideas are listened to more than others, and certain people can speak with a greater authority. That kind of power can be rather subtle and can be either empowering or disempowering.

It makes sense in certain traditions. In many Native American societies elders have a great deal of that kind of power. When the elders speak, people will listen because the people respect them. They know who the elders are and what their experience has been.

But it can also be very negative if certain people's voices are always heard and other people's aren't. Or where that influence is determined by somebody's skin color or their gender. Women in the feminist movement have reacted strongly to the sense that women as a whole are not listened to in the same way men are. Whatever happens to the formal structures of power, those informal structures remain. We saw that with Anita Hill.

DJ: In *Truth or Dare* you described what it means to work magic. Can magic be a way to change these informal structures of power?

S: Dion Fortune says, "Magic is the art of changing consciousness at will." You could also say magic is the art of evoking power-from-within.

Magic is first of all about an inner shift. That, in turn, may produce effects in the outside world. But the real focus is the inner change, the consciousness change.

When you do magic, one of the things you learn is to become responsible for your own mind. You learn how to take charge of it, how to concentrate, how to visualize, how to be aware of the energies around you, how to shift and change them.

In my tradition we do that particularly through ritual, which you could define as a set of actions designed to orchestrate a movement of energy.

In the Catholic mass, for example, a priest holds up a wafer and consecrates it. What that is meant to do is draw in the Christ energy, which presumably the priest has contact with, and infuse the wafer with it. Through the wafer, then, people can physically connect with that energy. It's a very powerful magical ritual if the people doing it are aware of what they are doing. If they're not, it's just some guy saying words and holding up a stale piece of cracker.

In the Goddess tradition, we have lots of different rituals. We do a ritual for the winter solstice where we stay up all night and keep a vigil, because it's the night the sun is symbolically reborn and the Goddess is in labor to bring forth the new year.

We know of course the sun isn't really rising, we're turning around. And we also know this would probably happen whether we did the ritual or not. But it's different if you view it symbolically.

We often start with a plunge in the ocean at sunset to cleanse and to let go of what we want to let go of in the year that's passed. We then stay up all night, which puts you in another state of consciousness. By the morning, when the sun rises, you have a very powerful relationship with it. You have a sense of that whole drama of light and warmth returning out of darkness. That evokes those changes within you, too.

DJ: I was struck that in the mass, the individual has access to the divine only through a certain learned person, and . . .

S: In our tradition, like in many other traditions, each individual has access to the Goddess. Some people may have training in how to do ritual, some people may have better concentration or more psychic ability or whatever, but each of us has our own ability to contact the source. And in fact our own obligation to do that.

DJ: Tell me more about how magic works.

S: We work magic a lot of different ways. It can be done just like praying, in the mind, something you say, some intention of the heart. But we believe it's most effective when connected with an action you take in the physical world.

Throughout the eighties I was involved in many actions around nuclear issues—blockading at Livermore, the Nevada test site, Vandenberg Air Force Base, Diablo Canyon nuclear plant. Each of those actions was a concrete political action with a concrete point to it.

Sometimes the point was symbolic. For example, if the action was to stand in front of a busload of workers at a nuclear plant to prevent them from going in, you knew you weren't going to prevent them very long. But at the same time it was to me an act of magic. The physical act embodies the inner intention and sets in motion forces to bring your ends about.

It's interesting now, ten years later, looking back on actions that at the time seemed almost hopeless in terms of really accomplishing what we wanted to, to see the enormous changes that have gone on. There was a little article in the newspaper the other day about a possible plan to convert Lawrence Livermore Lab into an environmental research facility.

Sometimes you do these things without really believing they're going to work, but one of the principles in magic is the principle of "as if." You may not really believe you can prevent nuclear war by going out with your little sign and marching around, but you act *as if* doing that could prevent nuclear war. You may not think you have any power to change the system, but if enough people act *as if* they can, sometimes things can change.

The Jesuits have the same idea. They say if you put yourself in the position of prayer, you'll start to feel like praying.

DJ: You have called this a culture of estrangement. Can you tell me about the importance of community?

S: A lot of us are faced with the need to create a community. People do it through their friends, through the people they know, sometimes through their work. A lot of people in this society, though, are lost, left out, alienated, without a sense of a body of people that cares about them and that they are accountable to.

When we talk about community, of course, that community includes not just the people but everything involved in that ecosystem—the plants, the animals, the rocks, the land that supports a certain community. Because of that, different places have different energies. People say San Francisco is tolerant and different from, say, Milwaukee or Chicago. Some of that is generated by the people who are here, but in another sense the place itself attracts a certain type of person. Perhaps if everyone from Milwaukee and San Francisco traded places, the culture might not trade with them.

DJ: You've said, "To value the mysteries we must describe the world in ways that make possible encounter with mystery."

S: The language we use frames the way we encounter the world, the way we encounter ourselves. One could describe the same experience as mystical or as a schizophrenic break. The two are going to have very different consequences on the person's self-esteem and on what happens to them.

So if we are limited to a language that has no room for the unknown, if we're still working out of that mechanistic model of the universe—that the universe is like a great machine that's completely knowable and controllable—it's going to be harder to break out and actually encounter the vast parts of the universe that aren't measurable or quantifiable.

And of course not having the language to describe a particular experience doesn't stop people from having that experience. What it often does is make them feel different, as though they're going crazy. Or it makes them deny the experience altogether, pretend it never happened.

DJ: Neil Evernden has written that in the long run the environmentalist must either capitulate or question his or her own sanity. Is it the same for anyone who relates to the world in a poetic fashion, or a mystical fashion, or a nonutilitarian fashion within this utilitarian culture?

S: All those people you mentioned, from the environmentalist to the mystic, are at this point trying to bring some new ideas into the collective mind. To do that you have to be willing to stand a little bit outside. That's why so many new movements and philosophies and ideas are brought in by people who are in some way different or marginal, why so many great thinkers were Jewish, for example, or people of color. But at the same time, if you're too far outside the collective mind, you run into *true* insanity, which is not at all the same thing as mystical enlightenment.

DJ: What's the difference?

S: One of the differences is the rigidity of its patterns. As well as not being in contact with collective reality, people who are really insane are also not in contact with outer reality. They're trapped in a system of thought that often has very little opening in it for shifting and changing.

DJ: You say people who are really insane are not in contact with outer reality. What is outer reality?

S: Everything is interconnected. That is the reality. It seems so obvious it's hard to even talk about it. Chernobyl should have taught us that, if nothing else.

There's no isolated part of the world anymore. There is no isolated biological system. There are no isolated species that are not interdependent with other species.

The same is true of human beings, too. We are involved and interdependent and connected with the rest of the world. To me that's what the Goddess tradition is really about. And that's what environmental science is really about. They're just different ways of going about the same understanding. One says let's figure this out, and the other says let's celebrate it. There are times when you need to do both.

REED NOSS

Conservation biology has been called a combat discipline. About it Reed Noss writes, "Most biologists do not think of themselves as soldiers. But war has been declared against wild Nature, and we best acquainted with that marvelous web of life have no moral choice but to defend our wild friends and relatives, the innocent victims of human greed, ignorance, and arrogance. Our defense is not contingent on probabilities of winning or losing; it is an absolute obligation."

Reed Noss has been fighting in defense of Nature for more than twenty years. He specializes in applications of community and landscape ecology to conservation problems. Much of his work is concerned with the resolution of conflicts between commodity production and protection of biodiversity. He is the author of more than one hundred papers and of the book Saving Nature's Legacy. *He is editor of the journal* Conservation Biology.

DERRICK JENSEN: You're known for your work protecting biodiversity. Why is biodiversity important?

REED NOSS: If human beings have value, and all ethical traditions accept that we do, there's no objective reason to say that other species don't have intrinsic value. It has always seemed crazy to me that we could think of ourselves as fundamentally superior to other living things.

We may be more intelligent than a peregrine falcon, but we sure can't fly as well. A falcon does just as well with its ability as we do with ours. Arguably, peregrine falcons do better, because we're destroying everything. They're just living.

I work for biodiversity to try to defend fellow creatures I believe have every right to exist. It's my obligation as a person and a scientist.

DJ: How does your defense of wildlife mesh with what you've called our culture's "mythology of purely objective, value-free science"?

RN: Applied sciences are goal oriented. In medicine, you have the goal of saving the patient's life. That goal is a value in itself.

It's the same with conservation biology. We have a job to do, which is to improve the health of the environment, to maintain or restore biodiversity. You still use the scientific process of testing hypotheses, but whenever there's any doubt about the right way to go, and there always is, you have the obligation to choose the action or strategy that minimizes risk to the species and ecosystem.

DJ: Some environmentalists are very critical of science . . .

RN: I don't have a lot of sympathy for science bashing, because science is a perfectly appropriate way for solving problems. Ecological science in particular has done far more good than harm. People who are interested in protecting or restoring biodiversity ought to use any ethical means available to do that.

What I'm doing, and what other conservation biologists with similar inclinations are doing, is trying to save the earth. We're using a body of scientific knowledge and techniques to do that. It's not very different from a poet or an environmental activist, except we're using different tools and techniques.

It's also true that science is one of the best ways we've found to determine the nature of things. Some other ways include meditation, spiritual approaches, and direct experience.

Science is not complete, of course. It has to be complemented by an ethic. That's the major point. In an ethical vacuum, science is incredibly dangerous.

It frustrates me that many of my fellow scientists, even the ones who have an appreciation of life for its own sake and inner feelings of biophilia, do not want to admit these feelings. It somehow taints them, makes them appear unscientific. That's a very dualistic way of looking at life. We need to recognize that a person can love nature and study nature at the same time.

DJ: Assuming the human population continues to grow—at least for a while—what hopes do you hold for the preservation of biodiversity?

RN: Even with the projected population increases over the next fifty to one hundred years, we can still do a helluva job in protecting biodiversity by limiting our resource consumption. Wood products make a good example. There was an internal Forest Service study of wood consumption that determined that if we in the United States recycled at the same rate as the Europeans, we wouldn't have to cut a stick from the national forests.

All public lands nationally contribute only 20 percent of our wood products, and some analyses have shown that an aggressive wood product conservation and recycling program could cut our consumption by as much as 50 percent. Our whole public lands system could then become reserves managed for biodiversity without any decline in our standard of living.

DJ: If you were given the job of chief of the Forest Service tomorrow, what would you do?

RN: I would tell Congress not to give us *any* money for road construction or timber sales. We wouldn't do timber sales except for restoration forestry, that is, to thin stands that are overly dense because of fire suppression, or plantations that are packed too tight.

We don't need to do commercial forestry in the national forests. It's destructive. Instead I would ask Congress for money for public works projects like road closures, revegetation of roads, fisheries restoration projects, thinning out plantations, helping plantations revert to more natural structures, that kind of thing. We could employ just as many people in the forests for the next several decades doing restoration work as we now do clearcutting. And it would give them something meaningful and positive to do with their lives.

DJ: How much would this cost?

RN: It wouldn't cost nearly as much as the $80 billion or so we spent for Desert Storm. Society has the money. It's just a question of how we spend it.

DJ: The concept of management has very bad connotations for many environmentalists, yet you state very strongly the need for management.

RN: I continually argue with those environmentalists who want us to sit back and let nature heal on her own. I think that would simply take too long; furthermore, some sites would never heal. Protective and restorative management is absolutely essential if we're going to maintain biodiversity.

For example, white-tailed deer are much more abundant now than previously over most of the eastern United States. That's partially due to the elimination of predators but even more to fragmentation of the original forest, which generally improves deer habitat. There are more than a hundred rare plants known to be adversely affected by deer. If we don't manage the deer by, say, shooting them, many of these plants may be extirpated. In fact, we're already having local extinctions due to deer in some regions.

Same thing with fire. Some of the species in fire-dependent communities, for example longleaf pine or ponderosa pine, will be eliminated without periodic fires to maintain open structures and reduce competing woody plants. In a fragmented landscape, the chunks of remaining forest won't burn as frequently as they did historically. It used to be that a single lightning strike would burn an area equivalent to several counties. In a fragmented landscape that doesn't happen, because roads, clearcuts, and developments are often effective firebreaks. So we have to use prescribed fire if we want to maintain the natural species composition. It's a regrettable situation, perhaps, but I don't think we have an alternative to active management if we want to preserve biodiversity.

A lot of the restoration can be done using human labor to expedite the recovery process. That's good, because there's a spiritual benefit in restoration—going out and repairing something that you or your society has damaged. It's a form of retribution.

President Clinton has spoken about increasing public works projects to provide jobs, but I haven't heard him mention restoration. I got a call from someone with the World Resources Institute who wanted to know how environmentalists could advise Clinton on ecologically beneficial public works projects. He asked me if we know enough about what needs to be done to get started soon.

I told him we know enough right now to keep people busy for many years. We can adjust priorities as we go along, but the list of what we know needs to be done—closing roads, removing dams, and so forth— is long.

DJ: Is your concept of management compatible with laws as they are currently written?

RN: The overall legal framework is reasonably adequate, but the laws are too vague. We need to strengthen them and make them more specific on a lot of points. There is too much misinterpretation going on, most of it intentional and politically motivated. We need to make clear which kinds of actions contribute to diversity and which don't. The latter cannot be allowed.

For example, the Forest Service might use biodiversity as an argument to cut down old-growth forest and create a patchwork of young plantations. If they do that, they *will* increase the biodiversity of that landscape—there would probably be more species or communities in the manipulated area than were there previously. The problem is that they would be managing for species and habitats that are common and would be impoverishing a community type that is rare and declining. So, the problem is one of *context*.

Many species have done extraordinarily well because of human activity. That's OK from the standpoint of those opportunistic species, but to argue we should continue to favor those species at the expense of others going extinct is insane. The net result is impoverishment on a global scale.

DJ: Do you think it's possible to manage a forest for resource extraction without killing it?

RN: I don't know. There are, in the history of intensive forest management, very few success stories. Some forests have been used by people for millennia while retaining most of their natural qualities. But now that many indigenous peoples have modern weapons and tools, we're seeing that even a hunter-gatherer lifestyle can result in severe depletion of certain species near settlements. So what looks like intact forest is impoverished of both animals and plants that are sought after.

I do think using wood is a legitimate activity. There's no reason why we shouldn't use wood and other natural resources in moderation. But we need to reduce consumption and therefore practice much less intense forestry. We need to tread lightly. We could go on managing many of the existing plantations for wood products, adjusting our practices to try to sustain the system over many rotations. And we can—and must—leave our natural forests alone, managing them only as necessary to substitute for missing natural processes.

DJ: What could we do to sustain a system over time? What does a sustainable culture look like?

RN: I don't think we know exactly. We're amazingly ignorant. We do know that our management goals have to change. The forests over much of the earth have gone from landscapes dominated by old forests to those dominated by young forests, from structurally rich stands to simplified stands, from large intact forests to smaller and more isolated forests. We've reduced fires, and we've built roads. As a consequence of these and other trends, more and more species are threatened with extinction.

It is possible to go in the reverse direction, to start managing for older forests and structurally rich stands. We can maintain large reserves that are interconnected. We can use prescribed fire or allow natural fires to burn. We can close roads, and we can recover populations of declining species. All those activities would move us in a desirable direction.

DJ: I doubt if the managers of big timber corporations want to hear this. The cry of timber companies used to be "we need good science" and now the cry seems to be . . .

RN: "Shut up the scientist." They say that because science isn't going the way they want it to.

Each time a committee of scientists is called together to offer recommendations about a conservation problem, the scientists are a little stronger in what they say. That's not what industry wants to hear.

DJ: Many scientists, like you, are recommending the preservation or restoration of larger and larger chunks of intact wilderness. Why is size important?

RN: If you only want to protect spotted owls or marbled murrelets or old-growth trees, you might have very modest reserves of 20,000 acres, provided you have enough of them. On the other hand, if you want to restore the full complexity of life in any region, to maintain large carnivores or to restore large carnivores where they've been extirpated—in other words, to manage for a whole ecosystem rather than an impoverished ecosystem—you need a lot more area, in much bigger networks.

Big carnivores have large home ranges, and they don't get along well with human activity, at least the way humans tend to behave these days, with their guns and off-road vehicles. If we want to maintain viable populations, we need millions of unfragmented acres, not necessarily in one piece, but in a connected network inaccessible to motorized human activity.

Here in Oregon's Coast Range, we've lost the grizzly bear, the wolf, and very recently, it appears, the wolverine and the Pacific fisher. If we want to restore these species, which I think we have an ethical obligation to do, we are going to have to maintain very large reserves. And they must be connected at a scale of millions of acres.

DJ: Say a person is really excited about the idea of restoration, but lives in a big city. What could this person do that would be more empowering than merely writing a check?

RN: A person could volunteer to spend vacations with a restoration project. Students can do internships. Older people, or people who are physically restricted, could still become politically active, advocating restoration, forest protection, and any other kind of conservation plan.

People can do a lot just through paper and phone calls. You don't have to be physically present on a site to have an impact. Anybody who cares can find something meaningful to do. You have to care first.

John Osborn

Activists worldwide are fighting desperate rearguard actions, hoping to main-
tain whatever wildness they can until the culture either undergoes a change
of heart or collapses. Every time activists preserve a run of salmon or a patch
of old-growth forest, they preserve that much beauty, wildness, and evolu-
tionary potential. If, one hundred years from now, there still survive grizzly
bear, fisher, marten, and great blue whales, it will be due in part to the de-
votion of these activists.

    John Osborn worked for seven years fighting fires as a seasonal employee
for the United States Forest Service. He later became interested in the his-
tory of the Forest Service, and extensively researched the early years of
the agency. In the early 1980s, while doing an internship as part of his
training in internal medicine, he formed the Spokane Resident Physicians
Action League to oppose the destruction of the forests within the Columbia
River Bioregion. This later evolved into the Inland Empire Public Lands
Council.

    Through educational programs, the journal Transitions, *and grassroots*
activism, the council has been pivotal in helping the public increasingly ac-
knowledge the transition that inevitably comes with the exhaustion of the
forests.

John Osborn: In the three hundred years we've been cutting the forests
of North America, we've always had one more great stand of native forest on the other side of the ridge. So it was in New England, so it was in
the Midwest, and so it seemed in the Northwest. But today on the other
side of the ridge lies the Pacific Ocean, and we are cutting the last stands
of ancient forest.

    We have an opportunity to save these stands, in part because our sys-
tem of government allows us to potentially influence decisions made
about our public lands. The situation in the United States is telling—if
we can't save the forests in the Pacific Northwest, where there are still
forests left to save and where the Constitution guarantees us freedom of
speech, where on earth can we do it?

    One obstacle to citizen influence in governmental decisions is what

Hedrick Smith, in *The Power Game*, calls "the iron triangle." Iron triangles, and there are many of them, are fundamental to the flow of power in Washington, D.C. With the forest issue, one point of the iron triangle would represent politicians, one would represent corporations, and the third point would be the Forest Service bureaucracy. Each of these three components benefits from cutting down the forests: politicians because of corporate contributions to their campaigns and because of the votes this money can buy; the corporations because of profits; and the Forest Service bureaucracy because for decades the budget of the U.S. Forest Service has been dependent on building roads and cutting down forests.

To save the forests you have to break the triangle by separating the three points. This probably has to be done simultaneously: politicians must receive pressure nationally, through publicizing the damage to the forests and by revealing the close connections between politicians and industry; the corporate component of this mess must be overhauled; and the Forest Service, particularly its budget, must be reformed. All of this is difficult, because we're faced not only with the enormous and entrenched forces of Congress, and not only with an entrenched Forest Service bureaucracy, but also with, in just the Pacific Northwest alone, well over $30 billion worth of timber corporate assets.

What's worse is that when you take on these timber companies, you find that they are not separable. Instead, they are linked by marriage and interlocking boards of directors, as well as by the common history of fraud and corruption associated with Congress's land-grant railroads. The wealth of four of the major timber corporations in the Northwest—Weyerhaeuser, Boise Cascade, Potlatch, and Plum Creek—is derived directly from land conditionally granted by Congress in 1864.

This means it's impossible to understand the forest crisis in the Northwest without considering the 1864 Northern Pacific land grant. This grant, signed by President Lincoln, was a contract or covenant creating the Northern Pacific Railroad Company, intending that it build and maintain a railroad between Lake Superior and Puget Sound. For this purpose, Congress and President Lincoln conditionally granted 40 million acres of public land. This land, originally intended for settlers, instead ended up establishing corporate empires, including those of the timber companies I just mentioned.

From the beginning to the present, the grant has been characterized by fraud and flagrant abuse of the public trust. There have been numerous attempts to revest part or all of the grant lands, the most recent of which occurred between 1924 and 1940, at the urging of President Coolidge. Another congressional investigation of the 1864 Northern Pacific land grant would be one way to get at this iron triangle.

DERRICK JENSEN: How did you get started on the railroad issue?

JO: I started this journey when I saw the first square-mile clearcut in a place I cared for deeply. After that, I watched as one square mile of forest after another went down. And I was helpless to stop it. I had read about this occurring during the last century in Minnesota, Michigan, and Wisconsin, but I couldn't believe it was happening in the watersheds of the Saint Joe and Clearwater Rivers of Idaho.

DJ: You've said before that many environmentalists begin by wanting to protect a piece of ground and end up questioning the foundations of Western civilization.

JO: I'm not alone in this. There are people all over the region who care deeply about the forest, who live in or near the forest, take their drinking water from the forest, who fish and hunt in the forest. When you see the forest being destroyed, and when you systematically set out to stop that destruction, you begin asking questions you never asked before and end up doing things you never thought you would do.

I remember holding my first news conference—reading my Sierra Club media handbook and then actually facing the reporters and cameras. I was so nervous. And I remember the first time I ever testified before a congressional subcommittee. Even though people had told me it wasn't like the Watergate hearings where the hearing rooms were packed, their assurances didn't allay my high levels of anxiety about testifying before Congress.

But more than just taking the concerns to the public and to the public's decision makers, the desperate nature of the issue—of trying to stop the relentless destruction—takes you on a journey.

In the physical context, I can tell you I started out with a few of those little cardboard filing boxes. And I had a typewriter. Today, I have twenty-two filing cabinets in my apartment and a laptop computer with a modem.

Beyond just the physical appurtenances, I have come to understand that the threats are really symptomatic of a much more serious underlying process. I have realized we are not dealing just with Forest Service bureaucrats and profit-driven corporate executives, but instead with the symptoms of an enormous historic transition. How else can we explain the senseless destruction? Why does the Forest Service spend millions of dollars building roads to nowhere? Why do corporations want to cut down the forests in the backcountry, in wildlands that are not even the good growing sites? Questions such as these, that I couldn't answer before, became comprehensible after I had come to understand the transition.

Let me give you an example of how the concept of this historic transition helps explain otherwise inexplicable, tumultuous events here in the Pacific Northwest. During the 1980s, I was the lead author of the appeal of the Forest Service's plan for the Idaho Panhandle National Forests. As part of that appeal we asked for a stay of further activities in roadless areas. The Forest Service had never granted broad-based stay requests during this nationwide forest planning process. But in 1988, on the Idaho Panhandle, the federal agency granted our request for a stay. The Forest Service agreed to stop further timber activities on 800,000 acres of roadless lands on the Idaho Panhandle. This decision was significant, although you have to remember that the Forest Service had already trashed the Panhandle's watershed with ten thousand miles of logging roads and had clearcut away most of the commercially valuable forest.

The timber industry's response to our stay was entirely unexpected. In reaction to our efforts on the Idaho Panhandle and to other challenges by environmentalists in the region, the companies orchestrated a huge logging-truck convoy down Montana's Bitterroot Valley. It became the timber industry's most successful media event of the 1980s. As I watched the media buildup and anger among the workers, I felt the awesome power of these huge timber corporations.

There are many reasons for the industry's extreme reaction. The first and most basic is that the overcutting of the forests had created a timber supply squeeze. The second reason, and I think a more fundamental one, is that the industry, which had largely controlled the region for more than a century, was being challenged. Timber interests felt compelled to crush even the tiniest threat to their hegemony, tolerating nothing that might jeopardize their historic influence and control.

But the trees are gone. The forests are overcut. The timber industry's tactics were extreme. For what? For the roadless areas? For the least productive tree-growing sites, for the remnants, the little pieces of what was once the fabric of a forest? The timber industry's unwillingness to publicly acknowledge the transition left me troubled.

The media didn't help. The timber lobby has always been extremely effective at choreographing media events, at manipulating timber workers, and at manipulating the public. During the logging-truck convoy I talked with a reporter about the inaccuracy of what the timber industry representatives were saying, effectively making environmentalists scapegoats for the transition. I suggested that the lack of critical reporting by the media was extremely misleading for the public. The reporter responded that in these kinds of cases facts aren't particularly important. That wasn't the first time I'd heard the refrain, "Don't confuse us with the facts."

DJ: Where do we go from here?

JO: I think the goal, or at least the challenge, is to continue to focus on the discrete problems—the clearcuts, the effects overcutting has on our forests and on our communities—and to continue to help people understand the connection between overcutting and how it affects people on a personal level, on every level from economic dislocation to the destruction of the natural world around us.

During the past ten years I've seen a marked increase in concern about overcutting. That is heartening. I know, however, that a hundred years ago there also was a national outpouring of concern about the forests, which led to the creation of America's National Forest System.

The public memory is altogether too short. If we as a community could have remembered the magnificent forests of New England, if our collective memory included the tremendous white pine forests of the upper Mississippi River Valley, and if we could have remembered the devastation of those forests, we would not have allowed our national forests to be devastated in the same way.

I often ask myself, how could this have happened? We created the National Forest System as a response to the devastation of the forests of the Great Lakes region. And what did we do to the National Forest System? I know what we did. I've walked those watersheds. I've driven those logging roads. I've photographed clearcut after clearcut. I've watched those forests go down. And I know firsthand that not only has there been a tremendous betrayal of the public trust by the U.S. Forest Service, but that the public either didn't know or didn't care and couldn't remember that there was a time when people fought very hard to protect these forests as National Forests.

DJ: Is it so hard to remember? We can go downtown and see Spokane Falls. The Indians used to put boxes under the falls, and 100-pound salmon would fall into them. The salmon are gone. But we can see the dams. We can see Grand Coulee Dam. We can see the clearcuts.

JO: I think in terms of a human lifetime the changes are so gradual that we don't see them. If you could imagine the Columbia River Bioregion as it was when Lewis and Clark walked into it, and then look at it today, you would be horrified at what has happened here: the liquidation of the forests, the destruction of the greatest salmon runs on earth, some of the worst nuclear and mining contamination on earth. If we look at the Columbia River Bioregion as a microcosm of life on earth, it demonstrates our lack of clarity and capacity to recognize the extremity of these problems.

DJ: How did you commit yourself to conservation work?

JO: I am a physician, and I originally went into medicine expecting to work in the third world. I worked for a time at a mission hospital in northern Thailand, and after that I worked at another mission hospital in western Kenya, near the border with Uganda.

But at the time I left Spokane for Kenya I was very deeply troubled by what was happening here. The timber lobby was going after the Idaho Department of Fish and Game, attempting to dismantle the agency in the Idaho legislature. Resource specialists in the Forest Service were under enormous pressure to overcut the forests. And it was becoming increasingly clear to me that then-Senator McClure of Idaho, who later became a director of Boise Cascade Timber Corporation, was manipulating the forest plans for north Idaho.

I really struggled with all of this during the time I was at the hospital at Lugulu. I can remember one night when a runner came and dropped a message through the screen and woke me up. The message read, "Daktari, come quickly," which usually meant that a patient was seriously ill. And I remember walking into the pediatric ward, which was an open ward of about forty beds, with a single lightbulb hanging from the ceiling. At night oftentimes many members of the same family shared the same bed, and since the treatment area was in the middle of the ward, there was a sense of being on stage, being surrounded by 150 people, all watching you, underneath this one bare lightbulb hanging from the rafters.

A child had been brought in who probably had pneumonia from measles. She was gasping, and her nostrils were flaring. It was clear she was going to die. I called for a nurse to bring over the oxygen, which she did. But perhaps because she was so used to death as a daily occurrence, she brought it in a less-than-prompt manner.

I remember as this little girl was dying we tried to get the oxygen hooked up. We finally did that, and we got ready to do mouth-to-mouth. We turned the oxygen bottle on. The oxygen bottle was empty. The little girl died in her father's arms.

After she died, I remember going outside. It was about three in the morning. I struggled with this whole issue, and just sat and thought about which way to go, whether to come back and make some sort of sense of this whole mess here, or to continue my commitment to third world medicine.

I suppose that each of us has a point in our life where we've made a conscious decision to follow a certain path. And I made a decision that night to try to stop the insanity of the destruction of the forests here in the region.

DJ: What is the prognosis for the forests?

JO: I think the prognosis is not good.

I take care of people with chronic, multisystem diseases. Many of my patients are nearing the end of their lives. At some point in the dying process, a moment comes when the hospital chaplain should be at the bedside. That's because, although there are some things for which I can be helpful, my patients have spiritual needs as well. If I were the physician managing this larger case—the transition underway in the Northwest, which also is a multisystem case—I would be calling for the chaplain.

DJ: How do you deal with the pain?

JO: In many ways my environmental work is an extension of my work with patients. As a physician my responsibility is to do the best I can to diagnose and to recommend treatment options. There are times when people I care about reject my advice. They continue to do things that are damaging—they continue to smoke, they continue to drink—and put their lives at risk. And so too my work on the environment. Ultimately, all I can do is present the information and make recommendations. People continue to do things which are destructive to themselves, to our communities, to future generations, and to life on earth. Ultimately all I can do is find solace from doing the best job I can possibly do.

DJ: Are you happy?

JO: I feel a sense of peace that comes from knowing my work is the right thing to do. Yes, the problems may be overwhelming, and at times they seem absolutely insurmountable, but working on them provides a sense of peace. To not work on them would be very difficult.

DJ: What is point B? Where are we trying to go?

JO: I don't know. I think we'll get to point B by a series of approximations. We may not know what *will* work, but we will know pretty quickly what *won't* work. We know that overcutting the forests, destroying diversity, continuing to increase the numbers of our own species on this planet will get us to where we don't want to go. It's the old saying, "If you don't change directions, you'll end up getting where you're going." Another way to say this is that people who care, and who are willing to act, can make a difference. Collectively that difference may not be enough. But I have come to understand that if people who care don't act, then assuredly it will never be enough.

PETER BERG

Peter Berg has written, "Wherever you live, the place where you live is alive, and you are part of the life of that place."

Founder (1973) and director of Planet Drum Foundation—an organization helping people to become "native to a place through becoming aware of the particular ecological relationships that operate in and around it"—Peter Berg is a noted ecologist, speaker, activist, and writer. He is acknowledged as an originator of the use of the word bioregion to describe land areas in terms of their interdependent plant, animal, and human life. He believes that the relationships between humans and the rest of nature point to the importance of supporting cultural diversity as a component of biodiversity.

PETER BERG: The bioregional perspective, the one I've worked with for nearly twenty years, recognizes that people simply don't know where they live. Generally when you ask people what their location is, they give it in terms of a number on a house on a street in a city in a county in a state in a nation-state in some political division of the world. But if you were to answer in bioregional or ecological terms you might say, "I'm at the confluence of the Sacramento and San Joaquin Rivers and San Francisco Bay in the North Pacific Rim of the Pacific Basin of the planetary biosphere in the Universe." Very few people know where they live, and fewer think it's important.

But unless we think it is important, we're going to destroy the places we live. If you destroy the place you live, you have to move someplace else. And there isn't someplace else left anymore. Unless you understand the place where you live in terms of its natural system, you're not going to understand anything, anyplace.

Is this a big problem? Yes, because 75 percent of Americans live in cities, and the biggest human migration in history in the shortest time has been since 1950 from the old industrial Northeast to the Sunbelt. Towns have to pass out pamphlets telling people, "You're now a resident of Tucson, Arizona, and what we have here are saguaro cactus and mesquite. We don't have English lawns here, and if you try to have one, you're going to run us all out of water in the next five years. So don't do that. Love your jojoba tree."

This process of finding out who you are in terms of place is probably the principal consideration of contemporary civilization. Who am I, where am I, and what am I going to do about it? I am a member of the human species. I am in the Shasta Bioregion, roughly northern California. And what am I going to do about it? I am going to attempt to reinhabit the place where I live, attempt to become an inhabitant again.

There are a lot of ways to do this. Through natural sciences. Through stories of native peoples. Through early settlers' records. Through experience, which is probably the best way. What happens on the summer solstice in Shasta Bioregion? What happens when the rains come, in our Mediterranean winter-wet/summer-dry climate form? What happens to various soils? What's the role of earthquakes here?

A lot of this is understandable to somebody who lives in the country, because rural people tend to be more in contact with elements and natural situations and systems. If somebody says it's called Goose Valley, it's because geese go through it, whereas if you ask somebody in Los Angeles, "Why is this called Chavez Ravine?" they might not even know there's a ravine there.

Not everything country people tend to do is divine. I've seen a lot of rural situations that couldn't exist without a hyperexploitation of energy sources. And in the past, people in the country were pretty much tied to resource exploitation, cutting down the trees, digging up the ground, taking out the minerals, killing the fish, and so on.

But that's not our problem anymore, from a bioregional perspective. Our problem now is city people. They are the majority population, and unless they agree with practices that are bioregionally coherent, bioregionally coherent practices just aren't ever going to be carried out, for voting and economic reasons.

So how do we go about persuading urban dwellers to know the place where they live in natural terms? That's difficult, because urban dwellers are so divorced from the sources of their fundamental requirements of life. For example, if you ask somebody from the city where the water comes from, they say . . .

DERRICK JENSEN: The faucet.

PB: And where does the water go?

DJ: Down the drain.

PB: When you flush the toilet where does the stuff go?

DJ: Away.

PB: Where does the garbage go? Out. Food comes from—the store. So our task is to try to engage urban dwellers in activities that lead them to greater perception of how they are involved with interdependence in the planetary biosphere. What we at Planet Drum have been doing, besides publishing books and issues of our review, *Raise the Stakes*, is undertaking various activities here in the San Francisco Bay Area under the title Green City.

We've realized that city people want to do things to not feel guilty about their relationship with ecology. So we've established something called the Volunteer Network. Interested people can call us to find out about the activities of 240 Bay Area groups that work in areas ranging from urban wild habitat to recycling to transportation to neighborhood empowerment. The callers say what they want to do, whether it's rescue marine mammals, replant native vegetation, recycle, participate in transportation coalitions or bicycle demonstrations, whatever. Our service raises ecological consciousness.

But we also have to raise consciousness within the groups themselves, because they may not feel as though they're all connected the way *we* think they are. We see Green City as a big umbrella—urban sustainability as a new kind of consciousness. The people who collect the curbside recycling in San Francisco are hired by the garbage company, and they may not think they have anything to do with restoring wild habitat. We think they do, and we want to convince them of that fact.

Another thing we've done is to develop a Green City Calendar of activities going on in San Francisco and the Bay Area, activities you can join on your own. We've also developed a youth directory to connect high school and middle school students with activities.

That's all in the area of public information. The second realm of this is what we call workshop/workdays, where in the morning we give a talk about bioregionalism and about a specific project we'll work on that day. Then we have lunch together. In the afternoon we all go out and work on the project. Things like taking garbage out of a creek, pulling up in-vasive plants, digging up asphalt to free the headwaters of an urban creek in Berkeley. We dug out scotch broom and put in native grasses on a piece of city-owned land. And we're going to build planter boxes for rooftop gardens in the Tenderloin District, which has about the highest unemployment and homeless rates in the city.

DJ: You've used the word *bioregional* several times. Can you say more about what bioregionalism is?

PB: The bioregional concept has three main goals. One is to restore and maintain local natural systems. The next is to find sustainable ways to satisfy basic human needs—food, shelter, energy, water, culture. The third is to support the work of reinhabitation, of people becoming native to the places where they live. These goals are very simple, and not overtly radical, but satisfying basic human needs in sustainable ways has a lot of social, political, and economic implications about sharing and cooperation and carrying capacities, and judgments as to what is too much.

In addition, supporting the work of reinhabitation doesn't only mean growing some of your own food. It also means, for example, preventing offshore oil drilling, stopping things that will destroy the possibility of reinhabitation.

DJ: And reinhabitation seems to be accomplished at least partly through making personal connections to a sense of life, even in the midst of a city.

PB: To be disassociated from the rest of life is totally alien to our species. To urbanites, though, nature is like a frightened bird that flies through the window into the living room, something you encounter by accident. Urbanites have to begin making the connections—this house is made of Sonoma County redwood, the electricity that comes into this house is from a hydroelectric plant on a tributary of the Sacramento River, and we use natural gas from Canada. The place where the nonrecyclable gar-bage goes is a horrifying landfill in Altamont. Our food is increasingly standardized and regimented and poisoned.

In the history of human civilization, the sustainability of cities has seldom been an issue. Cities have destroyed themselves and the coun-tryside around them. That's why there are magnificent ruins in jungles—the people who lived there stripped the capacity of the land to support them.

Sustainability of cities has to become a major gauge for whether or not we're succeeding at becoming harmonious in the planetary biosphere. In fact, I believe urban sustainability is *the* environmental issue of the nineties and the next century, because not only have cities generally been unsustainable, *no* American cities are presently sustainable. And major infrastructure collapses of cities are already happening.

City governments have to take the ecological sustainability of the city as their *central* topic of governance. And city dwellers have to look at being an urban person differently than they did previously. They have to think about providing some of their own food, some of their own energy, participating in local decentralized neighborhood government, undertaking different modes of transportation, carrying out different activities to make a living.

DJ: Can you get more specific on sustainable practices cities can undertake?

PB: In most Asian cities, human waste is collected daily and carried to nearby farms to be used as fertilizer on the fields. That's a sustainable agricultural practice.

Another is for every urban household to have a dual water system. One of fresh water for cooking and bathing, and the other of gray water—water left over from bathing—for other purposes such as flushing toilets, watering lawns and gardens, washing cars, et cetera. We could reduce water use in the average American household by probably 75 percent.

Gray water is already used this way in most third world countries. Most water, whether gray or not, is undrinkable in Mexico. But people have practices for dealing with that, such as boiling water before they use it or putting a drop of iodine in water used for soaking vegetables overnight. Rather than having a huge plant that pours hundreds of pounds of chlorine and fluoride into water so that the substance I flush down the toilet is nearly the equivalent of bottled water, we should be asking ourselves why we don't use our shower water to flush the toilets.

Similarly with electricity, or any of the energy that's consumed. If city governments would decide that public buildings should feature renewable energy, not only would taxpayers save money in the long run—not that much, between 5 and 10 percent of the energy used—but the agencies would be making a wonderful statement, much as when governments print on their agencies' letterhead, "We are an equal opportunity employer."

And food production in the city could be hugely amplified by a couple of simple techniques. One is greenhouses. Another is that every open space could feature some aspect of gardening, such as a community garden, cooperative gardens, privately owned gardens, and so on. This includes rooftops and planter boxes. In some third world cities it's not unusual to see fava beans coming over the sides of the roof or to see a goat eating grass on top of the building. These goats are going to be milked and eaten, and those fava beans are going to go into stews.

I feel you shouldn't give a permit for constructing a building unless 10 percent of the space bought for construction is designated as garden space—gardens, orchards, grape and other arbors of various kinds, whatever.

DJ: Two themes connect all these practices. One is the idea of reducing waste, and the other is the importance of self-sufficiency.

PB: Those seem to me to be design principles. And while, for example, it interests me that a Japanese sliding door saves space over Western hinged doors, probably five or ten apartments' worth in an apartment building, I'm much more interested in examining what our sense of limitless resources has done to us.

For example, we drive a car to have fun. Well, sure, I think everybody has driven in a car and had fun at some point. But driving a car for fun should be on the same level as taking a roller coaster ride for fun. It should be the kind of thing you pay for. And not just at the pump. If you're having fun driving the car, then it's an amusement park event. Go to an amusement park, pay some guy two bucks, and drive a car. But the idea that the price of fossil fuels should be kept at less than two dollars a gallon so that you can take a Sunday drive is inane. It's not even that much fun.

Hiking is fun. Hiking in the country would be a revelation to most urbanites. Most inner-city people don't know there is a naturally governed world outside the human domain. And if they did, they might find more reasons to live. I have taken inner-city kids out where they wouldn't get off the path because they were sure something huge and horrible would eat them.

Which takes us back to consciousness, and how to change consciousness. I have a story about that. Urban sustainability is especially important in Mexico, because Mexico City is the most polluted and overcrowded city on the planet. One day I asked one of the brave people trying to make Mexico City into Ciudad Verde (Green City), "How do you reach all these people driving these Volkswagen vans without exhaust pipes, and all of these homeless people burning railroad ties full of creosote to cook their dinner?"

She responded, "To reach them, you show them a man and a woman in a kitchen making dinner, and show that the water comes from a waterfall, the energy comes from a forest, the food comes from the soil, and the garbage goes back to being compost. Show them that the dinner they make is the earth's, that the earth gave them that dinner. You tell them, 'Your kitchen is the earth. Your grandmother knows this. She knows the kitchen is the place where you worship the earth.'" That's a wonderful perception.

DJ: That seems very similar to everything you've described you're doing here.

PB: We're trying to. The fact that we're all connected is a planetary reality. The fact that we don't know it is a huge condition of disability. We're in a hospital, and we're not getting better. The way to get better is to start finding out what these things are and relating to them again.

It was the popularity of physics in the industrial era that removed people from thinking that relatedness to natural systems was important. People have been enamored of physics because of what it could do to natural systems. What physicists told people was, "We no longer have to be bound by what nature gives us."

And this is a trick, an illusion, the fossil fuel illusion, the industrial era illusion. And we're coming to the end of it. When you have a hole in the ozone layer, that's like saying there's a hole in the milk pail. And it doesn't matter how much milk you put in the pail, it's going to run out.

So wake up. We've got to do something about that hole. And the way to mend that hole is to mend our consciousness.

DJ: Does restoring wildlife habitat to cities help mend consciousness, by allowing people quick access to the natural world?

PB: Typical of all the other mistakes urban dwelling has caused is the presumption that wildlife does not belong in the city. Human beings have a kind of prescription for living in an urban environment, and that's to systematically destroy invasions by other species or systems. We should be doing just the opposite. If there are other systems in the place, plants and animals, the place is viable. Without them it isn't. Just to begin with, plants and animals are fantastic biological monitors. Keeping birds from dropping dead or moving out means keeping an environment you can live in.

But it's more than that. Human brains need the interaction of other kinds of squiggly, furry, many-legged, able-to-fly, fierce, slinky species. Our brains need this, not just for metaphors, but for stimulation. If we're surrounded by sheetrock walls all the time, we dry up. If we're surrounded by other kinds of creatures, they start to fill our consciousness.

Think about what I said a while ago about being in a hospital. Whenever patients are allowed to sit in the sun or on the grass, cure rates go up tremendously. Ask any honest doctor in a hospital and he'll say, "The best thing you could possibly do is get the hell out of here." Cities make people sick, the way hospitals make people sick.

So the value of urban wild habitat is that it's our legacy. It's not that we should allow it to be. It's that we deserve it. That is the highest level we can operate at. It's silly to say it's a question of anthropocentrism or biocentrism. It's mutually interactive. We need each other.

For better or worse, I have a bird feeder in the back yard. Now that it's spring, no birds come near it. They don't need it now. And besides, I wasn't *saving* the birds last winter. I was just trying to help them, because I like them. A friendly gesture on my part. I'm encouraged by the way they look, their beauty, the way they move, their migrations through here. Cedar waxwings were just through. Yellow-breasted finches are here. It's marvelous to watch these tides of animals.

It's a democracy of species. It's not a situation where we save them or they save us.

DJ: Say a person lives in New York City and doesn't have access to an organization like Planet Drum. How would this person go about reinhabiting place?

PB: Find a couple of other people like him- or herself. They can be found among fishermen, naturalists, teachers, artists. Start a study group to find out what the natural systems are and begin to understand how they relate together, as well as what the priorities are for restoring and maintaining that place.

And find out what issues are most pressing. For example, in northern California, the thing that really galvanized the bioregional movement was the state's proposal in the late 1970s to transfer a million acre-feet per year of the Sacramento River down to the southern Central Valley and Los Angeles. We encouraged people to oppose it, to look at what effect it would have on San Francisco Bay. We even encouraged them to quit the Sierra Club if the Sierra Club didn't oppose it.

Ninety percent of the people in the Bay Area voted against the proposal. It was the biggest one-sided vote on any issue for an area in the state's history. This means we really hit a chord of consciousness. A sociology professor at the University of California at Davis was asked afterwards, "Why did the people vote against it?" He said, "We just don't want to pay to support their lifestyle anymore." That's a hell of a comment. Very bioregional.

DJ: And very encouraging.

PB: Afterwards there was no stopping us, in terms of confidence that this is an appropriate point of view. People all over northern California— the Shasta Bioregion—say, "This is our watershed. We want to restore and maintain native animals and plants and native systems here." This is a new language for grassroots politics.

So, people interested in reinhabiting their place can find a galvanizing issue, and they can find out facts about where they live. They can decide not to move, regardless of the real estate values or the winters. They can decide to live there, decide that people *do* live there, and they can have a different consciousness, an inhabitory consciousness, and they can realize there are inhabitory rights that come with that, and they can strive to get those rights.

In northern California, for example, I would require that people do a weekend's worth of ecosystem restoration activity per month for six months before they are allowed to have a driver's license. The restoration work would qualify them to be inhabitants. I'm not suggesting that as a restriction. Instead it's a trade-off. You want to drive on the stuff, you've got to find out what it is. After everybody got through groaning and moaning about it, you would notice a tremendous shift in consciousness. People would start saying, "I don't want a freeway to go through there. It would disrupt too much of the native vegetation." They're going to know what it is and how rare it is.

And we need to begin teaching bioregional studies in schools K-12 as an accredited course along with literature and mathematics. Bioregional Studies 101. Make it required. If you're going to go to school here, you've got to find out about the place. Graduates would be inflamed with a desire to protect natural systems where they are, and to relate to them.

Even little things like that would shock people out of their disinhabitory coma. It would let people know they are a part of the place where they live. And that it's their true legacy.

MAX OELSCHLAEGER

What does it mean to be an animal? Having evolved in what is now called wilderness—but which not very long ago was merely called home—does humanity have a future in increasingly domesticated and fabricated surroundings? What is the relationship between an environmental ethic and Thoreau's line, "In wildness lies the preservation of the world"?

These questions drive much of Max Oelschlaeger's writing, which includes The Idea of Wilderness (*nominated for the Pulitzer Prize and the National Book Award*), Caring for Creation: An Ecumenical Approach to the Environmental Crisis, *and* The Environmental Imperative, *as well as the many books he has edited, such as* The Wilderness Condition, After Earth Day, *and* Postmodernism and Environmental Ethics.

Max Oelschlaeger teaches graduate courses in the philosophy of ecology, postmodern thought, political ecology, and ecofeminism in the Environmental Ethics Program at the University of North Texas. In addition to his teaching and research, he participates in a variety of workshops and conferences in Texas and across the nation. He was recently appointed by the Texas Natural Resource Conservation Commission as a member of the State of Texas Environmental Priorities Project.

MAX OELSCHLAEGER: It seems the pernicious aggressive behavior we display toward nature arises from the fact that we've become economic man, *Homo oeconomicus*. Nature has become just a standing reserve that we economically conceptualize and technologically attempt to dominate.

One of the problems with this approach is that economics, if we think of it as a set of categories, is blind to crucially important questions that surround it. On the one end it's blind to questions of ecology, the second law of thermodynamics, and biology. On the other end it's blind to the ultimate questions of religion and philosophy, as well as to questions raised by sociology, psychology, and anthropology.

Neoclassical economics is basically modeled on mechanistic materialism. Ernst Mayr, the noted historian of biology, observes in his book *The Growth of Biological Thought* that such an atomistic philosophy, where wholes are no more than the sums of the parts, is fatally flawed. The joke is on us, he says, because our institutions, political economy, and conception of ourselves as moral agents are predicated on the notion that we're little atoms, when the overwhelming evidence from anthropology, psychology, sociology, philosophy, and religion leads in another direction. We are all part of the fabric of natural ecology and social ecology.

Neoclassical economics is a sterile and dying paradigm. While of course we can't exist without economic categories, we need economic categories that have some reason to exist. Our current categories have no rational support. They carry on because there are powerful political constituencies that continue to legitimate them. Intellectually, though, they are bankrupt.

DERRICK JENSEN: Are there alternatives to *Homo oeconomicus?*

MO: Certainly. People could, for example, enter into sacral relations with the earth, viewing themselves as *Homo religiosis*—one of the roots of the word *religion* being *religiare*, or relinking.

It's possible for people to reawaken this sense of sacrality through reading philosophers, poets, and ecologists such as Aldo Leopold, Gary Snyder, Robinson Jeffers, and E. O. Wilson. But most people, to be honest about it, don't read these writers.

The question then becomes: How do we reach these people? It *is* necessary to reach them, because if we don't, if not enough people reawaken their own sense of the sacred, we will not be able to address the difficult but necessary political questions, such as those concerning equity, and we simply won't have a world in three or four generations.

It seems to me that insofar as people still have moral sensibility, for most people it grows out of their religion. The question I ask in *Caring for Creation* is: What are the possibilities for people who are in the religious middle in America to find within their own faith reasons to love and care for the earth and its creatures?

Ghillean Prance, director of the Royal Botanical Gardens at Kew, England, and one of the leading Amazonian rain forest scientists in the world, is one example of a person whose care for the earth derives from Christianity. He makes basically the same set of recommendations for

Amazonia as does E. O. Wilson, yet the ethical grounds by which these are reached are totally different. E. O. Wilson's environmental ethic has its source in biophilia, which traces back to his early childhood and the opportunity to *be* in the woods. Prance, on the other hand, is a conservative Christian and says he cares for the earth because God made it.

DJ: Others take a dimmer view of the possibility of salvaging an environmental ethic out of Christianity. You have quoted Ortega y Gasset as writing about Christianity: "What had seemed real—nature and ourselves as part of it—now turns out to be unreal, pure phantasmagoria; and that which had seemed unreal—our concern with the absolute or God—that is the true reality.

"This paradox, this complete inversion of perspective, is the basis of Christianity. The problems of natural man have no solution: to live, to be in the world, is perdition, constitutional and unchangeable. Man must be saved by the supernatural."

MO: To Ortega, Christianity represents the belief that the embeddedness of the human person and the human group in nature is mere appearance. The reality of human experience becomes associated with the human soul and its transcendence, or the quest for the afterlife.

For Christians, at least as Ortega reads them, there is no solution to life in its immediacy, in its ongoing rhythms and cycles and processes of production and reproduction. You might say life is but a vale of tears. And so we attempt to escape this life, to rise above or beyond.

DJ: I have a hard time seeing life itself as something to be risen above or beyond.

MO: Think of it this way. When Christians were being thrown by the Romans to the lions, the Christians were capable of singing as the lions slaughtered them. What gave these people their equanimity when they were about to be gobbled up by lions?

DJ: So Christianity, with its complete inversion of perspective, is one response to the fact that we all die.

MO: Precisely. But you can trace the idea that earthly existence is meaningless and irrelevant further back into history. Socrates had an almost total and cavalier disdain for physical existence. He said in the *Phaedo*, for example, that "the true philosopher is always seeking death," meaning that the body is but an illusion.

This leaves us confused. We have a compulsive attraction to our body, our corporality, our *being* in the world, that in some senses is biologically determined. At the same time we live in a culture that has developed traditions which cause in us a kind of fear and loathing of our corporality.

DJ: To fear and loathe one's corporality would seem to be a denial of one's own experience of being alive. R. D. Laing wrote, "Our behavior is a function of our experience. We act according to the way we see things. If our experience is destroyed, our behavior will be destructive. If our experience is destroyed, we have lost our own selves."

MO: An example of how transcendentalism can cause you to lose yourself is Ralph Waldo Emerson. When Emerson looked at Nature, spelled with a capital N, he saw an expression of the oversoul, the Transcendental Ego. He saw Nature as a lawfully ordered system designed by a transcendent creator and in which Man, capital M, was perfectly at home.

Let's contrast that with Thoreau. We can see the difference immediately just in how they titled their works. Emerson's *Nature* is universal and abstract. Thoreau's *Walden* is a particular place. The magic of *Walden* is not that we escape the immediacy of experience in order to reach some eternal unchanging definition of the human condition, but that we're continually exposed to the vivid immediacy of Thoreau's experiences in a particular place.

DJ: Perhaps then a way to resacralize the world is to help people reconnect to their own experience. I'm thinking about Thoreau's words from *Maine Woods*: "Think of our life in nature,—daily to be shown matter, to come in contact with it,—rocks, trees, wind on our cheeks! the *solid* earth! the *actual* world! the *common sense! Contact! Contact! Who* are we? *Where* are we?"

MO: Thoreau's piece was written about his climb up Ktaadn's Ridge, on his first trip to Maine. He got up early that morning and left his partners in camp. He climbed to about 4500 feet, with the fog swirling around him. The jagged rocks were probably slippery and wet, and at that moment he realized his ass could be grass any second. *This* is wildness. *This* is primeval chaos. He's just here, facing the realization that this place is not made for him. He may be a part of this place, but it's not written into the fundamental design that everything is going to be peachy keen and wonderful.

Later, John Muir said: "I can't understand the attitude of Lord Man who thinks that everything has been put here for his use, when the simple fact is that we could very well wind up to be the meal of a lion or a tiger."

The world is not our oyster. That's the illusion of the transcendental mind. We are trying, as a culture, as a civilization, to get over some of our myopia. Transcendentalism, like the economics we were talking about, is myopic. Both are tied to mechanistic materialism—we are the transcendental spectator, the earth has been designed for us, our economic categories define the total possibility of human experience.

We've got to jettison that and instead attempt to get our categories—our belief systems, our ways of looking at the world—back in line with what is permitted for human beings on this planet, to live in a way where we can still produce the basic wherewithal for life without totally cratering the world.

Part of this involves ecological economics. It's Thoreauvian economics. Thoreau was a pivot point. It occurred to him that this worldview, this culture, this civilizational complex could not hold together. This allowed him to flop into a different way of conceptualizing his place in the scheme of things.

Whatever the insufficiencies of organic existence, the terrors of death, the failings of flesh, it is a delusion to think we can find solutions in that which is beyond or above. This is not to say we don't need principles and ideals, but we have to realize the point of our principles and ideals is not to escape our organic condition, but merely to make it possible for us to live an existence that is a fuller realization of our human potentials.

DJ: How does that relate to a quote from Thoreau that forms a theme throughout *The Idea of Wilderness*: "In wildness lies the preservation of the world"?

MO: What world is he talking about? The human world. Why is wildness the preservation of the human world? Because the human world is suffering from a pernicious disease. Let's call it, to speak metaphorically, hardening of the categories. Human beings die because our arteries fill up and we can no longer pump blood. Cultures die because their categories fill up, become ossified, and can no longer carry the sustaining nutrients of life. It's like the economic categories we were talking about.

What's the antidote to this? Wildness. Wildness represents the possibility of renewal, of vigorous action, of expansion, of chaos, of chaos out of which new order . . .

You can go back to *Walden* for another way to look at this. There, in the bean field, Thoreau wrote about the kinds of people you can grow, in analogy to the kinds of beans you can grow. If you plant seeds that are old and worm-eaten, you're going to have a poor crop. If humans are being raised up on seeds—categories, in this sense—that are old and worm-eaten, you're going to get a weak crop as well. So what you need, if you're going to have a good bean field, is healthy, vital seed stock that's lively and full of energy. And similarly if you're going to have a healthy culture, and now think of categories as seeds, you need to have new stock, new seeds that are full of energy and possibility.

The old categories of neoclassical economics are worm-eaten. Anybody can see through them. We determine our success as a culture by measuring the gross national product. The real question, though, is not: "Are we growing, in terms of the gross national product?" but instead: "How gross *is* the gross national product?" It's very gross, as literally thousands of people know. But it lives on, and we continue to wither as a culture. The seeds, the basic set of categories, are worm-eaten.

Back to ecological economics. It's chaos now, it's new stock, it's vital. It's imperfect, it's going to be unruly, it's going to have some branches that need to be pruned, but that's the road to the future, insofar as we can see right now. In wildness lies the preservation of the world.

This phrase also speaks directly to individuals. Insofar as anyone is going to serve in any meaningful capacity, they've got to continue to be venturesome. I always want to be pushing out there as far as I can at any one time.

DJ: Let's put Thoreau back on Ktaadn's Ridge, standing amidst the fog and slippery rocks, and speak more to those moments of encounter, to the recognition of our human beingness in the presence of the other-than-human.

MO: Florence Krall teaches what are essentially autobiographical narrative forms of writing that are related to place. Human beings discover their psyche, their self, their character, their persona *in* place. Any autobiographical account, and of course we are all continually writing our own biographies by living our lives, must take this into account. Krall's thesis seems to be that any person who defines himself or herself independent of place has defined himself or herself in a very truncated, artificial way.

Another way to think about this is to look at the losers in the Greek tradition, people like Diotima, who appears as a minor character in *The Symposium*. Diotima teaches that the truth, with a small *t*, is not logos, some transcendental system of concepts, but eros, an erotic, pulsing dynamic of life. People who have championed the erotic, which has nothing to do with the lewd or the vulgar or *merely* sensual, have been the losers in terms of the mainstream tradition.

Logos, once again, is the attempt to escape from that which is situated, embedded, pulsing, concrete, immediate, into that which is constrained, logical, classified, lawful, ordered, universalized.

Either logos or eros, taken to the extreme, becomes a parody of itself. Right now our culture is at risk because we're too restricted. We suffer from hardening of the categories. Logos rules. That, for example, is why the old-growth forests are in jeopardy. Within our current categories, the value of old-growth forests lies in board feet, in jobs for human beings, and so on.

Nor would a culture swung totally toward the erotic be able to sustain itself. One reason is that human beings are biologically underdetermined. Whatever we once were as protohumanoids we are no longer.

This doesn't alter the fact that we need to loosen up, which is why the erotic is so important.

This brings us to Thoreau on Ktaadn's Ridge. As he went up the ridge, he went across the boundary into what Hans Peter Duerr calls dreamtime. Thoreau saw the contingency of what he had been, the Harvard student, the man who made pencils, the American scholar—as Emerson liked to think of him—and he became an entirely different Thoreau. Remember, Thoreau took this trip during his Walden sojourn. And he'd gone to Walden, at least in part, because he'd realized—while he was in New York City—that the Emersonian plan for his life was not authentic. So he went to Walden, and also to Ktaadn, to cross over—to find a place where he could just maybe glimpse the cultural cocoon in which he lived.

This is what all of us who love wildness and who go to the wilderness continually seek. I can be sitting in my favorite spot in the mountains, and all of a sudden realize it's dark. Time has stopped. Max the university professor, who's got appointments to keep and places to go and papers to write, has disappeared. I've gone across a line and become part of the rhythm of the play of the cloud shadows on the mountains, the dappling of the surface of the lake by the nymphs, the trouts' rise—I disappear into the whole phenomenal field. I get out of my Western self and go somewhere. Time stops, and perhaps when I catch it, ten hours have gone by. It's an incredible experience. Dreamtime. Alcheringa. To pass over or through.

There is no predictability to this. You can't go up there and expect it, nor can you make it happen. There's no technology of dreamtime.

DJ: Does *Homo sapiens* have a future without wild wilderness?

MO: To steal a phrase, such a future would be increasingly robotic, pre-posterous, and crass. Anybody who thinks very deeply about what is most meaningful about their lives would not want to live in that world.

Buckminster Fuller wrote that he could feed, house, and clothe the entire human population on the main island of Japan. That seems to me typical of the kind of technologically arrogant, ecologically illiterate, bureaucratic, scientific mentality that rules the modern world. I call it the Managing Planet Earth mentality, and I view it as a danger, a threat to everything I hold dear and to everything meaningful in being human. Psychologically we would be so profoundly altered that we would be-come different kinds of human beings.

And this bureaucratic, scientific mentality is insane. John Fivor, for-mer director of special research projects at the National Center for At-mospheric Research, finds this high-technology managerial path we are embarked upon the height of arrogance. The supposition of the mana-gerial path is that we can replace biophysical processes and ecosystemic arrangements that have evolved over 3.2 billion years of history with technological inventions and engineering designs produced in the last ten or fifteen years and that at the same time we will have a viable culture capable of maintaining itself. Of course he finds that ridiculous. Further, he says, looking at what we have done as an engineering species and the consequences of the technologies we have actually been using, the outcomes have always been disasters. The overwhelming evidence is that we're already failing. We've gone too far from nature's way.

Let's turn, then, and look in a different direction, the direction where we begin attempting to preserve these natural ecosystems and biophysical processes and maintain at least the opportunity for people to escape the bounds of culture. We then need to ask what we need to be doing in terms of engineering design and technology.

I like to think in terms of technologies that are mimetic rather than arrogant, technologies which are not designed to dominate nature but are based on the observation of how things work in nature. How do bees work? What are the teachings of the bees' economy for the human economy? How does nature channel water? Does nature build dams? Canals? Channels? Or is the hydraulic engineering of nature based on different principles and orders? If we look we will find that indeed it *is* based on different principles and orders.

Sure, we can envision a technological world in which the entire surface of the earth has been humanized. But I am radically and unalterably opposed to that future. I perceive my own project as doing everything I can to redirect the human experiment away from that outcome.

Unfortunately, there aren't very many of us yet who are speaking with this subversive voice. The managerial approach is by far the governing mentality.

DJ: I don't understand why the managerial ethos is the governing mentality when it clearly doesn't work. Even the Forest Service admitted on the first page of the *Blue Mountains Forest Health Report* that "scientific evidence suggests that we have encouraged conditions that may result in catastrophic levels of tree mortality."

The Exxon *Valdez*, Chernobyl, Three Mile Island, catastrophic decline of fisheries, desertification. Everywhere you look the managerial ethos fails.

MO: We stick with it because the categories have hardened.

There is also another answer as to why the bureaucratic, engineering mentality prevails. Pogo of course gave us this answer, "We have met the enemy, and he is us."

As an example of how this works, think about a program like the EPA Superfund. We spend literally billions of dollars. On what? We provide hundreds of millions of grant dollars to universities to produce environmental scientists and engineers and technicians, and we provide contracts worth hundreds of millions of dollars to giant construction companies like Brown and Root. Of course Brown and Root also works for the U.S. Army Corps of Engineers—they'll work for anybody. So the Superfund is enormously profitable, and it creates the appearance to society that we're actually doing something about the dire predicament into which we're pushing the earth. But it's a shell game without a pea. It's nearly a total fraud, in the sense that the illusion has been created in the lay public's mind that the Superfund cleanups will restore ecosystem health. The truth is entirely different. But the Superfund is just the kind of predictable, technologically arrogant, bureaucratic response you would expect—given the dominant economic paradigm.

Contrast that with the Pollution Prevention Act. A dollar spent on pollution prevention will save between ten and a hundred dollars, depending on what you're trying to prevent. Total expenditure in fiscal 1991 on the Pollution Prevention Act? $16 million.

The managerial ethos springs from our cultural narrative. Each culture has a dominant narrative, with little dissident traditions within it. Only when the dominant cultural narrative is in such overwhelming crisis that everybody can see it's going to collapse is there really any possibility of revamping it. We're possibly reaching such a point right now. We're caught between a failed story and a future powerless to be born. It is the lot of the dissidents to do everything they can to help ensure we find our way onto a path which is socially and naturally viable.

DJ: What you said about mimetic technologies seems to tie to something else that Thoreau said: "The highest we can attain to is not knowledge, but sympathy with intelligence."

MO: Most humans delude themselves in believing they know what they do not. And they act in terms of that. Thoreau on the other hand deconstructed that conventional wisdom and reconstructed the idea that we need a willingness to be humble, to admit that we're ignorant.

"The highest we can attain to is not knowledge, but sympathy with intelligence." The intelligence I believe he's referring to is that which is embedded in the organic natural order that surrounds us. That's an intelligence that's been authored, but not by human beings. It's our mission, then, first to grasp the fact that we deceive ourselves continually by thinking we know what we do not know and by becoming pumped up with pride in our theories and categories. Once we've found our way through that, it's our mission to achieve a sympathy with the intelligence in nature. In other words, to open ourselves to it so we can resonate with it or vibrate with it. I'm sure bees have taught you as much about beekeeping as all the manuals you've read.

DJ: Far more. Far more about everything.

MO: That's a sympathy with intelligence. The intelligence is the order and structure of the bees, their processes of communication, how they locate flowers and communicate that, how they establish the pathways and operations of the hive. Now extend that more generally to the entire cultural order. That's the goal, to achieve a sympathy with intelligence.

When we feel we're in control, that we're active knowers who impose an order upon the world, we've reduced the world to what Martin Buber called an "It." When we enter into a relationship where we are learning from the world, we've moved into I-You relationships. From this perspective we view knowledge, with a small k, as a participatory occasion, an interactive, dynamic exchange, a realization that we come to consciousness in a situation that inevitably eludes any categorical frame or net we could put upon it.

Even those cultures that people like myself like to valorize, such as the indigenous peoples of the southwestern part of Turtle Island, often exhausted the soil, had too many babies, and put too much demand on the ecosystem. This serves to remind me that *any* human frame of reference is no more and no less than that—a human frame of reference.

I want to be clear on all of this. Or as clear as possible here. What Thoreau sees is that a viable culture is one that has a certain wildness to it, so that it remains flexible. It also has a humility to it, so that it is seeking a sympathy with intelligence. What he envisioned as ideal, and what I envision as ideal, is a society that is, in these ways, the opposite of the society we already have. We're not humble, we're arrogant, and we're not open, we're closed.

DJ: What does the word *sacred* mean to you?

MO: It's the relinking, the rediscovery, the reconnection of the little point of light, the sentience that you are, with the totality. On the one hand this sounds impossible, but on the other it has been uttered in 1001 different ways in 1001 different religious traditions.

If you are open, if you can somehow keep clear in your mind how much of your being has been socially defined, then you can continually slip through the cracks of that social definition and encounter the sacred. You can see the sacred in a baby's smile and in the caress of a mother's lips on a baby's forehead. You can see the sacred in the glimmer of satisfaction that comes when a student suddenly makes a breakthrough in a problem in logic. You can encounter the sacred in the tinkle of a wind chime in the wind. You can experience the sacred by raising your vision from the horizon and seeing Venus perched on the end of the new moon. It's all around us, it's just we get so caught up in the artifice of our cultural conditioning that it eludes us.

It's really nice being here at Castle Rock Lake. The sun was already nicely up when I got up this morning at about 5:30. I came out and sat on this porch. It was so quiet, and so green. I felt like I was in the forest. The hummingbirds started coming to the feeder, and this beautiful little yellow nuthatch, this incredible little bird, was feeding over here. God, it was so good to be alive, so rich.

DJ: If you could have the readers of this conversation take away one thing to know in their heart, what would it be?

MO: I would like readers to remember that technology is never neutral. By the very act of reading, the readers have been situated. They have been situated in a culture that is very new and that may very well not endure, and one of the reasons it may not endure is because we have become literate. Not only are they reading as literates read, but they are reading that which has been produced by typography, which of course is another form of technology. In that sense they are doubly situated.

I would suggest to the readers, as they become aware of that fact, that they look again at the conversations in this book. I would imagine that many of these conversations have either directly or implicitly encouraged them to lay down books and find themselves in an organic place where they are no longer reading, but where they instead have attempted to open up the pores of their skin and their pupils and allowed the earth and the creatures of the earth to intermingle with them. I would hope they would then in a certain sense escape the logos, which is the world literate people inhabit, and cross the line into the eros, which is the world in which our bodies are situated. And I would hope this corporeal dimension of our being, which has increasingly been hidden from us by cultural convention, could be renewed, reawakened, reaffirmed.

Get outside, escape the logos, encounter the other, and let the other begin to influence you. The other will empower you. We tend to get caught up in the idea that our projects are our own. I've been lucky enough to know that our projects are indeed *partly* our own. But our projects are given to us, and we find ourselves in them. I feel blessed. I often laugh at myself, because we take ourselves so seriously in our cultural definitions, the social places that overdetermine our self-conceptions. Increasingly I find myself to be an instrument being played by destiny. The more I let go of any sense of ego, the more empowered I am.

When you open yourself to wildness, to eros, you can find yourself on a path with a heart. You don't create the path, but you recognize this *is* a path with a heart. People, particularly students, always want to know what it is I'm *doing*, and how it is I know what to do. I always tell them I just have enough courage or faith to know all I need to do is walk to the end of this path. When I get to the end of this path, I'll see where I need to go next.

It's a little bit like climbing in the mountains, where you can't see to go until you next *need* to see to go. The mountain continually reveals itself. It unfolds. A path with a heart is like that. But it only opens up to you when you're not being fraudulent, where you have the faith to go with the flow, the Tao.

Most people today are conditioned to be butchers, bakers, candlestick makers. Mothers and fathers, who are always vitally interested in their children, say, "What do you want to be when you grow up? Do you want to be a doctor? A lawyer? Do you want to be this, or do you want to be that?" That's the way the world of convention operates, and that's why we have so many people who are damn miserable. A path with a heart is a path with freedom.

That's one of the reasons Robinson Jeffers always uses the hawk in his poetry. It's such a powerful symbol. The hawk is wild and free. Yet it's on a path. The path is invisible—the path and the energy come from the air and the sun and the play of the wind. Of course the hawk beats its wings occasionally. If you want to be an intellectual you've got to beat your wings, you've got to pay your dues, you've got to study a lot, you've got to write a lot, and so on. But before long you're able to ride some wind currents.

I'm sure any career counselor who found their way to this would say, "That Oelschlaeger is one crazy dude. That's a sure path to economic ruination and a life where you wind up a hopeless vagabond."

But I can't conceive of living life any other way.

DJ: Things happen when you open up.

MO: To learn to be wild and free. I struggled with that for quite a while, I tried to fight it off, and then grew up enough to follow the invisible path.

SANDRA LOPEZ

Sandra Lopez is a book artist, that is, a person whose work considers the physical form of the book. She had been making books for years, and, as she has written, "One day, I simply noticed that I was no longer focusing on words as the main point of a book. I began to see the book as a container for ideas, and to ask myself how we had shaped our ideas by the form in which we had chosen to preserve them. I had begun to ask myself what sorts of strictures the Western book puts on the knowledge it contains."

Who do books serve? Who do they exclude? What is the relationship between literacy and environmental degradation? Between literacy and a fear of the body, a fear of death?

Sandra Lopez explores questions such as these through her work. Her books, including Winged Book, Epiphany, and CLEARCUT, are in both public and private collections, and she has exhibited nationally. Since 1970 she has lived in the McKenzie River Valley in Oregon with her husband, Barry Lopez.

SANDRA LOPEZ: A container's shape determines what you can put in it. If you put water into an oval bowl, the water takes the shape of an oval. If you have something too big for the bowl, the bowl won't take it.

Books are containers that comfortably hold only certain kinds of information and that hold certain other kinds of information only in translation. To put into a book the way an animal behaves in the wild, I have to watch the animal as it acts in a non-human-language way, translate that behavior into human thought, into human language, and then into language which fits into a book. Out of all I've seen, that translation determines what I will discard and what I will keep. This then determines what the person who reads the book will receive.

Two images come to mind. One is what you see outside this window, a complex landscape of forest and river, in which your eyes move up here, down here, over here, and sometimes unfocus to allow you to take in the whole pattern. The other image consists of neatly shaped letters coming together in linear fashion on the printed page.

Books are sequential; you must go word-by-word, line-by-line, page-by-page. Perhaps in the early evolution of books people thought about the effects of such things. But we've stopped questioning the form, and so automatically translate into that form information we want to preserve and pass on.

DERRICK JENSEN: But isn't life itself sequential? Isn't time sequential?

SL: A digital watch is certainly sequential, but a clock with hands is cyclical. More important, you know from experience that some minutes are longer than others. Sometimes time rushes ahead of itself, and sometimes it lags behind. And sometimes you step entirely out of time, when you're in that state of creating or that state of *being* in the world where you entirely cease to experience time. So experientially I would say time is *not* strictly sequential.

It's important to remember sequence is different from change. Change happens, but not in measured, regular periods. Day and night, for example, breathe across the seasons.

Each of the two images I mentioned a moment ago has a sequence. In a landscape the sequence is determined by the seer; you can read a landscape randomly and have it make sense. In a book the sequence is predetermined by the print, the shape of the language, the way it goes on a page; we expect one thing to follow another toward a goal. We've taken the landscape and abstracted it into words, and have simultaneously taken on the goal of expecting one thing to lead to another and ultimately come to an end. Those of us who were raised with books as the source of knowledge have unconsciously absorbed the idea that knowledge has a beginning, middle, and end.

DJ: And that it's repeatable. I once asked a friend, who now has a Ph.D. in physics, of what human use it is to me to know equations for physical phenomena such as lightning or the changing of leaves' colors. He told me the theories of physics were superior to other perhaps commonsense explanations because they lead to repeatability.

SL: I don't think there is repeatability. Your friend knows one description of lightning. There are also mythical descriptions of lightning and poetic descriptions of lightning.

Americans have a touching faith in the idea that if you know how something works you know what it means. When there is an airplane accident, the first thing people want to do is find the black box, which will supposedly tell them why the plane went down. But knowing why the plane went down doesn't prevent this accident and doesn't make the people any less dead. It may in the future prevent other accidents, but that's highly unlikely. There is a difference between understanding how something works and understanding something. A knowledge of the sequence of events does not necessarily lead to a comprehension of meaning.

This is related to another question. Why do some people shy away from mystery as if it's a terrible thing, as if it's something to be feared, as opposed to something that simply is acknowledged? There's nothing wrong with a physicist saying lightning is xyz, but if he says that's all it is, I feel sorry for him. It's the same as saying anything you can't translate into English is not worth knowing.

DJ: If you've been raised on books, how can you know there are other forms of knowledge?

SL: Years ago I read a book with the unfortunate title of *A Male Guide to Women's Liberation*. This book taught me that if you fit the norm in your culture, whatever that norm is, it rarely occurs to you that not everyone is like you. If you are a white male within our culture, the structures of knowledge, language, education, and power are things you are more likely to feel comfortable with, because they are languages made by those who probably are similar to you. A person in that position, or even an acculturated person like a white educated woman, can only begin the questioning if something happens in life and he or she is outside for just one second. If that happens, this person *may* suddenly realize everything doesn't have to be this way.

Once you've experienced one other way of seeing, you begin to realize there are many different ways to describe the universe, many different ways to transmit knowledge. And then you may begin to think about the fact that while our methods of transmitting knowledge are very good, they can also exclude a great many things which could be of importance to us. Thinking about this, you may begin to ask whether many of these things were willfully excluded, not on a level of individual but cultural will. Was the exclusion necessary to allow and maintain dominance over those whose voices were and are excluded?

In trying to change the structure of books so they accept voices that have been up to now excluded, I have had to imagine what it was about books that kept these voices silent. For example, women were excluded from books at one time because they could not read or write. This is still true for the majority of people in the world, women and men. The voices of nature are excluded for the same reason. The progressive nature of books is critical to the exclusion of some voices; many Native American cultures seem to know the world in a nonlinear fashion, and it is perhaps significant that their stories are often oral, as opposed to written.

DJ: How do you maintain an openness to these other voices, for example, the voices of the natural world?

SL: I would describe hearing the voices as a reciprocity and not necessarily something you do. It is, after all, a dialogue. If you are not merely forcing your ego onto the world, sometimes you have to be patient until the world is ready to speak to you.

But there are things you can do. A practice of attentiveness and an attitude of respect can be important. And these require a lack of distraction in an important place inside of you.

That's how I made the work called *Daybook*. I wanted to see what would happen if I collected an object each day for a year. So I constructed a heavy paper grid that divided a large box into twelve rows— one for each month—with thirty-one spaces to each row, even though that meant that some of the rows would not be completed to the end. Beginning on February 17, 1991, every day I went into the world with the idea that at some point I would encounter something to put in that box. During that year, I was in a state of constant attentiveness. Some of the things that appeared were extraordinary. There were, of course, lichens and mosses, small stones, fir cones and cedar, shed dog fur. It was a year for moths—pale green, intricate brown, furry glowing white, velvet rust. Summer had mosquito hawks and paint chipped from the house as we cleaned it for new paint. A small wasp nest from under the eaves. A transparent bird feather. There were flower petals of every kind and color, green glass, coins, one of my first gray hairs. Harlequin beetles appeared like jewels. And there was a place up the hill where snail shells always seemed to present themselves, but only in that year, not before or since. On Christmas Day, I bit into a mussel and found a pearl. This collecting, this gathering was all an attempt to understand recognition, to cultivate it, and to maintain an openness so that when the object appeared, I would know it.

To stay in that state of open attentiveness is really a discipline, one in which you have to go prepared to receive a gift. It becomes a way of life, and everything that comes out of the world reinforces that sense of exchange and the rightness of the openness. The delight in the exchange, the delight of the small pearl in the mussel shell, becomes part of the process too.

Did you see the leaf pinned on the bulletin board over my desk in the back room? It's there to remind me there's no reason the world has to be beautiful, but again and again it is. Why is this? Does the beauty only come from our projections? Is the leaf only beautiful because I see and recognize it? Or does something in the tree wish to be beautiful? I believe it's the latter. Just look at birds. Or look at anything.

One of the problems in moving in systems like this is to attempt to distinguish between ego and outside. It's possible to go into the world and have incredible experiences, never having interacted with the world. We so often strive to find meaning in the universe, but we have to realize that while some of our conclusions can come from the openness that allows for exchange, other conclusions come just from a projection of our ego. It's important to try to understand which you're engaged in at the time. If you feel a certain level of discomfort about an event, does that mean you don't understand it, you haven't behaved properly, or something else entirely? How do you know when you are actually in dialogue, as opposed to monologue? That's a central question in interacting with nonhumans, or humans for that matter. Think of the translations we have to go through just to talk to another human being, let alone to a dog we know, or to feel we've had some interaction with a tree.

Unfortunately, even as I talk about this, I can hear people saying, "Interaction with a tree?" But this is a very real thing that can happen.

I think that I can say I once knew a cottonwood tree. It lived on one bank of a creek at a place where I often sat on the opposite bank. One fall day, I was sitting there quietly when a leaf fell into my lap. I looked up to see this grand tree across from me, one I had never singled out before, and felt that it had gently said hello. I always greeted it after that and don't think it was my imagination that more leaves came my way after that greeting. I cannot describe the gentle humor of that touch, or how it opened my eyes to the beauty not only of this particular cottonwood tree, but through knowing this tree, watching it through the seasons, through the changing light and weathers of the years, watching its huge graceful dance in the winds that passed through, how this taught me about all other cottonwoods as well.

I was present at its death. One day Desert, our dog, and I were walking along the creek to the river. This was in a time when the place where we always walked had been logged badly. What had once been a deep rain forest was now stumps. Ancient cedars graceful as any in Japanese prints had been taken away. Now there was only devastation and mud. I was numb with the memory of the continual deep thuds of the trees falling on the hillside above.

This day, as we came down the creek, a man on the opposite bank motioned us out of the way. He had a chainsaw. Only partly comprehending, and fearing for Desert's safety, I turned and we moved away down the riverbank. Then, to my horror, he began to cut down the cottonwood. It is to my continuing shame that I did not move, but only sat on the riverbank, holding Desert beside me and weeping. If I were to number grave sins in my life, this would be one of them, the failure to save that tree that had been a companion.

The question becomes: How do you recognize these relationships and then convey them?

That is part of what I try to do when I make books. I have made a spider's book. It is obvious to anyone who comes to this house that I live happily with spiders. I watch them a lot, and I'm deeply moved by the structures they build. What happens when I put books—as containers of knowledge—and spiders together? How do spiders pass on knowledge? People can say that they believe the knowledge is passed on genetically, but if spiders had knowledge they wanted to pass on in something they made, how would they do it? Would they perhaps spin it out of their bodies, leaving some behind for others to read, taking some with them, scrolling it up to carry on?

I looked at spiderwebs for years—the different kinds that were built, the different shapes—and used that knowledge to make the book. I found a branch. A friend had given me sheets of glassine paper embossed with spiderwebs holding both spiders and flies. I embroidered fifteen or twenty of those spiders with silver thread until I understood the shape of the spider. I beaded one of the webs and sewed the translucent wing of a mosquito hawk to another page. The last thing to complete was a web of iridescent line in the branch. The web was the culmination of all the things I knew about spiders, and all that I had learned in the making of this book. I told my hand, "You know these things," and let it go.

DJ: What's the relationship between words and the power of naming? Between knowledge and power-over?

SL: When I first moved here twenty-three years ago, I learned the names of all the plants, and now I don't know them. Some people find that terrible, as though I haven't bothered to remember. But it would be closer to say the names were a box for me to put the plants in. Without the names I can actually see individual plants and see what the plant is doing.

That's one of the reasons I began to take words out of books. With the words gone you can focus on the structure. What do you have left, and what are the implications of what you have left? Years ago, a friend traveled to Alaska, where she found herself with friends hunting ducks. Because they were eating them, they threw most of the skins away. My friend could not bear to see this beauty tossed aside, and so saved some of it, bringing me a green-winged teal wing. It came early in my book-binding time, and at first I thought it would be a spectacular ornament on a traditional book. After a while, I began to see that the book, while still traditional, should have the shape of the wing. But I still didn't make the book. Then I encountered a book form in which the spine of the book was freed to open from narrow to very wide, and the pages inside could move in opposite directions when the book was opened. I can still remember the elation of that knowledge, of leaving the room in Manhattan where I had been working and walking uptown in a cold gray November city dusk, my feet barely touching the ground.

Then I made *Winged Book*. It is the shape of the green-winged teal wing, and not too much heavier. The papers are handmade, with flowers and feathers and thread in them. Each page opens in two directions and, as the top of the page passes over the bottom, there is the sound of wings, a sound I neither planned for nor anticipated but which was a gift found in the making.

The subject of the book is flight, but it doesn't use words. This in itself is part of the gesture. People are used to reading about flight in the sequential way we mentioned earlier, and as they read, they may be able to imagine or remember flight. But as you read it's easy to forget the levels of translation that have gone on. We begin to believe that this abstraction which is words on the page is the real thing. In the same way, we substitute photographs for experience or images in a catalog for the painting itself.

This goes to the core of my work. My work is about taking a familiar form, the book, and breaking it in the hope of causing people to ask why it is the way it is. What can it tell me, and what can it not tell me? What sorts of things will it completely fail to tell me, simply because what needs to be told can't be put into this format? These are questions we need to ask not only of books but of everything.

Once the questions start they never end. An important question is, who do books serve? You have to read to use a book, which eliminates many people. You have to have eyes to use a book, which eliminates more people, in the sense of plants and trees and other things. When you start to see what doesn't fit, when you start to see for whom the book isn't a natural form, a comfortable form, you begin to see who it does fit, and for whom it *is* comfortable. Capitalism, for example, a linear progressive form, is well-suited to books, as is the whole idea of unlimited growth.

Another question: How does this form—rectangular pages containing type—serve capitalism and at the same time produce a world so many-layered, so complex and complete as the one in the book *Middlemarch*? With all I say about removing words, it is still simply amazing to me that human beings who can read are able to translate those symbols on a flat page into a universe.

DJ: I'm wondering about the primacy of the word. I've read that the Six

Nations didn't write down their code of laws, because they felt as soon as they did, the laws would become more important than the people involved.

SL: There is a connection between literacy and memory, in that if you know where to find something written down you don't have to remember it. Sometimes I'll write down a dream, rather than holding it in my mind and making it a part of me. After it's written, though, it's gone in a way it wouldn't be if I'd tried to understand it.

It is also true that we are less likely to question something that is written on a page. If it's in a book we believe it's true, and final.

DJ: Just yesterday someone told me, "It doesn't matter what man wants; what's important is what God says in the Bible." There's that primacy of the word, which was written once and is unchanging through all time.

SL: Which is an astonishing concept. And of course one of the attributes of God is that he is unchanging. This unchanging nature also makes him outside anything we know. And there's a clear connection between this unchanging god and words. In the Bible we read, "In the beginning was the Word, and the Word was with God, and the Word was God."

DJ: What would you like to convey to those who see your work?

SL: That we die.

A lot of the work I've done with books, and a lot of what we've been talking about—the idea of the word as abstraction, the idea of the permanence of the word, the authority vested in the book—is an expression of one of the things leading us astray in our culture, which is a denial of death. Much of our culture has been a denial of death, and books are certainly representative of that. If this word gets into this book, it will be here forever. It will be permanent. It won't change. Much of my work is concerned with saying it's *not* permanent, there *is* change. We live in time.

The first book I made that I recognized as putting me on a path away from traditional bookbinding was triggered by reading a passage in a novel in which a poet dreamed about what might happen if her books were left on the forest floor. It was a beautiful image, calm, full of mosses and snail tracks and gentle decay. That image became *Moth Book*, a small birchbark-covered traditional book that rests on a bed of thick deep-green moss. The pages are a soft Japanese paper with moths laminated in some. A curve is torn out of the fore edge of the book, with a moth resting there, eating her way in, or finding shelter in a place already eaten by another. Since this book was made, in 1981, there have been many moths, all volunteers, each one beautiful, and each one appearing just as the last is near disintegration.

I was trained by a master bookbinder to use materials that would last for hundreds of years. Because it was so difficult for me to let go of this idea, to use materials that will decay, that will change, that won't be here in the same form for hundreds of years, I think I can understand something of the underlying implications tied to books. There is something about the abstraction of the world into the letter form that implies if we separate from the world, from the body, we will be immortal. Until we overcome that idea and accept that we will die, I don't think we will be able to understand or curb the tendencies in our culture that are contributing to what some environmentalists call the crash. I'm talking about ideas like unlimited growth, like the linear progression of time.

Taking the form of the book, this thing that is supposed to preserve the word and preserve our ideas unchanged throughout eternity, and saying it's an illusion is a step toward accepting death. Until we accept death we'll continue to make the same mistakes, because much of the motion of our culture, including the exclusion and denial of much of the feminine, has to do with a desperate attempt to distance ourselves from death.

Dolores LaChapelle and Julien Puzey

Terry Tempest Williams said of Dolores LaChapelle's book Sacred Land Sacred Sex Rapture of the Deep: Concerning Deep Ecology and Celebrating Life, *"That book is it. What more is there?" Jeannette Armstrong has said that Dolores LaChapelle is an elder for the twenty-first century. And Max Oelschlaeger has written, "If our dangerously out of control industrial growth society somehow finds its way to an age of deep ecology, to people living bioregionally, then* Sacred Land Sacred Sex *will be celebrated as one of the texts that helped us recover the old ways and invent the new."*

Dolores LaChapelle is a Phi Beta Kappa with a degree in History. She has been climbing mountains and skiing deep powder snow since she was seventeen. Her books come out of this interaction between the academic and wild nature in her life. LaChapelle directs the Way of the Mountain Center, 9300 feet high in the San Juan Mountains of Colorado. She is the author of Earth Festivals, Earth Wisdom, *and* Deep Powder Snow: 40 Years of Ecstatic Skiing, Avalanches, and Earth Wisdom.

When I contacted Dolores LaChapelle, she suggested we meet in Salt Lake City so Julien Puzey could take part in the conversation. Julien Puzey is a dedicated devolutionist and teacher whose thought has been crucial to Dolores LaChapelle's work and to the deep ecology movement. As well as teaching, Julien Puzey writes and presents workshops. Most recently she put together a workshop entitled Soul: In and of the World, *which was a gentle, affirming exploration of the individual soul in relationship to nature, to other humans, to the material possessions of our lives, to the world soul, and to personal sacred practices.*

JULIEN PUZEY: As a culture, we have withdrawn from the conversation with death. Last year the herbalist Susan Weed told us the one thing most missing in vegetarian diets is—you'd never guess—animal flesh. Susan is going to make a video on giving death, because she says you have no business calling yourself a healer unless you're willing to give death with the same celebration with which you observe birth.

It's the same with people who panic about the end of this civilization, saying, "It's all falling down. It's all falling down." It's time to celebrate

it's all falling down. You can't solve the problem with the same consciousness that created it. You can't go from this mess to a great new glo-
rious day without a period of transition. When you get fired, when you
don't have gas for your car, when the electricity is gone, you've got to
say, "Oh, good. It's finally changing. We're in a corrective state." You've
got to not take it personally.

My partner, Marie, talks about how far removed we are from our
source of nourishment, about how we fail to participate fully in the giveaway. Next summer we're going to have the first annual bunny bop and
barbecue. People will say, "Can I help with the barbecue?" and we will
say, "Yes, go pick your entree. They're the ones with the black arm-
bands." For those who are really squeamish, we'll have styrofoam trays
and plastic so they can kill their bunny, put it on the tray, cover it with
plastic . . .

DOLORES LACHAPELLE: Like the supermarket.

JP: . . . put it in the refrigerator, bring it out, and absolve themselves of
any relationship to death.

This is all important because a city in Florida passed a law making it
illegal within city limits to kill what you eat. It has to be done outside
the city limits by people who are licensed. You can't have anything fresh.
The flesh has to go through trays and plastics. Anyone who has a direct
connection with the source of life becomes suspect, reprehensible, *and*
subject to fine and illegal.

This abhorrence of death affects every part of our lives. For example,
our culture is set up to celebrate spring and summer. Beauty is only one
season. Worthwhile is only one season.

At the same time, to think you can kill in an ordinary state of consciousness is *totally* inappropriate. You really do have to sacralize the
kill.

DL: Gary Snyder wrote, "You sing to it. You pray to it. And then you enjoy it." That's why tribal people have certain rituals before they go out.
And real primitives don't hunt the animals. They do the rituals, then go
sit to wait for the animal to give itself to them. And the animal comes
walking down the trail.

JP: That's the conversation. Christianity, monotheism, civilization, has withdrawn from the conversation with death. All of Christianity is about preferring life, and even life eternal, over death. This is a setting up of the human as an exception to the giveaway.

DL: Ethologists have done a lot of work on the predator/prey relationship, which is *the* basic relationship. They've described how when the predator zeros in on the prey, the prey goes into a state of bliss, shall we say, and gives itself to the predator. We have an experiential account of this from Dr. Livingston, of "Dr. Livingston, I presume" fame. One day he was walking down the trail and surprised a lion. The lion came at him, and before the bearer shot it, it tore his arm to shreds. He later perfectly described the state in which he faced the lion. It was total bliss, and no problem to give himself up.

JP: This is a willingness to be a part of the pattern, rather than arrogantly setting up a system contrary to the pattern, and trying to change the pattern.

DERRICK JENSEN: What do you mean by "setting up a system contrary to the pattern"?

DL: One of the oldest ideas of Western civilization is that just as lawgivers enact codes of law to be obeyed by humans, so God laid down a series of laws which must be obeyed by plants, animals, minerals, and so on. This is a human construct imposed on nature.

The ancient Chinese, on the other hand, had no word in their documents for the idea of Natural Law as we in the West conceive it. Instead they had the word *li*, which is the pattern in things. A foot becomes a foot by following its *li*, to hold up the body. If it followed some other *li* it would no longer be a foot.

There is a different pattern—different *li*—for the rainy Northwest than for the dry Southwest. If you get to know the place you live, you can learn to recognize the patterns underneath. Each of us, each animal, plant, rock, or whatever has a *li* of our own, and develops the fullest potential of that *li* by conforming to the pattern or dance of the place as a whole. All animals know this, but *we* have to keep remembering we know.

I first became immersed in *li* when skiing powder snow. I discovered that I was not turning the skis, but that the snow and gravity together were turning the skis. Once this rhythmic relationship to snow and gravity is established on a steep slope, there is no longer an I and the snow and the mountain, but a continuous flowing interaction. This flowing process has no boundaries. I cannot tell exactly where my actions end and the snow takes over, or where or when the gravity takes over. Looking back up the hill I can see that the pattern the tracks make is dictated by snow and gravity.

The essence of this is simply that of following a pattern instead of imposing human ideas. And the place *will* show you the pattern.

DJ: What, then, are systems?

JP: Systems are attempts to change the patterns, attempts to use power to increase the part at the expense of the whole. A system is a mistaking of the part *for* the whole, and an attempt to impose the part *on* the whole, for personal gain.

DJ: Wouldn't this damage everyone involved?

JP: I often have tremendous anger about the way abuse shrivels us, like bleach poured on a corn plant. I can almost mark points in my life where if I had been celebrated in my wholeness I would now be celebrated for just doing what I naturally do. We have a whole system that attempts to compensate us materially for giving up our wholeness. But I don't think *anything* can compensate for that.

At a workshop, I recently asked the question, "Who would you be if you were who you actually are?" The responses were revealing. The younger people, those in the thirties group, said, "If I were who I actually am I would be destroyed. I cannot be who I am and continue to exist in this society." One of these women was trying to conceive, even though at the same time she was saying that in her life, her environment, she cannot express herself. That doesn't seem to me conducive to life and wholeness. Then we went to the forties and fifties group who, like me, are angry about having been thwarted. Finally, the older people, those in their fifties to seventies, said, "If that hadn't happened to me, I wouldn't be who I am today. I *am* the result of the bleach poured on me; it made me stronger. There are lessons I needed to learn this time around, and I am grateful these things happened and kept me from being who I really am. I *am* my pain."

There is a real refusal to acknowledge they could have developed some other way. We have a whole system of people identifying with their pain. "Hello, I am an alcoholic. Hello, I am coming from an incestuous relationship. Hello, I am dysfunctional." This identification comes from their lack. They have no notion who they would be if they were who they are whole.

DL: I'm trying to get Julien to start a new business, based on the title of Chellis Glendinning's new book, selling bumper stickers that say, "I'm in recovery from Western civilization."

JP: People who say "These are the lessons I needed this time around" assume they're going to come back to another world. If you actually got in touch with what you intend in your wholeness you wouldn't put up with this shit for a minute. And if you *do* think you're going to come around again, where do you think you'll come around to?

DL: I think the answer to "Who you would be if you were who you are?" is, "A lot of people." We have this crazy notion we're supposed to be only one person. We're not supposed to be quiet at one time and unruly at another.

But there's no reason to kill all these other people within you and be only one. Sigmund Kvaloy compares the person to a cosmic jazz band. Among the Pueblo peoples, every time there's a festival you're allowed to be whichever one of your different personalities you want. This allows you to celebrate those parts of you not generally acknowledged. Kvaloy says that he knows a head monk at a monastery in the Himalayas who has five personalities. "That actually makes him an unusually stable and courageous person. He consists of a little *society*, prepared for anything."

JP: I describe this by saying you can't ebelskibber the tango. Ebelskibbering is what you do when you work in a restaurant, you've got eleven cast-iron pans, and you're trying to do ebelskibbers in the oven. It becomes a real dance. If you did those same moves on a dance floor, they'd say, "You're nuts. We're playing a tango and you're ebelskibbering." Sometimes *this* self is not appropriate for *that* situation.

I co-create the situations I enter. When I meet someone new, I don't react to a fixed entity, I relate to potential. This is at the core of one of the main dysfunctions of this culture, that of regarding substance as more important than relationship.

So *my* answer to the question, "Who would I be if I were who I am?"

is that I would be in process. I would be open and flexible and being co-created.

DJ: There have been and are many cultures in which it's easier to be who you really are.

DL: The anthropologist Ruth Benedict began trying to define a "good" culture back in the thirties. She found that a good culture, a synergistic culture where nonaggression is high, is one where you cannot do something good for yourself without doing something good for the whole group. She says nonaggression is high in societies where "the individual by the same act and at the same time serves his own advantage and that of the group." She continues, "Nonaggression occurs not because people are unselfish and put social obligations above personal desires, but when social arrangements make the two identical."

That is absolutely the crux of it. It's real simple and we aren't doing it at all. A lot of so-called experts don't think people attempting to change this culture have an answer. But we *do* have an answer. Some people just don't want to do it.

DJ: How do we change our way of knowing, when everything we see every day points us in a different direction?

DL: How we see determines our relationship to the world. We have this delusion that, except for the animals, the world is dead. Mountains and rocks aren't living. That's because we have a totally invalid conception of seeing. It began with the Greeks, and with Plotinus looking through the eye of a dead ox and seeing an image on the retina. This gives us the idea that an image is a picture on a screen and feeds into the notion that the human, or knower, has to make sense of a nonsensical world. This is all wrong.

I first got a hint of this one day doing T'ai Chi on Panic Peak, surrounded by a glacier in the middle of the Olympics. I'd spent every summer there for sixteen years, and suddenly I saw a mountain I'd never seen before. At first I thought it must have been something magic about T'ai Chi, but then I learned about the work of James Gibson.

Gibson was an expert on seeing from Cornell University. For years while he was working on other projects he kept trying to write and rewrite his great book, *Ecological Theory of Vision*, which totally reexamines the way we see. When you do vision studies at a college, you sit a person in a chair, lock their head in place, and flash stuff by on a screen. They're supposed to say what they see. This follows most current theories of vision, in which, as Gibson said, "the eye sends, the nerve transmits, and a mind or spirit receives." These theories spring from the assumption that there is a mind separate from body.

Gibson turned that all around, saying, "Vision is moving eyes on a turning head on a world turning around the sun. And you're walking. All those different factors go into seeing. The whole world is moving." After you learn this, everything moves. Mountains slide behind other mountains. When you begin to see that way, you know all the other stuff you've been taught is wrong.

DJ: What do you think, Julien? How do we change our way of knowing when everything we see every day points us in a different direction?

JP: That question makes three assumptions: (1) knowing is an accumulation of information; (2) we base our behavior on how we accumulate information; and (3) the media and everything around us gives us information on which we base our behavior. This goes to the heart of the substance versus relationship question.

What if knowledge isn't what Western culture says it is—the amount of data I've accumulated in my great gray file—and instead is the capacity to be open to making connections between the is-ness that is going on? The way we change our way of knowing is to become open to process and to the making of connections.

Wes Jackson of the Land Institute talks about how we're undergoing an information implosion. We're losing information and collecting data.

DL: Data that doesn't fit together.

JP: The more data we have, the less informed we are. In Jackson's words, information "requires high eyes-to-acres ratio." And information is a very slow process because it's about becoming *in-formed*, connected *with*, and operating from the connections one has rather than with and from the knowledge one has abstracted from possibly another place.

This is a difference between Dolores and me. Dolores is an information freak, and my buzz is about connecting in the moment. Pulling things together, but maybe never saving them long enough even to get them down on paper.

DJ: Dolores quotes Tom Bender to that effect, "Our purposeful creation of such things as Art or Architecture belies our ignorance of their and our deeper natures. If we grow through a certain act or experience and reach deeper into the vast potentials of our nature, that in itself is good. Beyond that, what is produced and remains is like the cast-off skin of a molting snake—a sign, but only that—of its growth. If we are truly growing, our every act and every surrounding will be permeated with the beauty of that growth, and there will be no need or desire to cling to and hold separate some things as Art."

DL: The Inuit knew that. When the first whites started getting into Inuit country they found lots of tiny ivory carvings everywhere, even in the dumps. When these people were stuck inside during a storm, they carved these things to pass the time. And then they threw them out, because the activity was the thing.

JP: I never know what to say when people ask, "Do you think of yourself primarily as an artist?" I usually say, "No. I think of myself primarily as a person." I'm not an artist, and when I worked in a restaurant I wasn't a cook or a waitress. It's Julien doing art, Julien doing waitressing, and so on.

Since in this culture we believe reality is substance, we have to *become* an artist. But I've learned through my checkered career that whether I'm painting snakes on the floor or flipping eggs, the thing I'm building is neural connections within myself. I'm accessing other channels of connectedness with the pattern. That's a struggle for us.

DL: It's a struggle because we're so rational. If you think you've got to start learning through rationality, you'll never get out of our Western cultural trap, because rationality has already cut you off from the whole. Joel Kramer, who teaches Jnana Yoga, begins the session with a story about being in a room with no door and only a shadowy light from what might be a window. The only other thing in the room is a cobra. He then asks, "What would you do?" Almost no one gives the correct answer, which is, "You would watch it continually." And then Kramer says, well, that's where you are, exactly. You live with the rational hemisphere and it's out to kill you. Jnana Yoga is about ways to learn how to watch that deadly part of your brain.

You can't know just by the rational; you've got to know with the whole brainbody. Certain things work for this, and everybody knows they work. Real climbing or real deep powder skiing, or being stressed out in nature. These work. Nature really helps in all this. The rational hemisphere gives up, and everything else takes over. You're there, you know you're there, everybody else knows you're there, and later you congratulate one another on the fact that it happened.

Once you have that experience, you can no longer be caught in the system. You know how it is to be fully human, and nobody can do anything to you. They can kill you, but they can't get you because you've been there once.

Earlier you asked how we can know differently. We know differently through experiences like that. This may make no sense on the page, but we have to keep reminding one another we don't have words for this. The fact that we have no words for this is one of the crosses we labor under.

DJ: Can community help?

JP: Joe Meeker, in *The Comedy of Survival*, writes that the viability of a pattern depends on its tolerance for diversity. Yet in our social groups we seek out sameness. Somehow we have to develop a pattern of appreciation for diversity.

I've decided I don't need to create community, but instead to allow it, because I'm already in it. Marie and I have attempted to somehow make our difference valuable to other people. When we have food left over from a ceremony, we always take it to the most unlikely of our neighbors. Or, for example, my mother gave me a sewing machine I'm not going to use, so I gave it to somebody who needs it. Now that person can sew my ceremonial outfits for me. We enhance each other's being by our difference.

DJ: What if you don't like your neighbors?

JP: Just yesterday I realized community doesn't mean you have to like everybody. Over the years we've tried to create community and resolve our psychological, personal, and emotional issues. But Dolores told me, "That isn't why you have ceremony or why you drum. You do those things to make entrainments and right-brain connections so life can continue in that group."

DL: If a bunch of humans live near each other, they're going to hate one another at various times. If they don't resolve it, they end up killing one another. But festivals allow you to get out of the rational hemisphere and start over again.

JP: I've been in communities that come together to drum, and the same with Dolores for skiing. That drumming, that skiing, that rhythm, that movement—that entrainment—is far more important than our psychodramatic interactions, because this latter is just about ideas and ideals and systems. When you drum or ski you participate in a synchronous pattern.

DL: And you've got other living things there besides humans. The drums are alive after you've drummed a while. And the snow and the earth are certainly alive.

JP: It's the abstractions that get you in trouble.

DJ: The chief abstraction in this culture seems to be the distant Judeo-Christian god.

DL: I have here a very important book called *In Bluebeard's Castle*, by George Steiner. It was compiled from the T. S. Eliot Memorial Lectures for 1970 at Yale University. Listen to what he says about monotheism, "What we must recapture in our mind, as nakedly as we can, is the singularity, the brain-hammering strangeness of the monotheistic idea. Such a thing never sprang up at any other time or place. . . . The abruptness of the Mosaic revelation, the finality of the creed, tore up the human psyche by its most ancient roots. The break has never really knit." He continues, "The demands made on the mind are, like this god's name, unspeakable. Brain and conscience are commanded to vest belief, obedience, love in an abstraction purer, more inaccessible to ordinary sense, than the highest of mathematics."

The gods of the primitive tribes—rocks, desert—are right there. You see them and interact with them. The Judeo-Christian god is blank as the desert air, and we don't know what he wants or what he's doing. We don't know what we can do to please him. This leads to perfectionism and competition.

Since we can't see the god in the sky, we interiorize him. James Hillman says, "Self is the interiorization of the invisible god beyond. The inner divine." He says no matter how you disguise it, the Western concept of self is still a transcendent notion with theological implications, if not roots. He works toward a redefinition of self as the interiorization of community, a community that includes not just other people. He replaces Descartes's "I think, therefore I am" with "If I'm not in a psychic field with others—with people, buildings, animals, trees—I *am* not."

There's a phrase I used a long time ago. "I am loved; therefore and to that extent I am."

DJ: Can we return to the deities of primitive cultures for a moment?

DL: The rituals of the primitives are all about enlivening the whole place—the plants, the trees, the rocks, their own lives and the lives of the animals they prey on.

And the deities aren't this transcendent substance god. Bob Bunge is a Sioux who teaches both languages—Lakota and Dakota—at the University of South Dakota. We were both giving talks at a conference. I asked him for the real translation of *Waken Tanka*. Everybody had told me it means "the great spirit," but I knew that wasn't accurate. He said, "The best translation is 'the great mystery.'"

We imposed the great spirit because of our one-god European stupidity. All the ethnologists fell into the same trap, and everybody now who talks about the great spirit is in there, too. That's how hard it is to get out of those traps.

DJ: Like an addiction.

JP: Exactly. The main characteristic of an addiction—to one-god, to industrial growth, to cigarettes—is that it creates a need for itself that doesn't provide you with energy to do anything else. What you get from cigarettes is a craving for cigarettes, as well as the denial of a lot of other needs. With pathological obesity you eat because you're hungry, tired, bored, sick of being fat. A single substance comes to meet the needs of a lot of subtleties.

DL: Without fulfilling the real needs. There's another aspect of addiction. Eric Hoffer said, "You can never get enough of what you don't really want."

JP: In that way it becomes an end in itself. It may seem like the supermarket and Sounds Easy and the video store give us more choices, but, as Dolores says, we have the option of choosing the same thing over and over again. As we choose it over and over again, it has to become bigger and better and louder to meet the original need it satisfied. Substance becomes addictive.

Dolores is really helpful with this, because she says all these addictions are substitutes for real community. Any of the states you reach through substance you used to be able to meet through relationship. And the more of those needs they can get us to meet through substance, the less likely we are to *seek* relationship.

DL: A woman named Dorothy Lee worked with the Trobriand Islanders, who are relational to the extreme. When one of them goes to work in a field, he carries somebody's child—anybody's child—to keep him company. When the Trobriand Islanders are lured or conscripted away from home to work on a nearby island, they have to eat much more just to stay alive. In a fully functioning human community you can live on less food.

JP: In a nonfunctioning community, food is expected to meet your social and comfort needs.

DJ: How can we possibly have empowering relationships in a competitive culture?

DL: Paul Krapfel wrote a book called *Shifting*. By paying attention to the natural world he realized, as many other people have, that competition is not what's most important to survival. Natural selection is not about the survival of the fit but the survival of the fitness. How things fit together.

DJ: Thomas Berry defined a species as viable if its presence in the ecosystem benefits both itself and the ecosystem.

DL: That's also the definition for a good culture.

Here is what Krapfel wrote: "I once interpreted the survival of the fit, using fit as an adjective to describe the kind of life that survives, strong animals, well camouflaged. Now I think of fit as a noun. The survival of the fit. Both life and its environment might change, but the fit between them will survive."

DJ: I still don't understand the addiction. Our activities are benefiting neither the ecosystems nor ourselves. We are not becoming the people we really are.

JP: If you don't know who you are, you can be manipulated easily. The culture isn't serving the survival of the whole or wholeness in any way, but instead is serving somebody's system-control addiction. This goes back to the fear of death, because if you become big enough, powerful enough, have enough stuff, you will never be forgotten.

This also goes back to the myth of scarcity. If there isn't enough to go around, you may be afraid of starvation. The leader can promise you stuff if you do everything he says. That's the tree model, as opposed to the rhizome model.

DJ: What do you mean by that?

DL: The tree model is hierarchical, with a trunk leading to larger branches that lead to smaller branches. The trunk is more important than a branch and forms the connections between all the parts, limiting direct connections. According to the French philosophers Gilles Deleuze and Felix Guattari, "The tree has dominated Western reality, and all Western thought, from botany to biology and anatomy, and also gnosticism, theology, ontology, philosophy."

Rhizomes are different. Rhizomes are thickened stems that grow horizontally under the surface of the soil. They spread underground and come up wherever they want to. Cattails, bamboo, banana, taro—which feeds most of the South Pacific—iris, orchids, lily of the valley, and crabgrass are all rhizomes. With rhizomes you don't have to plow the soil or put in seeds. You just use a digging stick, break the rhizome off and eat it. You plant it and it goes off in all directions.

JP: The rhizome is the model of grassroots movements. It's not like a tree that can be killed by destroying the trunk. The more you cut up rhizomes the more they split.

DL: You don't know where or when a rhizome is going to come up. They pop up almost anywhere. Any part of the rhizome can be linked to any other part without having to go through the trunk.

It's a very good metaphor for the new way we've got to deal with the destruction of the earth. If we are all in one place and start a revolution, they're going to kill all of us. But if each place of the country develops its own bioregion and pays attention to its local government, they would never be able to stop all of us, no matter how well organized they are. It's just like crabgrass.

DJ: This is multiplicity again.

JP: Tolerance for diversity, celebration of diversity. That takes us back to Joe Meeker. In *The Comedy of Survival* he wrote that while all cultures in the world have comedy, only Western culture has tragedy. That's because we're the only culture that sets up things that ain't so, and then beats ourselves if we can't live up to them. That's not what survival is about. He says a heroic moth would refuse to change color as the smoke came from the coal mines. "I will not. I will stand firm." The comedy of survival says, "I'm going to adapt."

DL: He says the only suitable Western classic is *Felix Krull, Confidence Man*, by Thomas Mann. Felix Krull says, "If I really love the world I will fit myself to it, rather than make it fit to me."

DJ: Can you tell me about affordances? It seems a radically different way of looking at what you receive.

DL: That's out of Gibson again. Instead of forcing something or someone to do what we want, we try to find what it will allow us to do. A quick example is rock climbing. When you begin learning to climb, you find real quick that certain rock breaks in bad ways—it fractures erratically—as opposed to granite, which breaks in straight lines. Granite makes for real good climbing. It *allows* you to go up a much steeper route.

JP: Affordance and carrying capacity are almost the same thing. "I can't afford that" means "I don't have the capacity to hold it or take it in." "It can't afford me" means "it can't take me in."

DJ: Given that we are over carrying capacity, and given everything else, how do we get there from here?

DL: We keep hearing that it's hopeless. Great! Then we can go ahead and begin to live right. After all, hope is actually just another idea out of the rational hemisphere. Hope doesn't exist when one is totally living in the present, because hope is a projection into the future. When you are fully living in the moment there's no hope involved. So it's time we learn to really live in place, not following any ideas or ideals out of the human head. Instead follow the pattern that nature in your own place gives you.

JP: And we can go back to the tree and rhizome problem. Nobody at the top of the tree can change the whole thing.

DL: There's nothing any one of us can do.

JP: But there are little things that each person at the end of every rhizome can do.

DL: That's a real positive thing, especially for those of us who have been in this for a while. We get despairing. Or not despairing, but *astonished*. Astonished there's nothing we can do.

JP: I've been telling Dolores despair does not exist in nature. Despair is a human notion.

DL: So I don't have to despair?

DJ: Where does compromise fit in? Conflict?

JP: Danaan Perry says compromise means everybody has to give up a little, and as long as you have compromise you create more denial. People stuff more and more. What people have to do is give up that notion of compromise. We have to make the world safe *for* conflict, not safe *from* conflict. When all that conflict starts getting expressed, we'll find out what needs people are actually talking about. These needs are usually pretty basic. Susan Weed says violence comes from people feeling they've not been seen and not been heard. It has nothing to do with not being agreed with, it just has to do with not being heard.

We have to start giving up that hierarchical tree model, that myth of scarcity, and start to envision environments in which everybody's needs can be met. That takes us back to carrying capacity.

DJ: Which we're over, which means there's going to be some form of crash. What good does it do us to know these things?

DL: It's important to realize these problems are bigger than us. The building is ugly, not you. The culture is ugly, not you. When you wake up to these facts you can find comrades who see the same thing and work together toward doing something about it.

JP: Like what, create a new culture?

DL: Exactly. It's only been two thousand years. Human beings have been exactly the same people for fifty thousand years. Two thousand years is a mere nothing.

We're engaged in a cultural rescue attempt. Nils Faarland draws an analogy between what we are doing and mountain rescue efforts. If we try to do either one by ourselves and the avalanche buries us, we're dead. Avalanche victims don't live very long. But if we have comrades around and we get buried under the avalanche of horrors, our comrades can pull us out. We can keep going.

And when an avalanche happens, there's nothing you can do about it. You just have to be prepared.

That old Black Panther statement—"If you are not part of the solution you are part of the problem"—is especially true here. If you're not doing *something right now* for the earth you are part of the problem.

DJ: What is beyond hope and despair?

JP: The pattern lies beyond. It's the comedy of survival.

DJ: What would you hope the readers of this interview would do?

DL: Get their feet on the ground. Pay attention to real things, factual things, place stuff.

JP: I would hope they would be conscious of the choices they make that leave them empty. I have friends who are shopaholics, who try to get substance to compensate. They work at jobs they hate so they can be compensated with this abstract material reward so they can buy more stuff that continually leaves them empty.

I would hope they would look at the whole notion of compensation. Is there anything that can compensate for your not being all that you are, for the giving up of your wholeness?

I would hope they would have the courage of their own authenticity.

And I would hope they would realize if you move beyond hope and despair, you also move beyond fear. If we're already dead, what can anyone do or what can anyone take away?

The dead can dance. We're already dead but we can dance, and we can drum, and we can make music.

PAUL SHEPARD

Paul Shepard's work on environmental perception and human ecology spans more than forty years. A Missourian and a graduate of Missouri University, he took his Ph. D. at Yale University, where he studied the relationship of ecology and art at the cultural roots of American attitudes toward nature. He was a conservation activist in the 1950s, then a teacher and an author.

His books include Man in the Landscape: A Historic View of the Esthetics of Nature; *an anthology,* The Subversive Science; *a tract on primal cultures,* The Tender Carnivore and the Sacred Game; *and* Nature and Madness, *identifying the origins of the disease of environmental abuse in child rearing, or ontogeny. In recent years his work has explored the roles of animals in modern culture, notably in dreams and the development of personal identity. From this has come* Thinking Animals—Animals in the Development of Human Intelligence *and (with Barry Sanders)* The Sacred Paw: The Bear in Nature, Myth and Literature.

DERRICK JENSEN: If the destruction of the natural world isn't making us happy, why are we doing it?

PAUL SHEPARD: Each year for thirty-five years I've started a college course with this question, and I still haven't any answer. But I can tell you the two main directions my thought has gone.

The first is that historical experiences with the natural environment condition our responses to it and our ideas of it. What are the cultural and ecological antecedents of Western attitudes and ideas? One is our belief in a future world that's better than this one; another is the "necessity" of dominating nature; a third is those sharp divisions between the human and the nonhuman, between the spiritual and the bodily. These beliefs emerge from a legacy of catastrophic destruction by people we now identify as Sumerian, Mesopotamian, Persian, Indo-European, Hebrew, Greek, and Roman. Their ideas of themselves emerged in a place where soils were depleted, forests had already been seriously damaged, and the environment was increasingly subject to drought, flooding, and outbreaks of pests.

If the world in which one lives is rotten, impoverished, unsustaining, if it seems to be exhausted and to offer no hope and no connections, one's hopes would be placed in another life or another world. If the earth has not been nourishing, as is happening today in Africa and many other parts of the world where there are too many people and not enough resources, there is no reason one should be concerned about sustaining that earth. The cycle of despair, rejection, and abuse of the planet feeds on itself.

My second direction takes up the processes of personal development. Everything we know about early individual experience in life tends to suggest that much of what we think we know and the ways we understand experience have already been set for us by the time we are ten years old. We are profoundly committed psychologically very early in life, so that our adult concepts and ideas later articulate these early experiences, giving logic to the motives that run beneath our consciousness. The question—to which I attempted a preliminary answer in *Nature and Madness*—becomes: What can we identify that is characteristic of early childhood in the Western world that would lead us as adults to perceive the natural world as hostile to ourselves, as something requiring control and domination, as something to be afraid of, and as something we reject for some mythic world that is better than this one?

Another way to ask this is: How are children raised differently in small-scale societies that are not highly technologically developed, particularly the primal societies in which we evolved, as opposed to the way they are raised in pastoral, highly developed agricultural, or urban societies? What differences between civilized and tribal child rearing might predispose civilized children to be more fearful and controlling of their world as adults?

These two lines of thought ultimately come together. If the people in the Tigris and Euphrates valleys, and in the "holy lands" of the world religions, lived in an increasingly overcrowded, threatening, dangerous, impoverished world, this would have affected the way they reared their children and the children's imprint of adult emotions.

Add to this the fact that a pastoral life especially creates a sense of alienation from the natural world that is even more extreme than that of farming peoples, perhaps even than that of urban peoples. The terror created by horse-riding cultures distorted the ways in which children are reared and in which men and women relate to one another. The equestrians created the traumatic sense of doom.

DJ: What would cause this alienation among pastoral peoples?

PS: First, the lack of clear dependence on the soil cuts them off from the sort of cosmology planting peoples tend to have. The pastoral peoples are oriented to the sky; their principal concerns are with celestial phenomena—weather, storms—which tend to diminish a belief in the spiritual power of the earth and of the manifestation of the sacred in terrestrial landforms. Mounted pastoralism is a source of various forms of monotheism that place the sacred somewhere other than on earth and that tend, because of their unequal gender relationships, to diminish the idea of an earth mother or of the feminine principle in the earth, replacing it with attention to some kind of sky or sun god. These people could then see themselves in their essence as nonearthly beings, having a heavenly home from which they come and to which they return. Does this sound familiar?

A second cause of ecological alienation among pastoralists is the interposition of domestic animals between themselves and all other animals. This skews their perception of the meaning and nature of animals.

Third, the kind of mobility involved is very different from the nomadic mobility of hunter-gatherers. Pastoralists in subtropical semiarid environments constantly glean and move on in a world of limited grass and water. Since they are intensely competitive among themselves with respect to these resources, their social groups tend to be organized on a semimilitary basis. And the more nomadic these societies are, the more hierarchic and patriarchal they are, the more one-sided their gender relationships, and the more they are involved in a world of organized aggression and defense against other groups and the wild world. Also, the more numerous their numbers and therefore the more bellicose they are, the more the range is overgrazed and reduced in its biodiversity and complexity.

Life in a degraded environment, once again, doesn't make you feel at home. And if your environment doesn't sustain you, there is no reason you should participate in sustaining it or joining with those who do. This makes clear why concerns today for such things as biodiversity and "nature" can be seen as mere luxuries of the rich. Only those who are confident and secure can afford to be concerned about the existence of a great many kinds of creatures in the world, whereas we—whoever "we" happens to be—always need more space, energy, resource materials, land, water. After all, what has the California condor ever done for me?

DJ: What *has* the condor ever done for you?

PS: It has given me, and continues to give me, a sense of the diverse forms creation can take and of my own limited place in an enormously complex other world that was not created for me. The condor, along with the frogs and salamanders that are vanishing, is a constant reminder that I am not the center of it all.

Once they are gone, and we have nothing in their place but our sheep and stupid cows and horses—horses that became our model for horsepower and therefore for dominance—when we have nothing left but those, there will be no evidence that we are not actually the purpose of the whole thing—a delusion. There will be no true otherness in the world to keep us both sane and small.

DJ: Is this culture then on a preconscious level intentionally destroying biodiversity? Is the Forest Service intentionally destroying the last of this country's forests?

PS: They would be the first to object that they are not destroying the forests but are preserving them. What they are actually doing, though, is continuing a process of domestication begun about ten thousand years ago. Forestry schools still foster the substitution of tree plantations for forests worldwide, on the assumption that a plantation of trees *is* a forest. They are, on a preconscious level as you say, replacing wild forests with something that more and more approximates the domesticated plants and animals with which we have become all too familiar.

I see the process of domestication in somewhat different ways than a lot of people do. My view largely goes back to the work of the geneticist Helen Spurway, who identified domestication as the production of what she called goofies, greatly diminished organisms that have been radically changed through genetic manipulation from what their wild ancestors were like. As we increasingly domesticate wild communities, thereby reducing their tremendous vitality, strength, intelligence, and complex behaviors, we increasingly create the kind of world our philosophy leads us to believe is out there, one subordinate to our own desires and in effect created for our own use.

Once you begin to domesticate plants and animals, you move into a different cosmology, value system, and cultural set of assumptions. The best evidence for this is what's happened to the !Kung in southern Africa. When they were forcibly transformed from hunting-gathering to agriculture, the number of children per woman increased, suggesting that agricultural-based societies promote population growth. A money economy and the social and physical ills of civilization made their appearance.

In the past it was assumed that populations increased historically because more food was available, and that primal peoples would have been more numerous had not some kind of natural limitation—disease or food—prohibited it. That apparently is not the case. Something else happens to cause the human drive toward fecundity to break out like a disease once you get into sedentary life associated with domestic plants and animals.

The whole business of nomadic versus sedentary life can be seen in terms of what people can carry. If you've got four children and no domestic animals, it's going to be a lot more difficult to be nomadic. It's been sometimes argued that it is for this reason that nomadic hunters and gatherers don't have more children, but once again I don't think it's that simple. For example, another important factor is the interspecies use of milk. Having an extra milk supply facilitates having extra children.

Milk is the short-term gain at the expense of long-term misery. We've thought of cow's milk as a very healthy and good thing, but we're discovering at the end of the twentieth century that milk is not so good for you after all. We've had to go through all kinds of human suffering to find what primal peoples already knew—although cow's milk may be all right for cows, it's not so good for us; stay out of social relationships with animals.

There is a growing body of evidence that since we are essentially Paleolithic—being Pleistocene in our later evolution, having Pleistocene bodies and psyches and physiologies—the best model for the way to live is one growing out of our understanding of how our ancestors lived fifty thousand years ago, whether it's exercise, nutrition, group size, inter-family relationships, gender relationships, the way children are raised, or the way in which people deal with the sense of the integrity of the nonhuman world around them.

DJ: How do you respond to someone who tells you we can't go back to being Pleistocene people?

PS: The reason you can't go back is you never left being a Pleistocene person. It's what you still are.

Going back culturally is not a matter of whole-cloth transformation, as a person who sees the world essentially as dichotomous might suppose. We are not *either* this or that. All cultures are mosaics. Culture, like our genome, like an ecosystem, is made up of a large number of components that are separable.

I recently tried to identify fifty or sixty mobile characteristics of Pleistocene life that can be dealt with more or less separately. Allowances and adjustments might have to be made, but that's no reason we can't begin to identify and recover at least aspects of what we truly are. To do that we need to know more about our heritage. Part of the crisis of the contemporary world, of course, is that peoples who are living in those kinds of cultures are disappearing. The need for protecting them is certainly as great as the need for protecting species from extinction.

DJ: What are some of these Pleistocene characteristics, and how do we recover them?

PS: A childhood in which the infant is constantly in touch with people and children are much more constantly in the presence of nonhuman living otherness, wildness, are both necessary preparations for a philosophy of shared being, as one species in many. We've long supposed that in some vague way nature is good for children, but there's been relatively little close examination of what goes on in the mind and heart of a child who may ramble in the presence of insects and the whole range of plant and animal life. In part it has to do with taxonomy, with the spontaneous emergence of speech in connection with naming a large number of kinds of things, living forms as the basis for the skills of cognition and categorization. If we understood that process better, as well as the way it facilitates all our thinking later in life, we would attend more to those experiences of biological diversity and free space in childhood. We would attend more to the need for identifying living forms, examining them closely, paying attention to their habits. This is indigenous to our being and a normal part of the growing up experiences of people in small-scale societies.

Another way in which we have obviously left our Pleistocene heritage would be diet. It turns out that wild meat is different biochemically from domestic meat and better for you. It's no wonder, at the very least because of the unhealthfulness of domestic meats, that we are becoming increasingly vegetarian.

I would also suggest we alter our use of space to take account of what's been called the twelve-adult group. This is the optimal size for making decisions, protecting people from authoritarian individuals, and allowing everyone to participate. There's no reason we can't design our living and working spaces to facilitate that kind of face-to-face small group decision making, even in the modern world.

Another interesting area is art. I recently had some conversations with Paul Winter about his thinking on participatory music, as opposed to music that divides the performer and the audience. Music symbolizes the way we socially submit to authoritarian regimes. Imagine the difference in social constructions that lead to the way we use, hear, and experience music. Take the symphonic performance, with its insular virtuosity of the composer, conductor, and soloist, with its silent audience, each person sitting in his or her own little isolated space, afraid to cough or to speak, as opposed to everything we know about "ethnic" participatory music, which isn't read from scripts and which doesn't follow autocratic leaders or ranked parts. Music in small-scale societies joins rather than separates. To isolate us from that by making most of us inert observers rather than participants seems one of those great breaks between what I would call our Pleistocene needs and the way we handle High Art in modern society.

Once again, the more we know about how people lived before ten thousand years ago and the way some small-scale societies still live, the clearer idea we have for a model with which to reorganize our own culture and our own society. The objection that you can't go back, which I've been hearing for twenty-five years, is the bigotry of history, merely an excuse not to look at the possibilities.

DJ: If life in a hunting-gathering community is more appropriate to being human than life in a dense and centralized society, why did we change?

PS: Because we learned to plant and protect. There is evidence that the earliest Neolithic villages, like the settlements of hunter-gatherers, had no walls against military aggressors. Conflict between primal groups tends toward highly individualized derring-do and occasional homicides, and as demonstrations of social display. These almost never involve occupying somebody else's land.

But as human density increased, bringing with it different economies and societies, people became increasingly desperate about land ownership, expansion, defense, and the exclusion of other people. Here were, on the one hand, cultures to whom it had not occurred to take other people's space and to convert these people forcibly to other ways of life and, on the other, societies with aggressive, controlling, and centralized power structures.

This happened, and continues to happen, time and again around the world. For the most part, the hunter-gatherers initially welcome strangers, on the assumption they are as generous as themselves. This eventuates in their being colonized and destroyed or enslaved.

This ties to some interesting ideas about primates by M. R. A. Chance. He sees the two types of societies I described above as already represented by different species of primates and argues that we have within our primate evolutionary background the potential for either of these ways of being. You can organize your life around control, conflict, competition, and the subordination of others, or you can organize it around cooperation, sharing, and mutuality. Both of these are present in the larger primate genome. As a flexible species, we may be able to call on either of these basic biological ways, depending on our circumstances, situation, psychology, and culture. At the same time, there is no guarantee that the logic apparent to some of us that the cooperative, sharing, and mutual way is better will convince everyone else.

Jane Goodall and her successors also showed that when chimpanzees are provided with more food than they can eat at one time, they become conflicting and competitive, with tyrants arising among them that threaten, intimidate, and injure others.

This suggests an analogy to agriculture's creation of storable supplies that somebody has to guard, control, and either dispense or hoard. Power becomes centralized in a world where nature is no longer your storehouse.

DJ: What are your views on the crash of which so many environmentalists speak? Do you have hope?

PS: I think that planetary, ecological disaster is a reality. But the popular imagination is in error. It is not something that may happen. We have been in the midst of it for the last century. Because of our biblical and Hollywood imagery of catastrophe, we suppose all such disasters to be a kind of Armageddon, with walls collapsing and people screaming. It's not like that at all. It's much worse, a creeping thing that we identify as something else—inflation, poverty, recession, levels of mental ill-health, suicide, crop failure, political upheaval, famine, social discontent—anything except its true nature, the disintegration of natural systems. It has nothing to do with the media question, "Will mankind survive?" because a species as tough as ours is not yet ready to join the cavalcade into eventual extinction.

Of course I have hope. Why not, it's cheap and available. It is also the last resort. It allows one to be seen as chipping away defiantly at "the problem" rather than taking one's sour misanthropy off into the rubble to await some final bell.

DJ: Different subject. In *Man in the Landscape* you wrote, "In all worthwhile travel, the search for god and reality and truth *must* occupy a center which is both philosophical and psychological." We can substitute other words for travel—conversation, relation, action, sexuality, leisure, exploration, art.

PS: Ever since the Renaissance, the arts have been disconnected from the rest of culture, particularly from religion. By the end of the nineteenth century they were even disconnecting themselves from content, so you had a body of experts which internally judged itself on purely abstract criteria, rather than on any kind of connectedness to the natural world, the ecological needs of being human, human economics, and human social life.

In increasingly disconnecting the arts from the rest of life, and particularly from psychological and religious belief, we have once again parted ways with our tribal background and human identity. The arts have always been part of the means by which people articulate and participate in those things central to what they believe. Art still does these kinds of things without our realizing it. Alienated pictorial forms speak to our larger alienation from nature, in the cosmos.

DJ: The separation of science, art, and the sacred from everyday life would seem to be a natural consequence of surrounding yourself with domesticated creatures and your own products, as well as the result of putting a monotheistic god "out there."

PS: It's a feedback system. Picture the circumstances of growing up today, surrounded not only by domestic as opposed to wild things but also being encased continuously in structures and landscapes that are the creations of human beings. Our lawns of domesticated plants, and the very laying out of streets and the enclosing of space by buildings, engenders the illusion we've created the world. That kind of imprint, using this word in the Lorenzian sense of semi-irreversible knowledge acquired extremely early in life, lends itself to the notion that indeed a humanlike deity somewhere created this world very much as we create towns. And did it for our use.

DJ: What does the word *sacred* mean to you?

PS: It refers to those inexplicable relationships and processes that govern existence. There is no reason sacredness cannot be manifest in *any* circumstances whatever, or in all circumstances, even if some are more numinous than others.

DJ: What's the connection between sacrality, ontogeny, and poetry?

PS: Until an individual is about eleven, twelve, or thirteen, he or she takes things extremely literally. God the Father means a literal father, someone who looks and acts like their father. At about fifteen, though, because of the kind of creature we are, something emerges in our mental timetable, and we reconsider the literal things already learned during the naming phase of early speech as having further reference than themselves. We spontaneously grow into poetry. It becomes possible to talk about aspects of the sacred that can only be conceived metaphorically. Reference to the ineffable aspect of the universe becomes a possibility in the individual ontogenesis at about puberty, when normally individuals are inculcated into a religious system. In other words, we utilize the first twelve years gaining the substance, the referents, which can then be used as an allegorical basis for representing in speech—and art—that which is not literal, tangible, or visible. In that sense cosmological matters come to be understood as some kind of an analogy to, but not the same thing as, the society and the familiar world.

I do not speak of the written or printed word here. Poetry is different from prose and other kinds of literature in that it is meant to be spoken, not as "literary," solitary High Culture, in isolation. Poetry is halfway to music. It brings us together rather than isolating us in our little solitary cell.

DJ: How do you interact with the other? How do trees signify?

PS: They are presences. I recently visited an enormous tree on the Upper Bitterroot in western Montana. I had a profound sense of a living presence, as I do especially among whales or elephants. That mystery of otherness—the fact that there is an unbridgeable gap between myself and the other—is extremely important. While we share common ground with any living thing, and to some extent with the nonliving world, it's not that ground which is necessarily the most interesting and beautiful quality of their presence.

DJ: Is seeing the other as other analogous to saying Martin Buber's sacred word *You*?

PS: Garrett Hardin feels "I-Thou" presumes too much about the Thou being like me and also that it doesn't sufficiently extend the awareness into the past and future. He's concerned—and I agree—about our failure to think backward and forward in time, especially in terms of the consequences of our actions. Buber's "I-Thou" is a bit too anthropomorphic.

DJ: I've grown to realize relationship *is* responsibility, which extends into the past and future.

PS: The trouble is that conventional Christian apologists for responsibility express this concern in terms of kindness and caring. The model for this responsibility is Noah's ark. Arrogance in the guise of love. Following this model, we therefore take control of their lives. With the idea that the planet's life is threatened comes the idea that we must somehow control the creatures. For instance, we put them into zoos in order to "protect" them from becoming extinct. This seems merely another way of setting up the authoritarian system in which we see ourselves as vice-roys of God in our superiority over the rest of life. The alternative, of course, is to live in such a way that the rest of life is not endangered.

DJ: The responsibility I mean is closer to R. D. Laing's line: "Love lets the other be, but with affection and concern."

PS: "Letting be" sounds a little too much the observer, the symphony-goer. What's important is to participate appropriately in the world, to limit ourselves, to acknowledge we are a part of world food chains. We have a long history of interaction with the rest of life; we should expect to house parasites in our bodies, to decay, to become food for others, and accept the responsibility of eating others and therefore of killing them in order to sustain our lives.

We need to have confidence in ourselves as organisms, neither as masters nor as mere voyeurs. Belief in ourselves as natural is critical, be-cause we will only enter into fully human social and cultural systems through compliance with and affirmation of what it means to be an or-ganism.

DJ: What does it mean to be an organism?

PS: It means accepting the world as given, rather than made, a world of limits, contingency, the courteous readiness of the sacramental reality of death. However much we pride ourselves on those magnificent things human beings have done and made, the final criterion by which all hu-man creations will be judged is the extent that they are consonant with the natural world, of which humans are a part.

We have scarcely begun to discover what it means to be an organism on a very small planet, from which there is no escape, no alternative.

ARNO GRUEN

In The Betrayal of the Self: The Fear of Autonomy in Men and Women *and* The Insanity of Normality—Realism as Sickness: Toward Understanding Human Destructiveness, *Arno Gruen points out that at the root of much human destructiveness lies self-hatred, a rage originating in childhood when we surrender our true feelings in exchange for the "love" of those who wield power over us. His work not only indicts modern culture and its self-alienation, but also directs the reader toward social responsibility, ecstasy, and joy.*

Arno Gruen was born in Germany and emigrated to the United States as a child in 1936. He has held many teaching posts, including seventeen years as a professor of psychology at Rutgers University. Since 1979 he has lived and practiced in Switzerland. As well as the two previously mentioned books, Arno Gruen has written about sixty scientific articles in psychological, psychiatric, neurological, and other journals and the books The Early Farewell, *a study of sudden infant death syndrome in the context of our social alienation, and* False Gods: On Love, Hate, and the Difficulty of Peace.

ARNO GRUEN: When a small child is at the mercy of those who mistreat it—when there is no one on whom it can fall back for security or comfort—the only way for the child to survive psychologically is to identify with the aggressors. If this happens, the child will begin to idealize them, and in that way will never form an identity of its own.

In order to understand what is going on in Yugoslavia, Russia, Germany, the United States, you have to understand the political implications of the identification with the aggressor, and you have to understand what happens when children grow up never having formed a full identity of their own. Those who hate foreigners, for example, or people of another race, or women, or children, or simply the world around them have always been ready to hate someone or something, because in effect they hate themselves.

Two years ago I gave a lecture in Berlin at the Akademie der Künste (Academy of Art) about what happens when people are not genuinely loved as children. Afterwards members of the audience, mainly sociologists and politicians from what was then still East Germany, told me that was exactly the situation they were facing in Hoyerswerda, the industrial town in which, one and a half years later, the racial riots against foreigners in Germany started. "We are afraid something will explode," they said, "because the youth we have in these high-rise complexes, complexes that were built simply to feed the factories, have no family life. They hate their mothers, and their mothers hate them." The politicians understood that these youths, who from their earliest childhood had not experienced genuine love, hated themselves and were ready to project their hatred outward.

DERRICK JENSEN: What is the genesis of this hatred?

AG: I would say the birth of this so-called civilization we live in, maybe five or seven thousand years ago, was the beginning of this drive for possession, for owning, for ruling, and for dominating other people. How that began I don't exactly know. Maybe it started with the first man who, feeling inadequate, found that if he could hit somebody on the head, if he could subjugate and dominate another person, for that one moment he could feel less inadequate. But then of course to continue feeling "adequate" he had to keep on doing it, not only because "adequacy" on that basis needs constant reinforcement, but also because of the fear so characteristic of such people, that right around the corner could be somebody else who could hit *him* on the head.

Many of the so-called primitives—I don't mean all of them; there are a lot of African tribal societies where power is almost as central as it is with us—are utterly different. With the Mbuti—the pygmies of the former Congo—for example, or many of the Native North or South Americans, what is of central importance is how people feel with one another, how they get along, how they can sustain and help one another.

The Jesuit missionaries who went into the Saint Lawrence River valley at the beginning of the seventeenth century left observations of the social structures of the local Indians, the Montagnais-Naskapi, which the American anthropologist Eleanor Burke Leacock has published in her book *Myths of Male Dominance*. The Jesuits were fascinated by the fact that these Indians had chiefs whom they respected, but whose orders they followed only when they made sense to them. And they were fascinated that these people never killed anybody to gain property or anything.

Groups with such social structures show child-care practices very different from ours. One sure sign of this is that in general you don't hear their children cry. To return to the Jesuit *paters*, LeJeune, the superior of the mission, complained that they couldn't get their schools going. Mission schools were based on the principle of punishment, but the moment a child cried the parents took them out of school. They could not stand to hear a child cry. "They will not tolerate the chastisement of their children," he wrote. "Whatever they may do they permit only a simple reprimand."

There is a description of a French drummer boy striking an adult Indian. His superiors wanted to whip him publicly, but one of the Indians said, "He's just a child. Hit me, and let him go."

To the Indians the idea that you can improve a child's behavior by hitting or otherwise harming him was ludicrous. It went against everything they understood about how human beings develop freely and in a loving context. They knew from their own experience that human beings don't develop that way.

Contrast that with our culture. We don't even hear our children cry. There is a Finnish study of the time it took for mothers to respond with the flow of milk in their breasts to the cries of their children. The glands of some mothers began to produce milk within two minutes, some within four, and there were some mothers who didn't produce milk even after seven minutes.

How different are the !Kung people from the western part of the Kalahari desert in Africa. Just three months ago I came across a study by a couple of anthropologists who happened to time the interval between a child beginning to fret and one of the mothers running to pick it up. The *average* time was six seconds. You can imagine what happens when children are immediately picked up. They feel the flow of a world that holds together, a world that is whole. So they don't have to cry.

We, on the other hand, deny early pain and that children suffer. That's where it begins. As long as we do that, we will keep on being violent, because people who deny their own pain, who cannot recall their own pain as children, are the ones who have to inflict pain on others.

DJ: How do these other groups teach their children?

AG: We all have it in us to become social beings on the basis of feeling empathically the pain and joy of the other. Erik Erikson described very poetically in his book about Luther how a mother teaches her nursing child to touch the world with his searching mouth and his probing senses. In this way, by its empathic awareness of its mother's attentions, the child becomes capable of sensing, and thereby giving form to its own feelings.

We perceive *immediately* what is going on in someone else, through touch or, for example, through the grimaces and changes in musculature someone makes. We perceive kinesthetically and therefore directly, provided the mother-child interaction has not been interfered with. Becoming human is simple. It only becomes complicated when this flow is interfered with.

A child who grows up connected with his perception of the other's joy and pain won't do anything that will make the other suffer. Just last night a friend told me that someone tried to repeat the Milgram experiment—in which the subjects are told to inflict pain on others "to help them learn"—with some chimpanzees, but the chimpanzees refused to inflict pain on their fellows. That's because they experience it themselves. And anyone who has a dog knows they immediately perceive when someone is in distress or pain. Of course, human beings have that capacity as well, but very quickly we cover it up, until in the end we don't recognize what's going on in someone else.

The neurologist Oliver Sacks describes an incident that speaks directly to this point. The incident took place on his aphasics ward. Aphasics are people who because of some neurological insult, defect, or injury have lost the capacity to understand words, for example, or numbers. Their cognitive capacities have dropped out. But they are perfectly able to understand what somebody is saying, because although they've lost the acculturated ways of perceiving, they still have their empathic perception. In fact, their empathic perception is freed, not inhibited as it is with us. One evening Sacks went into his aphasics ward and saw his patients watching a broadcast of then-president Ronald Reagan and rolling on the floor laughing. He thought, "What the hell can this be? People consider Reagan a talented and moving public speaker, yet they're laughing at him." After a while he understood. He quoted Nietzsche, "One can lie with the mouth, but with the accompanying grimace one nevertheless tells the truth." He believed these people experienced that Reagan presented himself as a very sweet and genuine person full of warm feelings, but also perceived kinesthetically the contempt in his facial musculature. It was clear that what he portrayed and what he really felt were diametrically opposed. So they thought he was a comedian.

We have become *absurd* in our perception of other people. We perceive them in terms of how we've been taught to relate to image and not to the real person. That's because very early on we lose contact to our empathic perception. By maybe three or four years of age these patterns become set. A lot of the boys have already become hostile and aggressive; they've learned that their fears are diminished by hitting somebody on the head. The girls don't do that so much, not because of biology, but because the pressure on most boys is to be "manly," which in this culture brings with it the fear of failing, thus inviting low self-esteem, thus anger, and then blind aggression.

When we lose track of our own pain and the pain of others, we begin to live in terms of finding security through the ways the culture offers. In our culture this has little to do with love and cooperation. What most of us take to be our true feelings are simply the way we've been taught to feel, or the kinds of feelings we think we ought to have in certain situations. We have to smile all the time and act as though anyone who is in pain is a softy or oversensitive. And people who respond to the pain of others are softies also.

But people who don't respond to the pain of others necessarily become destructive. This destructiveness doesn't have to be direct and overt. You don't have to be a criminal to be destructive. A lot of scientists are basically destructive, for example, when they declare that science and value are two different worlds. This not only distorts life, it is evil. The same is true of cognitive psychologists who think that cognition develops as if apart from love and hate. This obsession denies us our soul.

We can trace some of the violent aspects of modern science to Descartes, who in his *Methodology* wrote that man must learn to cut off his relationships to his childhood if he is to become a human being. In order to become what he called a human being he had to get rid of all kinds of false notions, by which he meant feelings. This is a pretty good description of how to turn yourself into a machine.

One of the most ironic things Descartes wrote was, "How terrible it is that a human being isn't clear from the first day, from his birth on." What he didn't understand is that a traditional Indian child *is* clear. Since the adults around the child have a clear relationship to him or her, what forms for the child is clarity.

I was very moved by accounts of Ishi, the last member of the Yahi Indian tribe in northern California. Ishi himself was a man of great dignity. He had a sense of who he was, and of his relatedness to others. When you read about him, you get a feeling of what human beings *can* be like. There are many similar accounts of the lives of other so-called primitives. And all of them have had very different upbringings than what we have had.

Jean Liedloff wrote of her time with a tribe of Indians in Venezuela, the Yequana. The children there develop in such a way that they are happy. This affects every part of their lives. For example, even though they bathe in rivers filled with piranhas, they don't get bitten by them. That's because they are aware of the danger, and they don't run looking for it. On the other hand, in our Western cultures children often get injured because they *seek* injury. There's an English report showing that many of the kids between two and eight who end up in hospital wards because of injuries come from families with terrible tensions between the parents.

DJ: Why do they seek injury?

AG: To punish themselves. I would say they seek death. I did a study on sudden infant death syndrome in Switzerland, in which I found some very upsetting patterns. Each of the mothers in the group with which I worked had had cold and rejecting mothers. They had then married men who were very motherly. These men, being part and parcel of a macho middle class, had used their motherliness to keep the women in their grasp. These women, trapped by their feelings in a culture that prevents free expression to a woman of her ambivalences, had no way to express their rage and hostility, and so their lives were filled with fantasies and dreams of death, including the deaths of their children. This doesn't mean, of course, that they wanted their children dead. But on the other hand, very few of them were able to relate to their children as individuals in terms of their own aliveness. I think part of what went on is that some of these children must have perceived this hostility and been unable to live with it. Other children develop other ways of escaping these difficulties, like autism or schizophrenia. Still others begin very early to simply conform to the expectations of the parents. These are the children I mentioned before, the ones who don't have a chance to develop a self of their own.

DJ: What can be done for this last group of children?

AG: There are some people in Germany, Monika Neanstedt and Arnim Westermann, who have done very important work in this area. They have placed about seven hundred of such severely traumatized children into families that are open to them and to their problems. Prior to their placement they were violent, not toward their aggressive parents but toward the outside, toward peaceful children especially. When given a chance to drop their personality formation on the basis of overadapting or identifying with the aggressor, these children changed. Once they found adults who gave them mirrors for their complaints, they could begin to see the source of their oppression, and begin to develop their own selves. And as their own creativity emerged, their destructiveness began to disappear.

When such violent children, however, remain in their original parental environment, reaching them later becomes more difficult. The destructive behavior itself begins to stand in the way of change. It reinforces their false identity. If you want to do something at a later stage you will have to proceed on two levels. On one hand you have to hold them responsible for the consequences of their deeds, and at the same time you have to open up ways for them to talk, to begin to have a discourse with themselves in order to get to the real source of their hatred. When the source of why we hate can't be confronted, we need to project it. We then have to destroy others in order to keep on living with ourselves. This necessitates living with a lie within our civilization. It is the lie that obscures the truth about who our parents really are.

DJ: What if you still cannot open a dialogue? What is an appropriate response to evil?

AG: If people are really cut off from the suffering of others, they are not reachable. I don't mean you have to stop them by force, but as long as you think you can change them, they can continue to play with your hopes and they have you in their power. By trying to reach the aggressor, whether he is a scientist or a politician or a murderer, you are still hoping to be accepted by that person, and in that way you remain enslaved.

DJ: Where do guilt and responsibility fit into this?

AG: Guilt is different from responsibility. We tend to confuse them. Guilt is a weapon used to make a child conform, to coerce it. This kind of guilt destroys self-esteem. Therefore guilt stands in the way of *truly* accepting responsibility for what you have done. There is a fundamental difference between feeling you are a *bad* person for having done something and facing the *pain* of what you have done.

When you internalize such guilt, self-esteem gets lowered, and you've left open no room to really change. You will only try to avoid feeling guilty, not face the suffering you have caused. And in an attempt to *not* feel this internalized guilt—to not feel like a bad person—you deny both the guilt and ultimately responsibility. This involves telling lies about yourself, never really facing what you are doing.

DJ: Let's go back to the children in this culture who seek death. Does continuing genocide, Mutually Assured Destruction, and the lack of general attention to worldwide ecocide lead you to believe this is an entire culture seeking death?

AG: Increasingly the people that determine political movement are people I call psychopaths. These are the ones who are most driven by this deathliness of which you speak. These people seemingly get themselves and others involved in schemes of greatness and so-called development—subduing nature and all that—but in essence they are driven by an inner drive toward destruction and death.

All great writers have understood that. I've used *Peer Gynt* in *The Insanity of Normality* as an example. Henrik Ibsen really understood that process. And Eugene O'Neill, in *More Stately Mansions*, gave a similar description of a magnate here in Massachusetts. O'Neill showed very clearly how this man, in being the product of an unloving family situation, dreamt only of conquest as compensation. The key role in this development was played by a mother who herself could find no self-realization, being oppressed by a dictatorial husband who couldn't stand a woman having equality.

It's easy to lose hope because so many revolutions have led to installing the old tyranny in new forms. It is necessary to look at who takes over revolutions. The people doing the fighting in Yugoslavia today are not Yugoslavs who want to stay alive and till the ground or do their job. They are people who in the name of ideology kill, murder, and rape, because destructiveness is their driving force. People who hate themselves because of a nonloving past must find victims for their hatred. It's the same elsewhere. The kind of people who came to the top in communist Russia or Nazi Germany, or who come to the top of most corporations, are essentially the same. They are all motivated by the drive to get ahead, to make things bigger, rarely to build better things. But if you look more closely, their motivation is always destructive, even if that is not their conscious intent. It doesn't make any difference whether they are scientists or politicians or businessmen, it's the same thing.

DJ: You wrote in *The Insanity of Normality* about the extreme external orientation of psychopaths. What's the relationship between cultural pyschopathology and large corporations?

AG: The reason corporations have taken over is that people who are external—who've almost entirely lost their connection to their inner feelings—choose to enter these organizations that are themselves entirely externally oriented. Our way of life supports such organizations and such individuals. That this culture values the corporation and gives it precedence over all individual lives is a symptom of that which gives the worst impetus to all that is destructive in our lives.

Eric Wolf described this. He wrote, in his introduction to Stanley Diamond's *In Search of the Primitive: A Critique of Civilization*: "The crisis in the Western world and its imperial hinterlands, which is also the crisis of humanity, cannot be confined to social, economic or technological 'problems'; it inheres in our definition, our very understanding of man. We live in what we pridefully call civilization, but our laws and machines have taken on a life of their own; they stand against our spiritual and physical survival."

DJ: If the majority of people just want to live, why do we put up with it?

AG: Since we can't tolerate pain, and since victims remind us of our own pain, we can't tolerate victims. We begin to hate the victim. But that also means the victim in all of us. Therefore, we can't think about these issues, can't work to resolve them. But since this has to do with the avoidance of fear and doubt, those of us who care can try to strengthen ourselves and others by insisting on the right to doubt and fear. The point is to reach the ones who have doubts to begin with. The more such people hear what we have to say, the stronger their humanity becomes. Our job is to strengthen them.

Those others, the ones who don't have doubts, are reachable only after their externally oriented personalities have collapsed. I spoke to a managerial group in Berlin recently. Afterwards I noticed that whenever people in that group introduced themselves to each other, by at least the third sentence they would say, "My yearly turnover in the business is so and so many million." These people were very certain, and very identified with the amount of money they made. It was almost as though they had signs around their necks that said "5 million" or "a trillion." I kept asking myself what that had to do with being a human being. Nothing will reach most such people until their kind of personal integration falls apart. That happens when they feel they have failed. But even then many of them won't be reachable because they are too afraid to become truly integrated. They prefer drugs, alcohol, consumerism, sex, or whatever it may be as a way out.

The only thing that slows down the destruction caused by such people is their fear of losing image. That at least forces them to be more careful about what they are doing. Their allegiance is always to authority and its consolidation—no matter what the political color.

DJ: Why?

AG: The American historian John Bushnell did a study of the behavior of the Russian army during the 1905 revolution. This army repeatedly changed its allegiance during that year, mutinied as well as put down rebellions. Their loyalty never had anything to do with their understanding of the situation, how they were being treated or whether they got more food. It simply had to do with what group they thought possessed the authority.

People who grow up without love and who therefore cannot develop a genuine identity go with the established way of seeing things. The moment the authority behind that established way of seeing things begins to shake, they are ready to join another group. Or, as in Russia in 1905, they are ready to return to the authority when they believe it has reconsolidated itself.

This, by the way, is part of the reason why there was less crime in communist Russia, fascist Germany, and Portugal. People's identities were produced and held together by the rigid framework of authoritarian societies. The moment that frame disintegrated, so did those identities based on it. When identity is external, that which might lead to freedom either threatens such an identity or "liberates" the destructiveness inherent in every such development.

DJ: Will the current social framework hold up?

AG: Although the earth clearly can't sustain this continual growth, there isn't an industrial nation in the world—nor for that matter a non-industrialized country—which doesn't solely see its success in terms of the growth of what they call the gross national product. This is the road to destruction.

In a certain sense the future depends on going backward. Am I optimistic? I think about what Erich Fromm said, "Basically I'm a pessimist, but if I weren't an optimist I would have to commit suicide." You've got to keep trying.

DJ: One thing that keeps me going is the knowledge that it doesn't have to be this way.

AG: Stanley Diamond made perfectly clear that while we call our civilization civilized, it actually is not. I haven't had one patient in Europe who hasn't been in some way assaulted or sexually misused by their own parents. This is hard to believe, but it is so.

The villagers in the Danube valley before the advent of our civilization had no defenses against enemies. It was our civilization that started building such defenses. We think of earlier peoples as being fearful, whereas in reality we constantly deny *our* fears and project them upon others. The American Indians' vision of the world didn't have to do with fear. They saw their mission in life as doing their part to keep the world balanced.

In *Memories, Dreams, and Reflections*, Jung cites a conversation with a Pueblo man, and I would like to quote this at length because it is right to the point. The Pueblo man said, "See how cruel the whites look. Their lips are thin, their noses sharp, their faces furrowed and distorted by folds. Their eyes have a staring expression; they are always seeking something. What are they seeking? The whites always want something; they are always uneasy and restless. We do not know what they want. We do not understand them. We think they are mad." Jung asked him why he thought the whites were all mad. The Pueblo man answered him, "They say that they think with their heads." Jung said, "Of course. What do you think with?" The Indian responded, "We think here," indicating his heart. This Pueblo man wasn't obsessed with fears of failure as we are, and which at the same time we deny.

John Collier, Commissioner of Indian Affairs under Franklin D. Roosevelt, wrote: "The Indian made it his business to have fullness of life within material meagerness, and within a deep insecurity which his wisdom did not even want to see terminated. . . . He made, through his social institution and social art, this *external insecurity* into the condition of *inward security*—individually inward and group inward."

DJ: What is your mission in life?

AG: To try to communicate what I feel to be the major hang-up in our civilization, the denial of pain, fear, and suffering. As long as we deny these feelings and experiences, we will keep being vicious and destructive, because if we don't know our own pain we have to create it in others.

My writing is mainly about alerting us to those who only feel alive when they can be destructive and to the way they try to lead us around by the nose in order to obscure their intentions. There isn't a primitive who when he comes amongst us doesn't see what's going on. A chieftain from a very peaceful and creative tribe from New Guinea was recently invited to Munich by the Max Planck Institute of Anthropology. The interesting thing is that this man had no trouble adapting. He took things in stride because of his inner flexibility. The first thing he said, and I repeat this concept because it's so important, was: "My God, I've never heard children cry as much as in this place. You all lie to your children." They see what is going on, and we can learn from them.

DJ: Do you have hope?

AG: I have to have hope, not only because I have children but because life is worth living, for us and for all living things. It's fascinating and beautiful. In order to enjoy it, though, we first have to knock down the obstacles we've built against perceiving what life is all about.

The most basic thing I can say about life is that from birth on, and perhaps even before that, we are exposed to suffering and pain, and also to ecstasy. As long as we can't feel these things we are lost.

The only kind of strength in man or woman that has any meaning is that which comes from passing through pain and suffering, because when you pass through, you find it's not going to kill you. That makes you ready for genuine joy. But instead of passing through pain, we try to escape from it by running from life, by plugging into a never-ending succession of ever-new and ever-more-rapidly-changing stimuli. The resulting frenzy makes us dependent on what we can buy or steal. At the same time we are fearful of the inner world, avoiding all contact with it. A vicious circle.

Another problem with being unable to accept pain is that you are then incapable of laughing at yourself. Without that kind of humor, life becomes very difficult. And true humor, the ability to laugh at oneself, is part of the essence of being a human.

DJ: What is the most important thing we can do?

AG: I would say two things. The first is, if we really want to change the way things are, we have to change the conditions under which our children grow up.

The second important thing we can do is hold on to the doubts we have. We don't have to be frightened of them. If we can find supportive friends who are asking the same sorts of questions, we might find that our doubts will become the basis of our true strength.

CATHERINE KELLER

On page one of her book From a Broken Web, *Catherine Keller states,* "Myth and religion, philosophy and psychology center our civilization on the assumption that an individual is a discrete being: I am cleanly divided from the surrounding world of persons and places; I remain essentially the same self from moment to moment." *In the next 250 pages, she shows not only the absurdity of this assumption but its personal and political implications. She shows also how separatism—the assumption that any subject is what it is only in clear division from everything else—and sexism—the assumption that men, by nature and by right, exercise the primary prerogatives of civilization—collaborate to perpetuate our culture's destructive worldview. She then proposes a different view of self and of mutual relations, relations that do not foster dependency, but instead test and nurture freedom.*

Catherine Keller is an associate professor of theology at Drew University in New Jersey.

CATHERINE KELLER: We have no reason to believe that in all times life has been based on the dominance of the weaker by the stronger, nor do we have any evidence that people have always lived in the defensive state of being that characterizes modern life.

Earlier Neolithic and pre-Neolithic tribal life seems to have been based on more subtle arrangements of power. But during the late Neolithic and early Bronze Age there were, for reasons that are not clearly understood, massive migratory movements and impingements of populations on one another in the Mediterranean Basin and the Near East. These movements, as well as worsening ecological conditions, led to increased friction between these different populations. Wars of conquest became more common. In contrast to, for example, much of the Native American experience, where so-called chiefs relied (and rely) solely on their persuasive arts, groups which were capable of exercising control through physical force began to do so. Heroes became dominant in mythology and iconography, and warriors began to exemplify what it meant to be most fully human.

Within a group in which warrior males are coming to the fore and

273

dominating the tribe or village, everyone in the group will begin to develop a sort of self that is different from that of earlier peoples, a self that reflects the defenses the society itself configures. I suspect even today that's what we see in situations where abuse communicates itself from one generation to the next—people construct defenses to protect themselves from those who are attempting to control them, and when there is no alternative community to which they can turn for support, they so internalize these defenses that no real mutual relatedness is possible.

Another way to put this is that if people are trying to control you, it will be very difficult for you—in part because of your fear—to maintain an openness to them or to others. Quite often the pain you received you will then pass on to other people. Over and over we see the causing of pain—destructiveness and abuse—flowing out of a prior woundedness.

We're left with an incredibly defensive fabric of selves that have emerged from this so-called patriarchal paradigm, which is, more broadly speaking, the paradigm of dominance. And because the people who embody the defensive persona will dominate these societies, this kind of self-damaging and community-destroying and ecology-killing defensiveness tends to proliferate cancerously.

DERRICK JENSEN: What do you mean by defensiveness?

CK: Alan Watts said one of the prime hallucinations of Western culture—and I would add of the paradigm of dominance—is the belief that who you are is a skin-encapsulated ego. And just as the skin defends you from the dangers of the physical world, the ego defends you from the dangers of the psychic world.

This leads to what I have termed the separative self. The etymology of the word *separate* is very revealing. It comes from the combination of the Latin for "self," *se*, meaning "on one's own," and *parare*, "to prepare." For our culture it is separation which prepares the way for selfhood.

There are many problems with this model, not the least of which is that it doesn't match reality. We know that on a physical level one is not "on one's own," that we have to breathe and eat and excrete, and that even on a molecular scale our boundaries are permeable. The same is true psychically. Life feeds off life, Whitehead says, and if we cut ourselves off from the way we psychically feed each other, the texture of our lives becomes very thin and flat. When we live in a state of defense, there is no moment-to-moment feeding from the richness of the endless relations in which we exist.

DJ: What are the alternatives to this defensive self? You began *From a Broken Web* by asking, "To be a self, must I be something separate and apart? How else could I be myself?"

CK: You could be yourself by recognizing the permeability of your personal boundaries. Probably the best way to talk about it is to talk about a sense of moment-to-moment presence to your experience, in which you understand your experience to be made up of everything that takes part in it. Everything that takes part in your experience is part of you. And the point isn't to dissolve who you are into that experience, but to recognize that who you are *is* that experience. It's not that I *am* the chair I'm sitting on; but that the chair is part of who I am at this moment, because it's part of my experience, like you are, and this candlelight and this sunset and these trees are part of what I experience right now, and therefore are part of me. That doesn't mean they're all I consist of. There's a part of me also that's my memory of all my other experiences. That memory—conscious and unconscious—gives a kind of foundation out of which I respond to the complexities in my experience. I sort and I sift. Out of the mix, I spontaneously compose who I am.

People can understand that they are influenced by everything happening, by the hardness of the chair, the rumblings of the tummy, the drift of the light and the rustle of the breeze. People can also understand they are influenced by everything that's ever happened to them before, even if the influence is very small. At the same time they can understand that who they are in the room influences directly and indirectly, through the vibes as well as through what is said, the other people and even the physical reality of the room. While a basic dimension of our being is this constant flow of influences, that which makes the self a self is the creative spontaneity that plays with the influences, puts them together in interesting ways. And the more alive one is to the complexity and play of those influences, the more interesting will be one's personal collage.

I think if people really hung close to their common sense, the sense we share in common, in the older sense of *sensus communis*, they would know there's a constant flow of influences, and there's a just-as-constant flame of freedom. People know in their moment-to-moment experience that they pick up the influences, and they also know they're always choosing between the influences, deemphasizing or reemphasizing, resisting or underlining. Living in the consciousness of that flow of influences, though, and at the same time carving out a stable, big, open place for the freedom of the self, is a challenge that lasts an entire lifetime. It all comes down to being present to the web of connections of which we *are* a part, whether we admit it or not.

DJ: In a society as destructive as ours, how do you maintain that openness?

CK: I believe that to have any chance of sustaining a permeable and interconnected self without simply dissipating like a dandelion we need to have a sense of strategic spiritual and communal accountability. Within a supportive and loving community we learn mutuality, and learn to hold one another accountable to this mutuality. Enriching one another through the sharing of our existences becomes a communal discipline. We often need help to think more critically and self-critically and socially critically about the consequences of our actions, and communities can provide this help.

It's instructive here to think about Jesus, which since I'm a theologian I must confess I sometimes do. A helpful book for me recently was John Dominic Crossan's book on the historical Jesus, in which Crossan viewed him as a peasant Jewish Cynic. The Cynics, who were nothing like the modern definition of the word, were philosophers whose writings of the time describe the ideal of wandering about owning absolutely nothing except what they could carry on their bodies, moving in utter freedom and joy, showing themselves to be much more content and whole in their lives than those who possessed kingdoms. The teachings of Jesus tell that same message.

The difference was that the Cynics tended to move around individually, and Jesus developed this interesting discipline of communality. His disciples moved around in pairs or groups, and were accountable to each other.

The combination of strategic community—that discipline of constant mutuality and loving accountability—with intense spiritual practice was probably part of the energy of the Christian movement in its early phase, before it got twisted into its opposite.

DJ: How do you think Christianity got twisted from a religion of love to one of empire?

CK: That's a really important question, because that sort of thing has happened over and over. Movements challenging the disconnective, competitive, destructive self with ideals of love, compassion, meditation, ecstasy, and the sharing of all worldly goods have repeatedly been co-opted and turned to the advantage of those already in power. How does that happen?

I think there are two parts to the answer. The first part is that for the system of dominance to perpetuate itself there must be clear rewards for those who manage to maintain a state of disconnection. People must be trained and initiated into that state, and they must be rewarded with a sense of dignity, indeed of manhood, if they are able to maintain a sense of self-control—as opposed to being present to their experience—and a sense of control over their surroundings, which would include as many people as possible.

When you have a society organized so that those at the top benefit from the labor of the majority, you have some strong incentives to develop the kind of selfhood that gets you there. The only kind of selfhood that gets you there is the kind of selfhood that allows you to numb your empathies. To maintain the system of dominance, it's crucial that the elite learns this empathic numbness, akin to what Robert Jay Lifton calls "psychic numbing," so its members can control and when necessary torture and kill without being undone. If its members are incapable of numbing, or if they have not been trained properly, the system of dominance will collapse.

This leads to the second part of the co-optation question. Members of these revolutionary movements that are based on love and compassion are often persecuted by those in power. Think of civil rights workers in the sixties, or more recently the members of Plowshares. When a movement is in a state of persecution, eventually those of its members who don't die or give up are likely to get pretty defensive. Those personalities or elements who can fight are going to come to the fore. Those are the personalities who can take the bruises, lead the charge, keep the revolutionary cadre together, and who have the guts perhaps to kill. Those are the ones who can institutionalize, who can create dogmas and systematic sets of social rules that allow an institution to stabilize itself. So, beginning with Peter and Paul, if early Christianity hadn't developed clear institutional disciplines, it probably would have dissolved under pressure.

As it was, those groups within Christianity that were able to organize in the face of persecution and hold together an institutional apparatus with a hierarchical leadership were best able to survive. They were ready to be co-opted by the emperor Constantine at the precise point when he needed a religion to unify his empire. Under the sign of the cross, he said, he would go forth and conquer. And he did.

The co-optation question is actually much more complex, because society as we know it may well need to live off of the energy of alternative movements. It needs to suck our blood in order to feed itself, in part because a system based on domination will always be undernourished.

DJ: How so?

CK: Once we unplug from our vital connections—connections which are more like the fiber of what we call nature where there aren't barriers between the relationships of things to each other—once we unplug from the way in which everything branches into everything, and instead we pursue the goals of civilization as we know it, the energy source has to come from somewhere else. To some extent it can come from sucking the labor of the poor, and to some extent it can come from exploiting the bodies of animals and people treated like animals. The exploiting of the bodies of women gives a lot of energy. But the parasitism of the dominant culture is endless, because once you cut yourself off from the free flow of mutually permeable life you have to get your life back somehow, artificially.

It is especially useful to plug into the energy of a vital countercultural movement. That's how Constantine used Christianity. That's how the princes of Germany used the Reformation. That's how Stalin used Marx. That's how "green" corporations use the environmental movement. That's how middle-class suburbanites use Native American spirituality. That's how, unless we are very careful, the dominant culture can use the efforts of all of us working for justice and love to not only maintain its deadened state but to further its own destructive ends. It is up to those of us on the margin to keep calling the center to accountability; and it is up to all of us to keep asking the critical questions of who our work really benefits, who it is we're really serving.

DJ: Different subject. Where does god fit into this permeable self?

CK: God is one of many possible metaphors for the spirit of that creative permeability. I'm more comfortable with the name *spirit*, but sometimes god is a powerful monosyllable.

By spirit I mean the way the life force blows. The word *spirit* is the same as the word for wind or breath. So talking about the spirit in things is a way of talking about the permeable power of life. It's in all of us and in everything, and it transcends all of us and everything because it's in everything *else*. It is one and many and immanent and transcendent. It is metaphoric and it is real. It's male, female, and nongendered. I think it has to do with what an old friend of mine, Nelle Morton, called in *The Journey Is Home* "the wisdom at the heart of the universe." To say that is just to say that the universe is full of purposefulness and knowledge that precedes and transcends human consciousness.

DJ: Knowledge that transcends human consciousness? Some would disagree such a thing exists. Many people have infinite faith in the ability of humans to know everything through the use of science. I know a physicist who believes that someday humans will know how the brain works.

CK: That's the eschatology of science. It's just as much a dogma of faith as the eschatology of Christianity. "What we now only see darkly, then we will see face to face." The truth will out, finally. What we don't have now we will have then. This means that somehow we can borrow on the privilege now of the knowledge we will supposedly have then, a sort of parasitism that feeds even off the future.

DJ: This ties back to mutuality. Frederick Turner has written that when the Europeans came to North America they tried to possess the land without being possessed by it. By the same token, don't many scientists attempt to know without being known? Isn't that a form of possessing without being possessed?

CK: Let's look at what it means to know. What you're saying is true if knowing is a form of unilateral intellectual mastery of an object, the laying of an object's machinery bare.

But what would it mean, if you live with a person and love a person, to say that now finally you fundamentally know her? Doesn't that mean she has stopped emerging, developing? How would you ever come to a point where you fully understand the other, unless the other had stopped becoming? Or unless you and your perception of her had put a stop to her becoming by putting her outside the realm of your subjectivity?

DJ: *If* knowledge is mastery.

CK: If it's not mastery, if knowledge is more akin to love, for example, then of course you wouldn't even try to exhaustively know; you would just try to keep the conversation going.

DJ: The idea of knowledge as mastery allows no sense of interpenetration or even penetration.

CK: The mutuality is necessarily lacking, because if mutuality is there, there isn't a moment at which the thing is known and the knowledge is in the past tense. You and the thing will keep interacting, and that interaction will create an indeterminacy, an unpredictability, and an influence on the knower. I'm going to be influenced by the thing that I'm knowing—at the very moment of the act of knowledge.

DJ: How is all of this philosophizing helpful?

CK: If all of this thinking about defensiveness and abuse somehow rehearses us to actually interrupt even one instance of abuse, hallelujah. Theorizing can of course just inoculate us, but I hope that by theorizing together we're getting clarity and strategy with which to act. We need to have some perspective from which we're acting, if our actions are part of an attempt to change anything.

And change is possible. It's important for people to know that by simply existing, they already make a difference. By knowing they make a difference, they can make even more of a difference and have fun in the bargain by sharing that interaction with others.

The logic behind that connects to everything we've been talking about. Because life *is* one great tapestry of influences, we are always influencing our environment and it is influencing us, our world and our people. By tuning in to that, we not only nourish ourselves on some influences and heal ourselves from the pains of other influences, but we also gather wisdom about how to direct the influencing process. There is a kind of mutual attunement that goes on as one becomes more sensitive to the interdependencies of things that allows one to be empowered by the process. That empowerment only really happens if we're working in groups, because it's a collective power to start with. It's the power of multiple mutual influences.

What's most important is that we not succumb to feeling helpless and overwhelmed. It's also important that whatever we do, we do out of love, and therefore with enjoyment, so that our lives are worthwhile whether or not we make some ultimate difference.

JEANNETTE ARMSTRONG

Jeannette Armstrong is Okanagan, residing on the Penticton Indian Reservation in British Columbia. A fluent speaker of the Okanagan language, she has studied under some of the most knowledgeable Elders of the Okanagan.

Jeannette Armstrong has a degree in Fine Arts from the University of Victoria. Her visual artistic works have been recognized through numerous awards. She is a recognized Canadian author, whose published works include two children's books, the critically acclaimed novel Slash, and a collection of poetry, Breath Tracks. She also collaborated with renowned Native architect Douglas Cardinal on the book Native Creative Process.

Her other creative works include two produced videoscripts and three produced poetry music collaborations. Her collaboration Indian Woman on the record Till the Bars Break was nominated for the Canadian Juno award.

Jeannette Armstrong is the director of the En'owkin International School of Writing, and also an appointed traditional council member of the Penticton Indian Band. She is an advocate of indigenous rights, recently appointed to the Council of Listeners in the International Testimonials on Violations of Indigenous Sovereignty, and was invited to attend the peace talks in Mexico as an international observer by the Continental Coordinating Commission of Indigenous Peoples. She is an advocate of a healthy environment and social change in which peace between all peoples is central.

JEANNETTE ARMSTRONG: One of the strongest and most powerful capacities we have as human beings is the ability to create understanding. When you create understanding you lay to waste all conflict.

The En'owkin Centre, originally called the Okanagan Indian Educational Resources Society and Curriculum Project, grew out of a capacity for this and also out of the real fear the Okanagans have for their continued existence as a people. In the late 1960s, as a result of the consciousness raising of the civil rights movement and the antiestablishment movement, those Okanagans who had been resisting assimilation began to voice their concerns about the dominant society's myth of vanishing Indian people.

One of the things Okanagan activists were saying is that we have something ourselves worth maintaining, perpetuating, and reestablishing, because we see things in society that aren't healthy or good for any human being.

The first step toward the establishment of the En'owkin Centre was the statement that we are *not* part of the dominant culture. That immediately led to the questions: What *are* we as Okanagan people? What do we stand for? What do we give our coming generations? How do we ensure a healthy lifestyle for them? How are we going to implement the changes that are necessary for the survival of our communities?

Education was recognized as a priority. We began to ask, what is education, besides schooling and skills acquisition? What are the important things we, as Okanagans, need to learn in terms of approach to life, to the environment, to our communities, and to other communities around us? How can we give these things to our children and grandchildren? What, historically, do we need to remember and relearn and reteach, and what are the values which go along with that?

We began doing research and developing curriculum and materials that would not only articulate the values but would help people understand the things that need to be changed and help them to be involved in that change.

At that point our elders, being well informed about the processes we use in our culture, bestowed upon us the word "En'owkin." This word, which corresponds to a conflict resolution approach developed by our people prior to contact, in action means, "I challenge you to give me the opposite perspective to mine. In that way I will understand how I need to change my thinking to accommodate your concerns and problems."

The En'owkin process also requires that *you* in a reciprocal fashion receive my most opposite point of view, thereby enhancing your understanding as well. In this way, our knowledge, our holistic understanding, is doubled every time we insist upon the use of this process.

Because it resonates with pacifism, the approach is sometimes seen as pacifist. Instead it should be seen as mutually respectful and active in terms of bringing about understanding.

One of the main reasons the elders gave us this concept is their understanding of the fact that we cannot continually live in the past.

While tradition is important to guide our future, we must always be fluid in terms of our interactions. Otherwise both personally and communally we will not survive as a distinct people.

En'owkin is a very simple principle to state. It comes down to a *willingness* to learn how to coexist and cooperate with others. However, it is a very difficult principle to implement as a community, if your oppressors cannot and will not work with it, and in fact will do everything they possibly can to subvert the process.

Another reason the elders said they gave us this concept is if it is not learned by humanity in general, humans may not survive. It is clear that the Okanagan people can only survive if humanity survives in a specific principled way, and so we at the En'owkin Centre have committed to and undertaken the responsibility of relearning this principle, implementing it in our communities, and instilling it in other communities around the world where we can.

When we began this talk, there was nothing in place that told us how to do that. Fortunately the En'owkin principle is one of the most powerful natural processes we know of and can be applied the world over without force. The question is, if we *don't* apply it, if we're not willing to understand something fully by looking at the other side, how can we accumulate knowledge? How can we proceed? We know we were given minds and abilities to accumulate understanding for a survival reason. We also know that when we depend on things such as physical strength or arms, we defeat ourselves in the long term.

Over the years the En'owkin has developed a full circle of programs. We have assisted our community to increase its capacity for incorporating old knowledge and values into the contemporary world; we are reestablishing those values in our children through language, cultural practice, and ceremonies.

On an individual level, I actively challenge the thinking in the dominant culture by going out and talking to communities. I end up in some pretty strange forums with some pretty strange thinkers. It is a continuous challenge for me that widens my own capacity and understanding.

This is good because there is so much I don't understand about Western philosophy or European colonialism. There is so much I don't understand about how the dominant society operates and perpetuates itself. To me it seems insane; it feels and looks like a mass psychosis. It's frightening, especially when you know it's not necessary and when you know that most people would be happier not being this way. Yet the colonizing society is like an insane machine that keeps churning out the things the society revolves around.

Seeing in this way has given me a lifelong commitment to try to make some sense of it with those people who want to be involved in the work of reestablishing sanity. In terms of my own process, I always go back to the En'owkin principle. It allowed my people to live in a coexistence pattern that was harmonious with the environment and with other living things and with other peoples.

The Okanagan were a peaceful people; they weren't caught up in the warfare and violence that occurred in other areas. At the same time, though, they would not back down when either the survival of the principles of En'owkin as a life process or the people who carry them were in jeopardy. The imperative is that they must maintain, and must find every way they can to maintain with nonviolence. However, if violence occurs and is the only resort to maintain the life principle, they *will* be involved. They were not pacifists. It is a concept that was misunderstood in Indian country by nonnative people who don't clearly understand that the nonviolence principle involved had to do with survival over the long term.

The question of violence is a serious one. Since contact, we as Okanagan people have not used violence. I don't think there is ever a point at which we would engage in violence, unless all of the Okanagan people were under siege. However, it is becoming more difficult to maintain because physically we *are* under siege, but not by guns or warfare. Instead the siege we are under promotes psychological manifestations that create sickness and as much death in our communities as if you took guns and shot people.

The defense of our people and their life principle is a large part of what we concern ourselves with at En'owkin Centre. Part of that defense is in creating allies who are willing to work with the principles of understanding and coexistence.

The last few years we have worked on international forums on environment and social change. One example is the Beyond Survival

Conference, which brought together indigenous writers, artists, and performers from various colonized countries to talk to each other about how the colonization of their artistic expressions and the silencing of their voices have occurred and what they have done to resist that.

We are now involved with an organization in Moscow called the Center for the Protection of Traditional Peoples in their Environment. It is concerned with the traditional ethnic peoples in northern and remote ethnic states of the Russian Union. Part of the work is to raise consciousness of people in North America about the very, very serious degradation of the environment and disintegration of peoples—culturally.

Another area of my work is my direct visits to other countries. I have had meetings with indigenous organizations and collectives like the Peasant Women's Organization in Bolivia.

Much of it is work that needs to happen in order to carry out what we have been talking about. At times the work is frustrating because we don't have enough support. Real support can be very difficult to get, especially when indigenous people are the ones who are asking. I think it has to do with a difference in values in the dominant society and its use of environment. You have a lot of people wanting to save the rain forest but not caring to listen to the people who live there. I think this happens because people in the dominant society think people are separate from the land. They think people can be removed from their lands, assimilated and educated, and still be OK. They also think the land can somehow survive in a healthy way without those people who are part of it. They don't understand that these people are natural and essential to that environment.

DERRICK JENSEN: Do you think it's exactly this idea, that people are separate from the land, that has fueled the conquest of indigenous peoples by Europeans?

JA: It seems to go back to the idea that human beings, and specifically human beings from the colonizing culture, are elevated above the rest of the natural world and that they have a prior right to use everything around them. It is a fundamental split in ideology that requires aggression. It advocates aggression as a principle of power and achievement. It is an ideology that advocates accumulation as a part of power and is central to the idea that the measurement of a person's worth is their economic and oppressive power. The consequences of that ideology, both internally and externally to all life forms, are very frightening.

I've been asking a lot of questions: How did that concept of power come to be, and how does it continue to manifest itself? How is it contained in all the things we see unquestioningly as an everyday process—in television, education, government institutions, societal customs and processes, and in the art forms?

If we look at some of the things that are articulated symbolically and metaphorically in the way we lay out cities, or in the way we construct means to get from here to there, we can recognize these as fundamental expressions of the thought and philosophy behind that concept of power.

How does that philosophy keep regenerating? Where does it begin in the individual? How is it possible to help that individual make a shift away from that philosophy, to help them recognize that their individual lives do not have to contribute to destruction? It seems this question is critical, because if we don't recognize the destruction around us, if we don't see it as destruction, if we see it as progress, or necessary, or something wonderful, then we're in terrible terrible danger because our lack of vision renders us helpless.

DJ: The way you talk about the dominant culture's concept of power makes me suspect the Okanagan view power differently.

JA: Power is a difficult concept and a difficult word to translate into Okanagan because of its connotations. In English it is very much related to coercion and confrontation or to the concept that someone is right and someone is wrong and that one must be less and one must be more. To be able to say that same thing in our language would be to say that the concept of supremacy or dominance exists in our society.

One of the things about the dominant culture's concept of power is that it suggests people who use aggressive force have no other power; it suggests that they are powerless. To translate the word *power*, I would have to suggest this in Okanagan. I would also have to suggest they could *only* accomplish their ends by force and that in fact they don't know how to do it any other way. In our language that means they are uncivilized, barbaric, and savage. They lack knowledge, systems, and history. Everything. They lack respect. To us as Okanagans, for a person to do any-thing in that way is unacceptable, unheard of. Not only is it unethical, but since you have so many other tools you can use, it doesn't make sense. If a child is sitting too close to a fire, why take a hammer and knock him over the head, when you can help him understand about fire and why he should move?

The English word I think about is *understanding*. When we accom-plish understanding, things happen in the physical world around us. New things replace old things, not by coercion or aggression, but by healthy, natural processes. That's power.

DJ: Different concepts of power would change our understanding and change the socialization of our children. When I taught at college, it always bothered me to give grades, because they're a form of coercion. No one ever gave me grades for learning how to fish or to play.

JA: At a workshop in Phoenix for indigenous people we looked at a tra-ditional process of acquisition of knowledge about the world around us, which is what education should be. Knowledge should prepare us in the best possible way to be the most excellent at the talents we were given and should prepare us to make a contribution to our community. We asked, "What is the human capacity for learning? How does a society or community acquire necessary knowledge?"

One of the interesting things that came out of this workshop was the idea of acquisition rather than teaching, acquisition of knowledge through mechanisms that motivate us, having fun at things, being in-terested or inquisitive about certain things, and having that kind of in-quisitiveness enhanced by certain kinds of people with certain kinds of skills. That seemed to be one of the most exciting and logical ways to look at learning, both for adults and for children.

A serious life principle is being happy at what we do; that is, fulfilled at what we do, internally whole at what we do, doing something because we love to participate in it and feeling that we need to do it or our lives are empty shells.

It's astounding how few people actually live that way. It's incredible that everybody isn't in an insane asylum. Everybody should be as happy and fulfilled as we know we could be.

We have to ask ourselves what motivates public schooling within this culture. What does it produce? We're told we're supposed to get an education so we can get a job, we can provide, we can make our parents or our community proud, we can do this or that. These become values that then replace the value of fulfillment of ourselves as entities conscious of our own internal being. We compromise the conscious beings we are, sacrifice them to the values of the society that surrounds us. We end up thinking, "I've got to do this or I've got to accomplish that. I've got to make this much money, and I've got to get this kind of recognition. If I don't, I'm a failure. I'm not successful unless I've done all those things according to that yardstick."

Much of what public schooling does is uphold the principles that create capitalistic society; the pretension that happiness is in having things; if you're not striving to own things, you're not happy.

It doesn't have to be this way. Education is a way to create understanding in the person that happiness does not equate to material things and that material wealth is a misplaced value, that happiness can be determined by ourselves, each individually.

Many Indian people know this. However, society has a big problem with the ones who say, "Ah, the hell with it. I don't have to work day in and day out. For what? I'm OK the way I am."

DJ: Let's go back to En'owkin process. What do you do when you're faced with someone who simply won't use that principle, when you're faced with physical or economic force?

JA: There seem to be two ways to approach it. One is to help in decolonizing ourselves by deconstructing the myths of the colonizing society. One of the myths we must deconstruct is the myth of what we, as indigenous people, would accomplish if we joined this society and did all the proper things. In its place we need to reconstruct a process that enhances the ability to cope with the economic and technological conditions that exist in the twentieth century as they relate to political systems and the use of aggression. This translates into resistance.

As well as resistance, survival requires advocacy. A large part of advocacy is to assist people with the learning process, not merely to help them decolonize but to heal their spirits, emotions, and souls, and to free their artistic, creative expression. One of the mechanisms for this, which we see as extremely important, is for people to give themselves the chance to be excellent at something.

As advocates we go into a community where there is severe alcoholism, really severe damage as a result of residential school abuse, or sexual abuse. Communities where suicides are on the rampage. In those communities we start the process of healing. Once that process begins, the people themselves see different routes they can implement in their communities or their families or in their own individual lives.

At the same time we support and assist one another. At any given time, here in the Okanagan you'll find people from the Six Nations, people from communities in the Southwest, and so on. We have become a center that people call on to help facilitate a process for community healing.

For instance, there was the Oka crisis two years ago in the Six Nations territory, in which Mohawks were being forcibly removed from land they were protecting. This land was on top of their ancestral graves, and the mayor of Oka wanted to cut down the trees to put in a golf course. The Canadian Armed Forces and the RCMP came in, until there were five thousand troops with their guns aimed at about fifty Mohawks.

The Mohawks said something like, "We're not moving. There's only so far you can push us, and you're not pushing us an inch more. You're gonna have to kill all of us."

Since the dominant culture owns the media machine, it went into explosions about how these people were criminals, and how they were Mohawk savages.

Our elders asked some of us to go in as interveners and assist in any way with their negotiation process. We sent a number of our people to try to help facilitate a peaceful ending to the siege.

The Okanagans initiated a consciousness-raising program called the Peace Run. A number of our young people went on foot across the country to inform other communities. It was really effective. At an international level, people informed the European Green Party and went to Geneva and the European Parliament.

Once our own native media machine got going and informed native communities across the country about what was happening, it became clear to the government that if something had happened to even one of those Mohawks, the government would have had to deal with every Indian nation across this country. As it was, roadblocks went up in many places, and railways were sealed off and rerouted through the United States. We weren't responsible for any of that. All we did was send out accurate information. Those people decided on their own how they could make their voices heard by the government.

DJ: So being committed to understanding the other side's position in no way implies compromise.

JA: One of the things that is predominant in my mind about the Oka crisis is how active the negotiators from the Six Nations were in informing as many people as they could. That was one of the ways of counteracting mis- or disinformation.

I know it was the concerted effort across the country that made a peaceful resolution to the conflict possible. It was difficult. The Mohawks were serious. They knew it would have to be the other side that moved to understand and that any compromise would defeat their whole purpose, because they had compromised for so many years.

DJ: Even when you're not willing to compromise, you are still willing to understand the other side.

JA: In a sense I saw that happening there. At the final hour, the chiefs and medicine people and warriors walked out and said they had accomplished what they came to accomplish—the place was not going to be turned into a golf course, and the trees were not going to be cut down. Their understanding of the government's position was evident when they said, "If their system demands we have to go behind bars for taking the position we have, we will still have done our duty." They were arrested and put through two years of trial, at the end of which they were acquitted.

DJ: I once talked to a Lakota holy man about duty. He said he understood duties and responsibilities, but did not understand the concept of rights.

JA: If I were to say "my right" in Okanagan, the word would translate as "my truth." This means if I accept my truth as being part of a family or a community or a land base, it translates into a responsibility. How am

I responsible to my family, to my community? How am I responsible as a thinking, choice-making entity? How can I carry out that choice-making in relation to my family, my community, and the land?

This translates in an overall sense like a right, but as far as the individual is concerned, it translates as a responsibility. It is the truth of the matter, which is why we call it a truth. It's a law.

It is more than just a law that somebody wrote, like a bill of rights; it's something so big that unless we understand that truth, we aren't human. Unless we understand our responsibility, we are something other than human. Part of our humanity requires us to be a family, a community, a certain way on the land. When we are not those things, what are we? We are a misplaced, displaced entity that can't be construed as being "a part of."

In a nonnative sense, I see "right" as being the capacity to live in a certain way, as being the specific freedoms that society offers you. But it still translates the same way, because the only way you can have a right is to be a part of that collective. And that collective requires that you be responsible to it.

In Bolivia I listened for four days through a translator to an Iamaran elder, who is one of the keepers of their knowledge. One of the things he said was, "When you are born Iamaran you are born into a community. And when you are born into that community, you are Iamaran *because* of that community. Because of that you receive a whole series of gifts in terms of the knowledge base the Iamaran have constructed over the years and millennia they have existed on the land. This knowledge base is articulated through the arts, language, ceremonies, lifestyles, customs, values, process, and so on."

That example can be used anywhere. You are always born with a connection, and unless you understand and are responsible to that connection, you become not a part of that community. You become disjointed. And to be disjointed means to not be whole.

It all revolves around how you react and interact with those things you are born into and how you view yourself in terms of what you're allowed or not allowed to do. You can call that rights if you want, but it really is responsibilities. It is a responsibility to understand and operate within the systems that are constructed around you, that you have had the opportunity to be born into.

I'm trying to untangle in my own mind what went wrong with Western society and its idea of rights. One of the things that occurred to me in a really clear vision is that a right is called a right not because it *is* a right, but because it is something that can be externally articulated and enforced. It is something that can be used to maintain a construct that doesn't have anything to do with rights; a construct that has to do with nonrights and that has to do with not having rights to begin with.

It is a serious concept to try to put together in a philosophical context that might be understood in terms of Western thought and society. I've been excited by the thought that nation-states and societies and the legal systems and governmental processes that say they are about rights are not about rights. They're about making sure the individual doesn't have the ability to be, in the true sense, responsible, that the individual can only be responsible for select things.

One of the difficulties in *talking* about this is that my mind doesn't work in words all the time. I'm a visual artist. My mind often makes sense out of things in a visual pattern that I then have to take the time to translate into words.

DJ: Can the visual arts help us to decolonize our selves?

JA: That's another difficult question, because the word *art* has been corrupted. Just as everything else has been commodified, art has changed from the expression of concepts in a visual symbolic form to a commodity to be marketed.

In original societies, the place of that kind of expression we call visual arts had nothing to do with buying and selling ideas. It had to do with how we construct our philosophical principles and how we manifest them.

For example, we can think about a philosophical principle that might be seen as a spiral, in terms of continually expanding thought that follows a clear pathway. The spiral is then a physical construct that refers to an abstract philosophical approach to things. You could incorporate that visual symbol in different ways in the functional things that you create, as well as in the things that are purely for pleasure. You could incorporate the spiral into your buildings and homes and tables and chairs, utensils and clothing, and so on.

DJ: I see you are wearing spiral earrings.

JA: We often dismiss such things as merely clothing, when in fact decorative art appeals to a part of our mind that is different from the analytical logic we use to create words.

In our indigenous ceremonies, we recognize that decorative art is a form of communication that is compacted much differently from the way word symbols are. Our experience gets compacted and stored in the place that creates symbols and metaphor and archetypes. We regenerate these back in purely symbolic constructs, using color or three-dimensional shapes, with whatever physical materials we have around us, and we display these as a result of our philosophy and our understanding of how things work in concert with each other and how things interrelate.

In a traditional sense all these forms of expression—visual and three-dimensional arts and music and sound and dance and ceremony—not only generate and express how things become changed as a result of new ideas, but also how things get incorporated into the old patterns and symbols to be re-created, with new experience and new materials. These forms of expression may form avenues by which we can access answers to those difficult questions we as human beings are beginning to face, and they may provide ways that society, on a subconscious level, can change direction.

Just to give a concrete example, all across North America Indian people meet in circles. A circle is a physical construct that empowers a certain kind of mutually respectful approach and a certain kind of action. When we say we want buildings like that and we want to do our ceremonies like that, our dances like that, and set up our communities like that, what we're saying and doing is empowering society to follow the principle we see, a way of manifesting and creating a continuous, eternal equal footing among all of us.

The idea of words and the analytical process is blown way out of proportion. We give it too much precedence over other communicative arts. The arts have been relegated to commodities, things we don't pay a lot of attention to in the sense of being legitimate forms of communication. They *are* legitimate forms of communication, enjoyable forms that bring internal fulfillment and external joy. It seems to me that within societies that suppress people's experience of these forms, whether the suppression is economic or ideological, the functioning and coping ability of the people within those societies begins to break down. I see that in Western societies, and I see that in pop culture.

DJ: What does it mean to be a human being?

JA: That's a serious question that seems to be at the center of some of the problems we're encountering as human beings in the governmental or political systems we construct. Our answer to that question seems to underlie how we allow our systems to operate.

Human beings are part of a community, the collective, humanity, the natural world, the earth. We are pieces of earth; our bodies are chemistry from the earth. That's what we are and that's what we go back to.

But something else occurs, and we know that something else occurs. We know there's a human consciousness that continues on as long as there's a human being that thinks and has children and passes that thinking on, and we know that that consciousness grows and grows and grows with each new generation. We know there's an *old, old* entity that we are all just minute parts of. We are all just disturbances on the surface of that old entity we could say is humanity. We add to that consciousness continuously. There are a few people who add more to it than others, and a few people who add less, but we all are a part of it, we all are a result of it, and we proceed as a result of it.

Sometimes it's difficult and painful to talk about this because of the condition we're in, in relation to that old entity.

Some people describe religion or spirituality as the practice of communing with that entity, connecting with it, drawing from it and connecting to it as our source. I think this happens from another capacity that we have, other than analytical logic or even the visual arts or artistic expression. We connect with this entity in what we call ceremony, ritual, worship. At the core of our being we have a belief system about humanity with which we connect, internally, in a very specific way, whether we say we are Catholics or Buddhists or atheists or something else. The connection gets carried on in things we do and in things we construct over generations.

What I'm trying to say is that this entity, the connection to it, affects individual humans in a much more powerful way than *anything* else does. I'm trying to say that in the individual, how we develop the connection, how we process it, and how we live it is a part of how humanity acts or interacts. In other words, we as individuals contribute to how we as a community manifest those belief systems in a real, fundamental, integral sense. When we lose understanding of and connection to that source in terms of health and well-being and happiness, when those connections are cut and we begin to reenact rituals for reasons *other* than those basic, integral reasons, then we lose our spirit. If, as individuals, we operate out of something other than this sense of connection, in a very serious way we damage humanity, damage us all. Connecting to our source is a spiritual process that requires abandonment of things we use in our daily lives, such as analytical, logical, consequential thought, and requires instead a reliance on that internal core that feels the connection, that connects in a way which is indescribable except through song or dance or through some kind of ceremonial recognition and acknowledgment of that big stream.

Spirituality is a word that is sometimes used to mean this connection, though sometimes spirituality is confused with ritual or dogma, or oppression through ritual or dogma. Institutionalized religion is one of those ways of oppression. However, we have the capacity, individually, to throw those shackles off; we have the right and the responsibility to be enlightened beings, to connect and to enjoy what life form we have while we're in the presence of the physical world.

Indian people experience a real reluctance to talk about the connection we make in a spiritual sense, because of the exploitation and commodification and misinterpretation. I *can* say that if a person is unwilling to abandon everything and look at spirituality and experience it, in the same way as is true for any other piece of knowledge, that person is missing out on a piece of learning that is critical to their existence and their survival. I have come to know that once you reconnect, your mind restructures all its processes. I see some things as a native person that Western society doesn't agree are possible, and which therefore to the colonized mind *are not* possible. But I have experienced such things. I have to ask myself: Who's right here? What's happening?

People are so afraid. There *is* more than just the individual mind. We know that. If people could feel themselves to be a part of the world in a real sense for just one moment, devoid of all the constraints that we've created and constructed around us that stop us from feeling that, from understanding and knowing it, if they could experience that, it would change their processes, their approaches to things, their approach to themselves.

I know it is that connection we seek as human beings, in terms of our reason for being, our essence of life. Even for a second to be a part of the eternal universe, even for a second to somehow experience that, is astounding. We as human beings were given one of the most profound gifts of creation, to be able to see ourselves and our part in the order of things, in the natural world. It's absolutely incredible. And to perceive even a piece of that, even momentarily, forces all things related to nations, racism, societies, land, environment, to fall into a different perspective.

People can make all sorts of justifications for not doing that, but the question I always ask is, what's stopping them?

DJ: The more we talk about the different concepts of power, the different uses of art, what it means to be a human being, the more angry I become. I feel impoverished by the language and culture of my birth. Linda Hogan told me, "We do not have words in English for our strongest feelings. It's not a language that can touch the depths of our passion, of our pain." That hurts. I feel that loss.

JA: Twenty or thirty years ago I read a short fiction piece that has stuck with me ever since. It was about going into a five-and-dime store and seeing all those ceramic and plastic knickknacks. The piece focused on ceramic green pigs with white daisies on them, and on the kind of society which could produce an artifact like that. What would be the philosophical ideals and values that would not only produce something like that, but would mass produce it for every shelf in every Woolworth's across the country? What kind of culture would produce people that would buy those things? Why would a culture do that to its members? It's a horrible concept to think about, for the future of that culture.

DJ: How can you help anyone who reads this to decolonize?

JA: One of the most important things in decolonizing is to challenge the givens of society, the things you take for granted. We all have cultural, learned behavior systems that have become embedded in our subconscious. These systems act as filters for the way we see the world. They affect our behaviors, our speech patterns and gestures, the words we use, and also the way we gather our thinking. We have to find ways to challenge that continuously. To see things from a different perspective is one of the most difficult things we have to do.

For me it is a necessary act. To be a practitioner of En'owkin process is to constantly school myself in deconstruction of what I believe and perceive to be the way things are, to continuously break down in my own mind what I believe, and continuously add to my knowledge and understanding. In other words, never to be satisfied that I'm satisfied. That sounds like I'm dissatisfied, but it doesn't mean that. It means never to be complacent and think I've come to a conclusion about things, to always question my own thinking. I always tell my writing class to start with and hold on to the attitude of saying "bullshit" to everything. And to be joyful and happy in that process. Because most of the time it's fear that brings out old behaviors and old conflicts. It's not necessarily that we believe those things, but we know them and so we continue those patterns and behaviors because they're familiar. Conversely, those things that are unfamiliar to us create fear, and our own logic and analytical processes end up working against us.

Another part of decolonization is the recognition that there must be some principles to operate under or else there will be anarchy. One of these principles has to do with nonaggression, nonviolence, not violating other things in the process of moving forward. It is a simple principle, but it's a very difficult principle to apply in our thinking and daily work. But to me it is a necessary part of decolonization, and important if I don't want to contribute more than necessary to the mess I'm trying to resolve.

DJ: How can I help you with your process?

JA: That's a really important question because disempowered peoples, indigenous peoples, have a common legacy of the inability to move communication in a market economy. Any time we articulate anything, whether it's valuable or not, it doesn't go anywhere. It moves only in a closed arena. This happens not because of any kind of well-thought-out plan but simply because of the way the market machine works.

A way you can help is to create space for our voice, advocate for it, add that voice in whatever ways are open to you. I make that challenge when I talk to different groups. I say: "You can ask for my thinking, but what are you prepared to do about it?" That's especially true for people who have any sort of power in the dominant society. I say to them: "There's no point in sharing this with you, if it's only going to excite you for a day and then you go your way. You're wasting my time and your time. If you're willing to do something I'm willing to talk with you."

Another way you can help is to always be an advocate of your own thinking. Without your own thinking you wouldn't be here talking to me, or you wouldn't be reading this. So it's very important that you give yourself credit and permission to be a powerful, beautiful human being. It's a mistake to think you always have to have permission from someone or have to be accredited by someone or recognized in some academic fashion in order to advocate your own thinking. You have a right to do that, by having been given your mind and your sense of understanding, your sense of compassion and love. That recognition in yourself and that empowerment of yourself is vitally important to the world. It's vitally important as well to the work we are doing, because after all, it is the same.

Susan Griffin

Susan Griffin is one of the most passionate, powerful, and well known writers and social thinkers working today. Her work, which includes Woman and Nature: The Roaring Inside Her, Pornography and Silence: Culture's Revenge against Nature, *and* A Chorus of Stones: The Private Life of War, *has shaped both ecological and feminist thought.* A Chorus of Stones *was nominated for a National Book Critics Circle Award, was a jury nominee for a Pulitzer Prize, and won the Bay Area Book Reviewers Award. Her most recent collection of poetry,* Unremembered Country, *won the Commonwealth Prize for Poetry. She has been the recipient of a MacArthur grant for Peace and International Cooperation, an NEA Fellowship, and an Emmy Award (for her play* Voices*). She lectures widely throughout the United States and Europe and lives and teaches writing in Berkeley, California. She is presently at work on a book of essays about ecofeminism, a book on society and the experience of illness, and a long narrative poem about her mother's death.*

DERRICK JENSEN: Does more than an economic imperative drive the destruction of the natural world?

SUSAN GRIFFIN: Absolutely. Economic motives are part of it, but if you go deeply into these motives, you don't find economics at the core. You find power.

The psychology of power is something we as ecologists need to understand, especially as it relates to the natural condition. We are a culture that can't admit death into our understanding. This leads to the core issue in the destruction of the natural world, which is a fear of nature and of the power of nature to change us. It is this fear that produces the distortions of gender and class. The issue is not money. Money is just a symbol.

Our economic perspectives are bound by a reductive idea of human psychology, which comes out of the rationalist tradition. These perspectives presume people do things for "reasonable" reasons and that acquiring a lot of wealth is reasonable.

The truth is, amassing wealth is not a reasonable thing to do. It's not necessarily in one's self-interest in a simple material way. The men, and it's usually men, who amass and manage these great empires are in fact owned by what they own. Management is a tremendous amount of work, for which one does not necessarily receive sensual pleasure.

Men in that sort of position often pervert the direct sensual experiences they receive. What others would consider simple pleasure—partaking of the earth or body through food, sexuality, intimacy—becomes instead a symbol of power.

The ideology of pornography, which is the real psychology of not only capitalism but of what has become of socialism, consists of the transformation of other forms of energy into schemes of power and domination. An example of this is pornography itself. Most feminists who criticize pornography are not criticizing explicit erotic materials or descriptions of sex. We are criticizing the turning of sexuality and sexual intimacy into an act of domination.

Let me say here, because often this is not heard, the ideology of pornography is not the same as explicit descriptions of sex. It is found in what is called "hard-core" pornography and in "soft-core" pornography (and believe me, even these names are revealing), but it is also found in advertisements using sex and films that depict conventional relationships between men women through a conventional lens. It is the pervasive way of viewing sexuality and gender in our culture. And it is also the underbelly, the not-quite-conscious side of a civilization bent on domination and control of nature. But it is not synonymous by any means with sexuality.

Sexuality, if it isn't an act of dominance, becomes not an act but an event. It's an event in which the participators are vulnerable, having moved away from the defenses of culture. This culture—European white culture—has within it a number of defenses against death, not just the end of your life but all the little deaths, such as aging, the sun going down, your children getting a little older and you realizing they're never going to be that age again, or the withering of the flowers you put in the vase. The French word for orgasm, *petit mort*, is "little death."

Saint Augustine said the penis is the most rebellious of organs, because it won't do what you tell it. Sexuality has a will of its own, and sexual experiences make us aware of our essential vulnerability and lack of control over outer as well as inner nature.

Pornography takes this experience and turns it inside out, perverts it so it becomes an expression not of vulnerability and participation but of domination and power. It also becomes an expression of difference and separation. That's why gender is so important to pornography; pornography can't exist without the belief that there are essential differences between men and women, which determine a hierarchy between them.

I'm going to develop an essay called "The Eros of Everyday Life." As we move closer to the heart of matter, instead of finding the hard and impenetrable objects a certain prejudice of mind had led us to look for, we are finding instead both movement and stillness. It's a wonderful paradox, and there's something erotic in it. The way I describe it in this essay is that the universe is always cooking and cleaning. It's always putting things together or separating them.

That separation is critical, and it is different from the separation essential to the pornographic mind. In pornography a false separation is imposed to create the illusion of power. But the universe has another kind of separation, more akin to discernment. Discernment is necessary in order to have meeting. There is continual meeting going on, and whenever there is meeting there is transformation. The elements don't remain the same, even though it may only be their trajectories that change. That meeting, that change, is eros.

DJ: Where does death fit in?

SG: I was my mother's primary family caretaker during her last months. I became part of her process of death. I was of course sad, not wanting to lose her, but at the same time there was a joy in all of us being present to that process. We knew we were sharing the labor, even when we were in another room talking to each other. That's where our consciousness was.

The more I've been around death, and I've experienced a number of deaths, the more I understand that consciousness is physical. While I don't believe in a heaven of Judeo-Christian dimensions, I do believe there is a dimension that we can feel though we can't see.

It's hard to speak about this and not have it immediately fall into that spirit/matter, mind/body split, which of course I do not agree with at all.

But there is, as is true of many of the false descriptions our culture holds, something real that's close by and which has its energy borrowed by the false description.

I find this in the New Age. New Age thinkers are some of the few people in America who, for example, are really talking about the experience of consciousness as an entity. We've all had experiences of consciousness not necessarily being located where we've been taught to believe it should be. But New Age thought takes this energy, which is as physical as radio waves, which are also invisible, and pours it into those old Judeo-Christian vessels—the mind/body duality and the spirit/matter duality. In so doing they borrow this energy—energy which points to a larger meaning—taking it away from the earth, and in this way distort the meaning of both materiality and spirituality by creating a separation and a polarity between them.

DJ: A theme of the pornographic mind, and thus Western culture, seems to be the creation of parodies. Judeo-Christian heaven is a parody of real mystery, pornography is a parody of real sexuality, tree farms are parodies of real forests.

SG: In *Pornography and Silence* I wrote how the witch-burners' descriptions of witches' activities were parodies of real natural rituals, those celebrating nature. That is, they were parodies of religious relationships to nature that include nature as part of spirituality and spirituality as part of nature.

DJ: Linda Hogan pointed out to me there was a coin with a buffalo on it at the same time buffalo were being exterminated, and the face of an Indian person at the same time there was a policy of genocide against Indians.

SG: Anyone described as other becomes the vessel of a part of yourself you've rejected. Whatever you've rejected in yourself you've also lost. This creates a longing, and you try to bring that rejected part back.

I didn't understand until recently that not only have you lost that projected part of yourself, you've also lost your connection to that other culture and to other people. That causes another mourning. The connections we have to each other as human beings, even to people we haven't met, are far more profound than we understand them to be. And necessary to us.

I'm not talking about necessity as reductive self-interest—even as a roof over your head or food. I'm talking about communion. One might look at power as the perversion of communion. This is another need that is not addressed at all by this culture. People don't understand communion is not just social gatherings where we meet somebody and get married. To be in communion is to have a way we can live out our collective consciousness together. Right now, our only options for mass gatherings are shopping malls, rock concerts, and churches.

DJ: Each of which has problems of its own. As you made clear in *Pornography and Silence*, Christianity and pornography are two sides of the same coin.

SG: Someone like Hugh Hefner is very understandable. He grew up in an incredibly restrictive, oppressive home and rebelled. But rebellion is often just a mirror image of what it's rebelling against, because the field has not been opened up enough to see other options. The same hierarchies and oppositions are played out in different ways, because there hasn't been enough self-knowledge and understanding to let go of the whole scheme and see that an entirely different way of organizing experience is possible.

DJ: How does one get to that entirely different way?

SG: Understanding is critical. I believe very much in democracy, which goes hand-in-hand with understanding. For me the preferred move regarding pornography, for example, is to clamor, press, demand education of every kind and for every age group about sexuality. Not just anatomical stuff, which is all very important, but also much deeper questions. We need to begin inviting people to think creatively about old models of masculinity and femininity and old ideas of dominating sexuality. What we think of as masculine is not primarily biological. It's a social construct, and the biological portion is malleable. Biological masculinity doesn't have to express itself either in rape or with an automatic handgun. There are a number of cultures that don't have violence of that nature at all, with guns or spears or anything.

DJ: In *A Chorus of Stones* you ask, "Why do some people inflict on others the suffering they have endured?"

SG: God, I wish I could answer that question. It seems clear to me if you've been abused, you are better off if you know it was abuse and are able to speak of it. The chances are much better that for the rest of your life you will be on the side of those who are treated unjustly.

Being unable to locate what happened to you and bring it to speech doesn't automatically mean you're going to be an abuser, but that event *does* have to be acted out in some way. Knowledge always tries to rise to the surface, to express itself through dreams, puns, jokes, slips of the tongue, supposed accidents, or direct actions. This is another reason I believe so strongly in understanding.

DJ: Viktor Frankl wrote of the importance of meaning to the survival of concentration camp inmates. Is it meaning that allows people to respond to their pain by opening out, as opposed to shutting down?

SG: Yes, I agree with Victor Frankl, and I have been influenced by his thought. What I would add here to what you have said is that the pain and meaning must be shared by a whole society. Because what happens to a stranger also in some sense happens to me. But when that is not understood in the social body, so that we are living a kind of atomized existence, pain, particularly pain coming from social injustice, is especially bitter. Unbearable. I am thinking of the pain, for instance, of South Central Los Angeles. The original verdict in the Rodney King case, which implied that no injustice had taken place, was an act of aggression against meaning and made a long and continued suffering, from countless such injustices, unbearable.

When people are able to understand within a larger fabric of meaning the harm that's come to them, as well as the mistakes they themselves have made, the pain becomes bearable enough for them to accept the truth and to therefore change. You can't change without accepting the truth, but when it is isolated away from the larger pattern of meaning, that kind of knowledge is crushing. Yet, for example, although the diagnosis of an illness is always saddening because it confirms the illness's existence, that sadness is balanced by the naming of your condition as part of a larger pattern of meaning. Naming is in itself redeeming, provided the larger pattern of meaning is grand and generous enough to hold the whole of existence.

This is another of the difficulties we face today. Most of our patterns of meaning are neither grand nor generous enough to serve this great need.

DJ: We were talking earlier about this culture's false descriptions borrowing energy from real experience. That ties to what you've written about a fundamental difference between images that open us up to reality and those that deny reality.

SG: We're so used to responding to images that deny reality—images and words that lie—that we forget the opposite can be true. There are also images, stories, words, poetry, language that can evoke and open up experience and point toward an exploration of what really is there.

Usually the images and experiences that are false, which bar you from reality, are also dead-ended, just like a dead-end street. You have to make a circle and do the same journey again. Not a circle of fruition, the life cycle, but a Sisyphean circle, a despairing circle that leads to addiction. The images of pornography always promise revelation, but the revelation isn't there because it's false, because eros isn't really in it.

DJ: Because the circle is not completed. Something central to relationship is what I call completing the circle . . .

SG: Yes.

DJ: Which is what you just did. "Yes, I heard you." If you objectify another, whether it's a tree or a human being, they *cannot* complete your circle because you've silenced their voice. You have to ever more desperately begin the circle again and again.

SG: Yes. The real experience of eros is in I-Thou. If you don't perceive thou, which is a very respectful word that understands the sacredness of another being, you have nothing.

I was abandoned over and over as a child, and I spent a lot of my life looking for and wanting love. It took a long time for me to understand love is a quality within you. It's not that I wasn't loving, far from it. But I didn't yet understand the very thing I wanted was already inside of me.

Pornographers are insatiably hungry, and they don't realize how simple it is to meet this appetite. The way to have a real life is through experience—not by possession, but by looking at another with respect, by understanding and accepting the subjectivity of experience. Perhaps when you look at another with respect, you possess them in a much deeper way. If you cage a bird, all you have is a caged bird. The only way you can have that beautiful creature that flies through the trees is through respect, and then you have it as much as you're supposed to have anything.

And the key here is perhaps not so much to possess as to be possessed. As I said earlier, the man who has amassed great wealth is possessed by it. But what we all need is to be possessed by the much greater wealth which is our birthright—existence itself.

DJ: Whether you are possessed by wealth, beauty, or existence, you *will* be possessed by something.

SG: Everything in the universe is possessed by something else. The very fact the earth is in an orbit means it's possessed by something. The cohesion of matter comes from possession. The nature of the universe is to be possessed.

DJ: Different subject. Why do people continue to believe lies about environmental destruction, when these lies are consistent neither internally nor with their own sensual experience?

SG: That's the question the ecology movement needs to ask, because it points to the irrationality of the defense mechanisms involved. People are not noticing the evidence of their own senses. You walk out the door and the air smells bad. Your eyes smart, you cough. You look into a river and see it's polluted. The harm we're doing ourselves is evident. Why are people not reacting more?

One of the answers is the old one—people are not sure what to do. But that's wrapped up in a curious way with the other answer, which is that from very early on this culture teaches a profound mechanism of denial. We learn almost from birth not to respond to what we really experience in our bodies. We learn to place our faith not with actual experience but with authorities who purport to control experience. Those in power of course cannot absolutely control experience, but they do control culture, and culture is very powerful in our lives. Parents are very powerful, and parents are the bearers of culture. Schools are very powerful, and schools are the bearers of culture. Culture controls the way we earn a living. Our survival has nothing to do with our own efforts, what we know how to do, and our ability to survive with our own senses. Survival has to do with filling out a job application, spelling your name right and putting the right numbers where it asks for your social security number. This is so divorced from direct experience that the power of whether you live or die appears to rest with culture, not with nature. Therefore truth belongs to cultural authority, and not to natural authority. Certainly not to one's own authority, which once again is natural authority.

You may have an experience of a sore throat or watery eyes, but then you'll hear some TV doctor say, "Statistically you've nothing to worry about. It's only six parts per liquid ounce. I'll drink this sulfuric acid right in front of your eyes and still be fine."

Part of our task as members of the ecology movement is to help people once again have and trust direct experience. This is really the next stage in the process of democratization.

There are so many parts of everyday life we don't have conversations with. We're not present. If there is such a thing as evolution in human consciousness, the time has come—it's imperative now—to honor our sensual life and to be physically present. We are on the verge of destroying material life. One of the ways I think we can avert that is to recognize the profundity of material existence, to deeply respect our own process of knowing in the world, knowing with heart and mind and body and sensuality all at the same time. This involves a deep self-respect for that process of knowledge that has evolved over millions, even billions of years, and it involves entering that process with full passion.

DJ: Which is eros.

SG: Eros has been narrowed in our culture to the genital area, which is certainly very important and wonderful and *part* of eros. But eros hasn't included an understanding of the whole range of sensuality. Because we've flattened it we say, "Oh, that's *just* sensuality." Democritus called sensual understanding a bastard understanding. This is a patrilineal comment, because a bastard is somebody without a legal father. In a way sensual perceptions *are* bastard understandings, because they aren't part of patriarchy.

Sensual knowledge, when you retrieve it from that hierarchical body-hating tradition, is full of meaning in and of itself. The New Age is onto this again, but they fall into the same Judeo-Christian traps. "I have a taste of lemon in my mouth, which must mean I'm bitter." Sensual experience is still secondary to a hierarchy of given cultural assumptions. To really honor sensual experience is to go into your mouth, taste lemon, and be open to understanding what it is. "What is this?" No limits. No reduction of experience.

I look at the red flowers over there. First I see red, then not quite red, then amber-red, and finally I begin to see, "My God, that such a thing exists, and that I have eyes. Newton's *Optics* says the red doesn't exist in the flower, but I know it *does* exist, because my eyes are taking it in. It doesn't matter if it's in the flower or my eye or somewhere in between. It's astonishing."

It's not what we would call *just* sensuality, because our hearts are engaged. There's a rejoicing and an awe, and all the feelings people describe as the experience of the divine. You look at the color red and it's all there, and much more. *That's* what we have robbed ourselves of in this civilization.

DJ: Beauty.

SG: Beauty. And beauty is not only beauty. It's not just what Alexander Pope described women as trying to create, something superficial like a decoration. It's not that at all. It's not separate from truth. It's not separate from love. It's not separate from the power that generates life.

DJ: It's not separate.

SG: It's not separate.

TERRY TEMPEST WILLIAMS

Terry Tempest Williams has written that "it's strange to feel change coming. It's easy to ignore. An underlying restlessness seems to accompany it like birds flocking before a storm. We go about our business with the usual alacrity, while in the pit of our stomach there is a sense of something tenuous."

Where, Terry Tempest Williams asked, can we find refuge in change? She has answered that question as well, "I am slowly, painfully discovering that my refuge is not found in my mother, my grandmother, or even the birds of Bear River. My refuge exists in my capacity to love. If I can learn to love death then I can begin to find refuge in change."

Terry Tempest Williams is Naturalist-in-Residence at the Utah Museum of Natural History in Salt Lake City. Her first book, Pieces of White Shell: A Journey to Navajoland, *received the 1984 Southwest Book Award. She is also the author of* Coyote's Canyon, Refuge: An Unnatural History of Family and Place, *two children's books, and most recently,* An Unspoken Hunger: Stories from the Field. *She is the recipient of the 1993 Lannan Literary Fellowship in creative nonfiction.*

DERRICK JENSEN: What does the erotic mean to you?

TERRY TEMPEST WILLIAMS: It means "in relation." Erotic is what those deep relations are and can be that engage the whole body—our heart, our mind, our spirit, our flesh. It is that moment of being exquisitely present.

It does not speak well for us as a people that we even have to make the distinction between what is erotic and what is not, because an erotic connection is a life-engaged, making love to the world that I think comes very naturally.

Eroticism, being in relation, calls the inner life into play. No longer numb, we feel the magnetic pull of our bodies toward something stronger, more vital than simply ourselves. Arousal becomes a dance with longing. We form a secret partnership with possibility.

The moment I realized that life is sexual, that death is sexual, *in relation*, was when Mother was dying, in those last hours. We were breathing together. It was a dialogue between mother and daughter, between two women, between human beings.

The permeability of the body was present. I felt her spirit disengage from the soles of her feet and move upward to leave out the top of her head. It was as though she was climbing through her body on a ladder of light. The only analogue I had for that feeling was in making love when you're moving toward orgasm. Again, you are walking up that ladder of light. It's almost like being inside a piece of music, moving up the scale, the pitch gets higher and higher and more intense, more intense. My mother's death was one of the most sensual, sexual, erotic encounters I have ever had.

I don't know why that should have surprised me. It is that immediacy of life, even in death.

That experience changed everything for me.

DJ: What did you do . . .

TTW: After Mother died, our family stayed with her body. Her spirit was very much present in that room. We all felt the peace of that moment, as well as the loss. But again, she was so present that grief was not yet a part of it. I remember when my husband, Brooke, and I finally left, my first impulse once outside was to look up. "Where are you?" How could something so full, so tangible, so alive, be gone and vanish into air? My only solace was to look at the full face of the moon and see my mother's face illumined.

I didn't articulate for a long time what that encounter had been for me. Then one morning, Brooke was waxing his skis and I went downstairs and started to explain to him what Mother and I had shared, what that landscape of death really meant to me.

He said, "I know exactly what you're talking about. I have the same experience whenever I go powder skiing."

I was incensed. At first I thought, what a sacrilege, here I am trying to talk about this profound moment and he's reduced it to powder skiing. And then, suddenly, I realized powder snow is his passion. That is where he lifts off from the face of the earth and moves through an ocean of snow—weight and release, weight and release. He becomes a bird, an

angel, mediating between two worlds. Each person has their own intimate connection to the erotic, to the sacred, to that movement. Once
again, it's that notion of surrendering to something greater than ourselves.

And of course, the erotic is about love, our deep hunger for communion, where issues of restraint and yearning, engagement and desire
enter us.

When I think about the moments in my life when I have felt engaged,
it's always about love. With my mother, I was loving a woman who gave
me life, realizing this was a dialogue, that here was the woman who not
only gave me my body, but helped to nurture and create my soul. I had
always felt my indebtedness to her, and suddenly in her moment of death
I felt her trust. I think that was the first time I really saw how much she
loved me, enough to trust me even with her life, enough that we could
breathe her, birth her, into the next world. She allowed me to be a mid-
wife to her soul.

A gift.

Erotic moments. Love. And I believe it is a two-way love, acts of reciprocity, where both parties involved are giving and receiving. When
love is only one-way, eventually it becomes pornographic, a body that is
used, rather than a body that is shared.

Without feeling. Perhaps these two words are the key, the only way
we can begin to turn our understanding toward our abuse of each other
and our abuse of the land. Could it be that what we fear most is our capacity to feel, and so we annihilate symbolically and physically that
which is beautiful and tender, anything that dares us to consider our creative selves? The erotic world is silenced, reduced to a collection of objects we can curate and control, be it a vase, a woman, or wilderness.
Our lives become a piece in the puzzle of pornography as we "go through
the motions" of daily intercourse without any engagement of the soul.

If I am honest, one reason the erotic is so intriguing to me is because
in the culture I was raised in eroticism is the ultimate taboo. It isn't your
body that is valued; it is your soul. Our souls could always be saved in
spite of our bodies. It's not this world that counts; it's the hereafter.

Why is that? What are we afraid of? That's the question I keep asking
myself. What is our culture afraid of? Why are we so afraid of the body?

I believe our most poignant lessons come through the body, the skin, the cells, our DNA. It's where our ancestral memory is. It's where the future will be changed. And what we take in we ultimately give away. If we stop the world from penetrating us, what does that mean? The body allows us to be human. It is through the body we feel the world, both its pain and its beauty.

DJ: If we stop the world from penetrating us, we're living in solitary confinement. The only love that can exist is one way.

TTW: I've been thinking about marriage, and what that is in terms of an institution. The oppression of marriage as well as the liberation of marriage, and how it's not something that people really share. Many people have facades of marriages. But are they engagements? Are they marriages in their bodies? Why don't we talk about what it means to be married? What it means to be married to our self? What it means to be married to a lover, a partner? What it means to be married to the earth, to our dreams, to community? What it means to be married to a politics of place that can both inform and inspire us?

When I think about Brooke and me making love, I often think of that deep peace that follows. That's the peace I would love to hold, because of those deep relations and that sense of connectedness, that sense that we are not alone in the world. Every time we make love to a human being, fully, we are making love to everything that lives and breathes. In that sense it becomes communion. It *is* a sacrament.

This has nothing to do with orthodoxy. Maybe religions have every reason to fear the erotic, because it would take the walls down. The erotic defies convention. Anything becomes possible.

DJ: What's the connection between eros and the land?

TTW: Brooke and I were recently in Spain, and in many ways that was all about erotic travel, about having the luxury of time and being in a landscape where you don't cast a shadow—you have no responsibilities or obligations.

We were gone almost a month and everything was sensual. Everything was erotic. It's the gift of travel, where everything is infused with meaning, compressed, so you begin to see the golden strand that weaves life together. You are in a constant state of awe.

We drove into Portugal, to a place called Sagres. If Portugal is the face of a woman, and Spain is her hair, Sagres is the tip of her chin. It's a very powerful place, with sea so relentless there is no ocean-beach transition. It's just ocean-cliff. Portuguese fishermen stand on the edge of the cliffs like herons, casting lines two hundred feet below with tremendous faith, both that they're not going to be blown off and also that their lines will lure fish that will provide food for their families. I sat next to the fishermen on the cliffs for hours. My body trembled at the beauty of it, at the peace of the fishermen, at their fierce attention, the precarious nature of their stance, the ritual, the dailiness of their lives.

The longer I sat, the more frightened I became. The seduction of the sea was alluring. The pounding waves, the sheer face of the continent, the immensity, the beauty, the fact that the depth of the ocean was unfathomable to me—the whole situation was so arousing it was all I could do not to step off. I had an insatiable, unexplainable desire to leap, to merge. I don't know why I didn't.

Had I walked off the cliff, it would not have been out of despair. It would have been out of beauty, out of my desire to be one with. I think about Rilke, when he speaks of beauty as the beginning of terror. That's the edge, that fine line between life and death, the erotic impulse that moves us beyond fear.

DJ: Matthew Fox also quotes Rilke, that beauty "serenely disdains to destroy us."

TTW: How do you make peace with those kinds of contradictions? At a pivotal moment in the wonderful novel *The Apprenticeship*, by Clarice Lispector, her main character, Lori, says, "I now know what I want: I want to remain standing still in the sea."

That's it. To be able to have that core of serenity in the middle of huge oscillations; to be present in those waves and emotional tides, but to possess a solidarity of soul. That's what I would like to hold for myself.

DJ: I have on my wall at home: "What do we do with contradictory impulses? We play with them. We accept them. Love them. Rejoice in them, and in the fact that we are alive, that we have choices, that the wind mingles with the branches and the snow kisses the soil."

TTW: That is lovely. It is what I so cherish about Great Salt Lake. It is Trickster. It is water in the desert that no one can drink. It is self-proclaimed wilderness with islands too stark, too remote to inhabit. It really is the liquid lie of the West. I love that. No one knows what to do with it.

I wonder why we have to do anything with it at all? Why can't it just be? Why are we always asking so much of ourselves or of these places of power? Is it not enough that they simply exist for their own right, whether it's Great Salt Lake, the ancient forests of the Northwest, or this ocean of sage that covers the Great Basin? Why must we always try to manipulate and control life?

It may be that our task now, as it has always been, is to listen. Simply that. If we really listen, the land will tell us what it wants, and tell us how we can live more responsively.

Just for fun, I made a spontaneous list of the lessons I have learned from the Great Basin. The Great Basin is about exposure. It's about austerity. It's about how nothing is as it appears and it's about aridity and the conservation of water. Again, in the Basin one finds deep relations with all their subtleties. I believe it is also about "deep time." John McPhee has created a beautiful canvas of these ideas in his book *Basin and Range.*

How can we take these qualities of the land and bring them to the table in terms of our politics and negotiations of how we as a people want to live in this desert landscape?

Exposure. Putting our cards on the table. Not being tactical. Not being hidden.

Aridity. Conservation. Conserving water. Conserving our energy. Perhaps living more lightly on this land that is not so forgiving. There is a history of human habitation in the Great Basin that spans ten thousand years. Perhaps we need to study our past to see what was known then that we may have forgotten.

The subtleties. Again, really listening. And time. It will take an enormous amount of time to really find out what habitation means in this country. We're just beginning to get a taste of it. And patience. We don't need to have all the answers right now. We may never have the answers, but as long as we keep driving the questions, or keep finding pockets of humility, maybe it won't seem so overwhelming or so difficult. Then maybe a rancher and an environmentalist can burn their labels and see each other as neighbors.

The environmental movement right now is not listening. We are engaged in a rhetoric as strong and as aggressive as the so-called opposition. I would love to see the whole notion of opposition dissolved, so there's no longer this shadow dance between "us" and "them." I would love for us to listen to one another and try to say, "What do we want as members of this community? What do we love? What do we fear? What are our concerns? How do we dream our future? How do we begin to define home?" Then we would have something to build from, rather than constantly turning one another into abstractions and stereotypes engaged in military combativeness.

I believe we all desire similar things. The real poison of our society right now is that everything is reduced to such a simplistic level. There is no tolerance or hunger for complexity or ambiguity. Do you want this or that? Black or white? Yes or no? It strips us to our lowest denominator, creating a physics that is irreconcilable just by the nature of polarity. As a result, we miss the richness we can bring to one another in our diverse points of view. It is not about agreement. It is about respect.

Again, when Brooke and I were in Spain, we found ourselves in the Doñana National Park, one of the last remaining wetlands in Europe. We were there during spring migration, so we were able to witness waves of birds from both the European and African continents.

The wetlands happen to be on the edge of a beautiful town called El Rocío. We went on a Sunday morning to see the flamingos and the spoonbills. On the edge of the marsh is a beautiful whitewashed adobe *santuario*. An old woman handed each person a large candle. She said, "Light this candle with your desire in mind, let your desire pierce your heart, and take it home with you."

The people lighted their candles with their desires in mind, then moved into an alcove to put their candle onto a huge iron rack. In this white-tiled room with a statue of the Mother of Dew, each person stood next to their candle and tended to their desire, watching while the wax melted. When the wax had melted sufficiently to make a ball of it, each person took the wax home as a talisman.

The room was searing—there had to be hundreds, even thousands of candles, all burning at the same time, with people attending to their individual desires. It was wonderful. Brooke said to me, "My desire is melting into everyone else's." And that was precisely the point. When you're in that collective space in a ritualistic way, there is no way your desire won't merge with everyone else's desire. They are the desires of our highest selves.

That gives me comfort. Our needs as human beings are really very simple—to love and be loved, a sense of connection and compassion, a desire to be heard. Health. Family. Home. Once again the dance, that sharing of breath, that merging with something larger than ourselves. One plus one equals three—that third thing.

DJ: That's a gift, and a contradiction. How does that relate to the houses that are being built in this canyon, to the trees in the Northwest that are going down now, and to women who are being raped right now? It's easy to tell myself to play with contradictions, but this is no spiritual game. Real canyons are ruined, real forests are destroyed, and real women are raped.

TTW: These are ultimately aggressions against ourselves. This is the blockage of time and the blockage of space. And it's building walls, it's building structure. It's whatever we can do to not be in that sacred space with our desires, to not be in that place of pilgrimage.

This is our addiction to speed and time. How can we have any sense of stillness when we have an insatiable appetite, when we have a big void inside because we've forgotten what we're connected to, we've forgotten where the source of our power lies? Everything becomes a substitution, with that hunger never being filled. So we build more houses, cut more trees, rape more women, thinking that will satisfy the yearning. But it only creates a deeper depression of the soul. Nothing is coming in—it's the one-way affection that becomes pornographic—because it's not a dance, it is an assault, an attack, the oppressor.

When we're in that space of oppression, we ultimately destroy that which we love. We fear that which we desire most.

The man who is building these houses in our canyon has more money than he knows what to do with. He is a man who has a deep desire for connection without knowing how to connect. I know this sounds judgmental. But I know him. I grew up with him. We played with his nine children, growing up in our neighborhood.

What if we were to hand this man a candle at El Rocío, on the edge of the migration of flamingos, and if he were to carry that candle into that room to sit with his desire? I'll bet his desire wouldn't have anything to do with money, greed, or power. I'll bet it would have to do with peace. It would have to do with being loved. It would have to do with trying to find his place in the world. One house. One self.

But we don't have time to even consider these things. So what we do is just engage in a speed of "development" that ultimately destroys both the land and ourselves.

To engage in the erotics of place means to engage in time.

DJ: And to engage in the erotics of personhood also means to engage in time.

TTW: We're not willing to give that time, because we might be affected. We might be altered, and that would force us to question the speed factor, the matrix of our very lives. Then what would happen? Would that be so terrible? Again, what are we afraid of?

I love how Edward Weston, the photographer, said he refused to drive faster than thirty-five miles an hour because he couldn't see. What does it mean that we zoom everywhere at seventy miles an hour? We are losing our ability to see.

DJ: If the ability to see and the ability to listen are not valued, what does this culture value?

TTW: My culture, if I were to define my culture as Mormon, values obedience, and adherence to the teachings of Jesus Christ. It values a work ethic. It values family, which means having children. And it values numbers.

Ultimately, my culture values control, a control which suppresses creative expression. That is necessary because creative expression threatens to undermine the status quo.

What does American culture value? In Washington, D.C., information is valued, because information is power.

DJ: And power within a patriarchy becomes eroticized. Marilyn French has written that women view sexuality primarily as a communication of pleasure, while men within a patriarchy view it primarily as an expression of power.

TTW: That's interesting. I understand what she is saying. Because it is about love, it's about exposure, it's about revealing who you are, and that is about having to change, having to be acted upon. Again, perhaps it is our different ways of defining power—the power with another human being versus power over another human being. One reveals love, the other reveals fear. We are frightened of engagement, of being fully present, because then we risk feeling pain and we feel grief, the grief inherent in life.

It comes back to the notion of time. If we are always busy, if we create an atmosphere of busyness around us, we don't have to penetrate anything in depth. We live on surfaces. We don't have time for connections.

But if we spend time with people, listen, see them for who they are, relationships develop, accountability arrives and stereotypes shatter. Power in the dark sense disappears in favor of cooperation. We face each other as human beings. Suddenly, the world is much more unpredictable, and that is very frightening.

That's why it's so much easier if everything remains an abstraction. "I hate ranchers." "Goddamn those environmentalists." "Don't tempt my heart."

Let's keep things simple.

DJ: I once had a friend who was a rancher. We've only spoken twice in the last couple of years, because each time we talk now he yells at me for being a nature writer. I'm not sure how to respond. We'd been friends for seven years.

TTW: We all feel schizophrenic. Here is a friendship that is being split apart because of an assumed ideology. How do we begin to break down these barriers? What candles can we light for one another to begin the healing? I believe all we can ask of ourselves is that we are as honest as we can be in our relations. I know I have personally been broken open a thousand times because of differing opinions or beliefs within my culture, with the people I love. And it is a very private pain. I don't think we are ever immune from being hurt by those we care about. For me, I must stay in my truth, my center, and that has everything to do with my relationship to the land.

That is also where my grief lies, because of what we are doing to the earth and its inhabitants. It's almost as though our own personal pain is so intolerable that if we destroy everything that is beautiful around us, we will no longer have a mirror to look at, to remind us of our impoverishment. If the world is only a strip mine, if the world is only a clear-cut, our own impoverishment is easier to bear—there's nothing to remind us of the richness of life, even our own. And again there is nothing to remind us where the true source of our power comes from. What we are doing as a species is an incredible mass abuse of our own spirit and of the spirit of life around us.

I don't think about hope much anymore. But I do think about imagination. That's where we have the capacity to shift.

And that's another aspect of eroticism.

DJ: When you feel love—for an individual person, for a place, for your self, for anything—everything becomes bearable.

TTW: It's in the context of love—love of the universe, in terms of a creation as divine as this, love between two people, the love we have toward our work, our families—that we can really allow ourselves to experience the full range of human emotion. We can experience the beauty and the terror, and we can be both fierce and compassionate at once. It is this honesty of spirit that is completely paradoxical. Once again, I think of Great Salt Lake as my mentor.

DJ: Are beauty and terror, fierceness and compassion, paradoxical?

TTW: Paradox is life. It's the same thing as balance. You can't have one without the other. There's always that creative third, which is where possibility lies. It's Jeannette Armstrong's En'owkin concept—give me your contraire, and we'll have something to talk about. Tell me what you fear most and then we can talk about what we desire most. Then this "third thing," which in this case is conversation or understanding, becomes the creative expression of an idea. Art. Story.

DJ: I'm thinking about grief and about hope. The mass abuse will undoubtedly get worse as we try to hold on to an industrial civilization that can't last. This transition will be very painful for humans and nonhumans alike. I've come to know that one of the most important things we can do through this transition is hold each other, including the land, while many beautiful things die.

TTW: I agree with you. And I've been thinking about what it means to bear witness. The past ten years I've been bearing witness to death, bearing witness to women I love, and bearing witness to the testing going on in the Nevada desert. I've been bearing witness to bombing runs on the edge of the Cabeza Prieta National Wildlife Refuge, bearing witness to the burning of yew trees and their healing secrets in slash piles in the Pacific Northwest and thinking this is not so unlike the burning of witches, who also held knowledge of healing within their bones. I've been bearing witness to traplines of coyotes being poisoned by the Animal Damage Control. And I've been bearing witness to beauty, beauty that strikes a chord so deep you can't stop the tears from flowing. At places as astonishing as Mono Lake, where I've stood knee-deep in saltwater to watch the fresh water of Lee Vining Creek flow over the top like oil on vinegar. . . . It's the space of angels. I've been bearing witness to dancing grouse on their leks up at Malheur in Oregon. Bearing witness to both the beauty and the pain of our world is a task I want to be part of. As a writer, this is my work. By bearing witness, the story that is told can provide a healing ground. Through the art of language, the art of story, alchemy can occur. And if we choose to turn our backs, we've walked away from what it means to be human.

DJ: Once you know what it means to be human, you never *can* finally turn your back. Your body won't let you.

TTW: If we don't get it, we keep having the same nightmare over and over. And then you can say, "It was just a dream. Even though I woke up in the night with an incredible sweat, I have no idea what that's about." But if we don't respond to those dreams, to those nightmares, to those numinous moments of our nightlife, the message will move into the body. It's a lot harder to ignore two ruptured discs or bleeding intestines. The body has its own voice and when it chooses to speak, it is very difficult to ignore.

DJ: I had a dream last night. I came upon a fiery car wreck, and as I tried to save whatever was inside, my hands kept catching on fire. Then I heard a voice say, "Beyond hope and despair is play." Waking up from the dream, I knew that each of us is reaching into the fire, trying to pull out whatever we can.

TTW: Yes. Exactly. The last three words of my grandmother's life were, "Dance, dance, dance." That's it. It's those grouse dancing on the sage flats, even in the rain, crazy with desire, their pumping breasts creating the sound of water. It's eros, it's love, that nurtures and feeds our soul.

We're so serious. We're so earnest. We forget, fear, and mistrust our own trickster energy because people don't have time to listen, to notice when we are playing, when we are provoking. Where are our clowns? Where are the Koshare of our tribes?

DJ: The exact moment I understood relationships was when I read a letter that said, "All there is to do is play."

TTW: Through play we develop relations and see each other whole. Through play tension is released, and joy is found. Humor emerges and that can be very intimate. This takes time. The culture at large views play as something frivolous, something that belongs to children. But that's how community is created. If we don't have time to play together, to eat meals together, to make love together, what holds us together? We drive fast in our cars, we have workloads that are unrealistic and horrendous and self-imposed for one reason or another, and we're not creating community. We're creating desperate, isolated, fast-paced lives that give us enormous excuse not to be engaged. We are lonely.

DJ: How can we live, and live in community, if we move every three years?

TTW: I was very fond of Wally Stegner. I always felt he was the one person who really understood what it meant to be Mormon, what it meant to be raised in this valley—both the gift and burden one carries with that.

A few years ago, I was driving Wally and Mary, his wife, to the airport. As we drove down South Temple he gave us a wonderful annotated narration: "This is where your grandfather and I played tennis. This is where I used to go for milkshakes at Snelgrove's. This is where I wrote *Recapitulation*." We parked at the airport, and as I helped them with their bags, I turned to Wally and said, "Thank you so much for coming." He looked at me dead-eye center and responded, "Thank you for staying."

I've never forgotten that. It's given me great courage to live in a place I both love and at times find great difficulty in.

This is my place. It just may be that the most radical act we can commit is to stay home. What does that mean to finally commit to a place, to a people, to a community?

It doesn't mean it's easy, but it does mean you can live with patience, because you're not going to go away. It also means making a commitment to bear witness, and engaging in "casserole diplomacy" by sharing food among neighbors, by playing with the children and mending feuds and caring for the sick. These kinds of commitments are real. They are tangible. They are not esoteric or idealistic, but are rooted in a bedrock existence of where we choose to maintain our lives.

That way we begin to know the predictability of a place. We anticipate a species long before we see them. We can chart the changes, because we have a memory of cycles and seasons; we gain a capacity for both pleasure and pain, and we find the strength within ourselves and each other to hold these lines.

That's my definition of family. And that's my definition of love.

DJ: Bees have blessed me by bringing their relatives into my family. Through them I have become related to willows, dandelions, and wild roses in a very real way.

TTW: Isn't that a way to extend our notion of community to include all plants, animals, rocks, soils, rivers, and human beings? On Brooke's birthday a wonderful wave of Audubon's warblers flew in. "Hello. Happy Birthday." "Welcome home."

It's all so beautiful, so intensely beautiful.

DJ: How do the warblers, the stars, the trees speak to you?

TTW: For me, it has nothing to do with language.

Some people have a hard time picking flowers. I don't at all. There's so much underground, and they live in the land, and then one day it's all right to bring them inside. It's that permeability, the inner and the outer. I love bouquets of flowers in our home picked from our garden.

The doors of this house are always open. I can't tell you the animals that have inhabited our bedroom. Everything from porcupines to lizards to raccoons. We've had bats in this house, and hummingbirds. If we open our doors we receive a constant flow of visitations, or messengers. It's all about the pleasure and acknowledgment of sharing this place. It goes into our bodies, our hearts, our cells.

And I think there are times we rescue each other. When the hummingbird came in, I held her little body with cupped hands and felt her heart beating, beating, beating, beating. She became incredibly still. When I opened my hand outside she stayed for a few minutes to get her bearings, and then she flew.

Each time, it is a privilege to have that momentary encounter, that acknowledgment of other, those seconds of engagement.

It's those times, once again, when borders dissolve, when boundaries dissolve. It's that breath, that erotic moment, that third thing, that merging into something higher.

DJ: Merging, permeability, eros . . .

TTW: And mutability. If we're going to survive we have to learn how to be shape-shifters. This has nothing to do with inconsistency. It has to do with seizing the moment, perceiving what is necessary *in that moment*.

I remember the last time I was at the Nevada Test Site, before the moratorium. Chief Raymond Yowell, a Shoshone elder, was officiating. He stood before the three thousand or more people gathered together, chanting and drumming, chanting and drumming. We had brought huge baskets and bowls of flowers, with the idea that we can throw flowers against evil.

Throwing flowers against evil comes from the Yaqui Easter ceremony. For several weeks during Easter season, Yaqui people reenact the passion play, a ritual they adopted from the Jesuits in the fifteenth century. Imagine this: a slow, inexorable build-up of evil against the forces of good. The *fariseos*, or pharisees, are dressed in black cloaks. They are masked and they march to a slow, steady dirge, to the haunting flute music that is accompanying them. They are carrying the weight of evil that is leaning against the village. In their long black capes they forcefully make their way through the crowd of onlookers. Their goal is to literally penetrate the church. They have stolen the body of Christ, they have violated every sense of decency within the community, they have marred and destroyed the sacred.

The *fariseos* charge the church in full run. As they do this, they are showered with flower petals thrown against evil by the children, by the women on both sides of the human gauntlet. The young girls—five, six, seven years old—are adorned in crisp white dresses. They are the final barrier to the community's holy altar that the *fariseos* must penetrate. The *fariseos* charge again. The girls raise boughs of cottonwood and mesquite and wave them over the *fariseos*. The *fariseos* are repelled.

They retreat, take off their black capes and return to the *santuario* in confession.

A deer—the Deer Dancer—the most peaceful of animals, covered with flower petals, dances in the middle of the *fariseos*. The *fariseos* have been "changed to good" and are "forgiven." The universe is restored, health and peace have been returned to the village.

This story was told to me by Richard Nelson, an anthropologist who has attended the Yaqui ceremonies. I asked him if it would be all right to carry this story with me to the Test Site. He felt it would be appropriate, saying, "I think these stories exist for all of us as a means of understanding how to behave in the world."

A few days before the demonstration, my nieces, Callie, Sara, and I decided we would visit all the florists in town and ask if they had flowers they would like to donate to heal the Test Site. The florists opened their arms to us and within a few hours, the car was completely filled with flowers: roses, dahlias, daisies, tulips, irises, lilies, chrysanthemums, every type of bloom imaginable.

We brought the flowers home, laid them out on a white sheet in the middle of our living room, and started plucking the petals. We placed the greenery outside and organized the flowers in big black bowls and baskets.

While we worked, we told stories. We talked about their grandmother, my mother, and their great-grandmothers, and what might have caused their deaths. We spoke about the Test Site, about the whole notion of war, the possibilities of peace, and that we could in fact throw flowers against evil, that something this delicate and beautiful could make an extraordinary difference. We discussed the power of gesture.

I never thought about how we would get the flowers to the Test Site given that we were flying to Nevada. But once we arrived at the airport and people saw the flowers, rules disappeared.

"Of course you can carry more than two pieces of luggage onto the plane," the flight attendants said. They happily (and a bit subversively) strapped baskets of flowers into empty seats.

When we arrived in Las Vegas, various passengers volunteered to carry the flowers outside. The beauty was intoxicating.

Finally, at the Test Site we placed the baskets of flowers around the barbed wire fences and on the platform where Chief Yowell was drumming. The story was retold of the Yaqui passion play and how the community threw flowers at evil. Chief Yowell never wavered, but continued drumming and chanting, drumming and chanting. The children from the audience spontaneously rose and walked toward the bowls and baskets of flowers. They took them into their arms and distributed the petals throughout the crowd. Chief Yowell stopped drumming and spoke, "We will now enter the land like water . . ."

En masse, people moved across the Test Site, ducked under the barbed wire fence, crossed the cattle guard, and infiltrated the desert, sprinkling flowers upon the contaminated landscape.

"There is something older than war," writes the poet Lyn Dalebout.

It's all about being shape-shifters, it's about permeability, it's about malleability, it's knowing what each occasion demands, standing our ground in the places we love. I have tremendous faith in these things.

Through an erotics of place, I believe anything is possible.

ACKNOWLEDGMENTS

THIS BOOK IS the product of community, and I am grateful to those without whom this book would perhaps never have been conceived, much less completed in its present form.

I would like to thank my mother, Mary Jensen, who by her support and encouragement has enabled me to discover a life of my own, a life based on love, and who by her patience and enthusiasm has taught me to never cease asking questions.

And I would like to thank other members of my family: Bruce Thoms, for his strength of heart; Royann Richardson, for her wisdom; Betty Lu Durham, who awakened me to life; Vicki Lopez, whose brilliance lights my path; Kathleen Malindez, for her constant support; John Osborn, for giving me direction; Claire and John Keeble, who live the questions directly and sincerely; Dana Elder, for his intelligence and guidance; Lori Clark, who taught me to believe in myself; Cathy Sinclair, who sees with the eyes of a child; Sara Folger, for the quality of her vision; Beth Clothier, for her ability to listen deeply; George Draffan, for being a friend; Sue and Jonathan Keeble, for their generosity; Charlotte Watson and Jane Treuhold, for their gentleness and compassion; Jeannette Armstrong, who consistently reveals the beauty that human beings are capable of; Terry Tempest Williams, whose ability to love has taught me awe; Sandra Lopez, who communicates deeply; Reneé Soule, whose thinking is not only dangerous but desperately needed; Beth Fries, for her courage.

The completion of this project would not have been possible without the generosity of many people who volunteered their houses, their vehicles, their time, and their love. These include: Tom, Mary, Jamie, and Josie Bunker; Mike Majesty and Paul Sousa; Jo and Eugene Lopez; Julien Puzey and Marie Fulmer; Sandra and Barry Lopez; Martha Brown; and Lucinda Soule. Richard Nelson, Felipe Molina, Felipe's mother Paula and his future wife Mimi checked facts for me. Jenia Walter made many clarifying suggestions.

My thanks to my agent, Lizzie Grossman, without whose faith this project would never have been undertaken, and who was able to place the book more quickly and in a more appropriate place than I would have believed possible. Thanks also to Barbara Ras for being the best editor a person could imagine, and for her unmatched ability to help everyone get what they want.

I would like to thank all of those people whose voices are in this book, as well as the other people who responded to my queries or with whom I talked. This gratitude is not only for the energy they put into the interviews and revisions but especially for the important work they do.

Perhaps most important, I am grateful to all of those nonhuman others—stars, bees, cranes, rivers, Crohn's Disease pathogens, pine trees, geese, coyotes, ducks—who by our interactions have taught me how to be a human being.